21
11:30

Zihuatanejo—Ixtapa
A Guide to Casas, Camas
Comidas, y Cosas

Best wishes,
Linda Fox

Hotel DORADO
011-52-755-112-1519

ISBN 13-978-1466449527
Printing History
1st edition – September 1989
2nd edition – September 1992
3rd edition – September 1998
4th edition – September 2003
5th edition – September 2005
6th edition – December 2011
Mini Revision – October 2012

Dedication

I'd like to offer my deepest gratitude to Anita Lapointe for her many years of friendship and encouragement when I was ready to "File 13" the whole project back in 1989 when I wrote the first edition of this book. I didn't know how to use a computer so Anita held my hand and taught me computer 101. Anita, like so many other "colorful characters" of Zihua is no longer with us and it is with great sadness that I dedicate my guidebook to her and all the other wonderful "colorful characters" we have lost over the past 12 years.

The book is also dedicated to the sisterhood—Tania, Esthela, Grace, Margo, and Isabel for making *Zihua* truly, the "Place of Women."

Table of Contents

Zihuatanejo

Ixtapa

Acknowledgements

I want to thank recently departed Dr. Anita Cowan for the use of her extensive research material from her book, "Tourism Development in a Mexican Coastal Community." Her contribution provides valuable insight into the history of Zihuatanejo.

Thank goodness Victoria Priani is still here—her editing help, especially with the Spanish translations, was so very important to the professionalism of this guidebook. Any and all errors are typos on my part.

I have also usurped some fascinating tidbits of knowledge from our wonderful but no longer published local magazine, *Another Day in Paradise*.

Special thanks to Ted Tate for writing such a fun short story book—*Wash Gently, Dry Slowly*.

A big thank you to friend Wendy Ogle, a professional photographer, who has allowed me to use one of the photographs she took while visiting the area for the front cover. Also a thank you to Tania Scales for the back cover photograph taken in her temple to the goddesses.

Introduction

In the spring of 1971, when I arrived in Zihuatanejo, there seemed to be little need for maps or guidebooks of the area. At that time, 40 odd years ago, there were only about 4,000 residents, a handful of single story buildings, and virtually no cars in this quintessential sleepy little fishing village. The streets were of packed dirt with potholes the size of small VW's and the buildings that now house the downtown stores were mostly private dwellings. Back in 1971 Ixtapa was nothing more than a virgin white-sand beach and a couple of coconut groves.

Naturally, there have been **huge** changes in the past four decades. Zihuatanejo de Azueta, which is now the official name of the municipality of which Zihuatanejo and Ixtapa and other areas form a part, is now a small city with a static population exceeding 130,000 inhabitants. Zihuatanejo is not as sleepy as it used to be and Ixtapa is a healthy and vibrant 30 something internationally known resort. And as for the need of maps and guidebooks? Time and a faithful readership have proven otherwise. My book is an attempt to chronicle, if you would, the many changes that have taken place since Ixtapa was "created" and Zihuatanejo was a fishing village.

Just over the hill from Zihuatanejo, Ixtapa is the resort area companion to the historic, traditional Zihuatanejo. Between the two there is a marriage of the old and the new. This matrimony is unique in Mexico, and perhaps could not have been consummated anywhere else in Mexico.

Ixtapa is neither a town nor a village but more like a place created for the recreational pursuits of people. It was hacked out of the palm groves that once stood as sentinels along the shoreline of this gorgeous stretch of beach. According to some, not all, Ixtapa is a *Náhuatl* term designating the white salt crust that once covered the surrounding dunes and hills.

Together, *Zihua* and Ixtapa form *ZI*, an ambidextrous sort of place or playground where one can tailor a holiday or vacation to fit his/her individual economic circumstances and recreational desires. It encompasses those extremes of contrast of Mexico about which so much is written. It is the strumming of guitars along the *paseo del pescador* or the ear-splitting bass of the music in a disco. It is an afternoon lazing away in a hammock or racing down zip-lines at breathtaking speeds. It is a freshly caught fish cooked in a humble adobe restaurant with dirt floors or a chateaubriand served with

7

imported wine while your feet rest on velvet cushions. Whatever your heart's desire for a vacation might be, ZI can probably provide it.

Times have greatly changed. The Internet and completed highway between Zihuatanejo and Morelia have let the world and 40 million Mexicans discover *Zihua,* resulting in some positive and negative influences.

A huge change occurred in 2010 when the state government paid for a much needed facelift for the aging *Zihua.* Unfortunately, as so often happens to women seeking perpetual youth, the facelift cannot be qualified as stellar. Anyone that has ever picked up a paintbrush knows that most of the work has already been done in the prepping for the project. In the case of *Zihua,* not much thought went into the prep work. As a result, huge stripes of paint are peeling and many of the newly erected protective overhangs are sagging or have collapsed and it will be interesting to see if any follow-up is done by the new state governor.

Ted Tate, a beloved long-time resident, wrote a marvelous guidebook in 1986. It was written, as he says, "to present a bit of history, a whole lot of the present and a touch of the future of Zihuatanejo-Ixtapa. It is one *gringo's* opinion of where things are, what they are called, and what is being offered." Ted's book, *Wash Gently, Dry Slowly,* is for sale via Amazon—there are from time to time copies offered for $99.95. Ted would be turning over in his grave if he knew his book would fetch that kind of money.

My desire is to follow in Ted's footsteps. I've tried very hard to listen to suggestions from my readers. As a result, the focus of this book is to impart some information that cannot be found on the Internet or through any readily available sources. I'm hoping to impart to you, the reader, tidbits of life in the tropics that, hopefully, will make your vacation more enjoyable and make you laugh.

In gathering material for this edition, I noticed that Ted Tate and I had almost identical stories about a variety of topics including the circus, Lauren Hutton, the movie theater, bus travel, the post office, and many other subjects. This edition, I'm using stories that haven't been published in my guidebooks before, with a few exceptions of my very favorites. I have purposely printed both of our stories about Dr. Bravo to let folks see just how parallel our stories are. I also left Ted's stories completely intact. I didn't change any verbiage or correct grammar or spelling.

Many have called the guidebook "the *Zihua* bible" and I do so hope this new edition lives up to such exalted expectations.

I've cut down on the number of maps but hopefully a glance will get you properly oriented. Zihuatanejo is quite spread out for a community of 130,000 with the focus of tourist activities located in and around *El Centro* and the beach areas.

Zihuatanejo, its history and services, will be discussed in the first part of the book with subsequent very short chapters devoted to the formation, development, and interesting aspects of Ixtapa.

Also included is information on beaches stretching from *Saladitas* to *Barra de Potosí* respectively north and south of Zihuatanejo-Ixtapa. I've also tried to address some of the special needs of the boating community.

In the first edition, I felt compelled to list every single restaurant, bar, and shop in the *Zihua* area. This was necessary in order to have at least a one-hundred page book. In preparing this edition I have purposely omitted dozens of shops, restaurants, and bars. Many of these places change names or formats as often as I change sheets. Bad publicity and a continuing economic crisis have caused many restaurants to close and bars to open. I try to be current; hence this mini-revision. I have tried to give a well-rounded picture of *Zihua* with price ranges to suit all budgets.

These days, some friends are saying the guidebook is obsolete due to the Internet. I tend to disagree. The world now has access to Zihuatanejo-Ixtapa through the Internet but there are so many sites, that one can spend days sifting through the tons of information being written about the area. Also, one must keep in mind, people wanting to sell you a product pay to put their sites on-line. Naturally, these sites are biased to say the least. Alas, I am opinionated but I have nothing to gain in giving one place accolades over others.

In the 2003 edition, I wrote "Furthermore, a guidebook can be stashed in a purse or backpack and referred to readily when looking for a specific location. I challenge anyone to carry around a laptop in the streets of Zihuatanejo!" Enough said. Well, gotta eat those words— now anyone can walk around *Zihua* with an I–Pad containing a GPS application and readily find any business that might strike their fancy.

I hope the folks reading this book will glean some new bit of knowledge from these pages. I've been accused of reading a lot of junk novels so in my own defense; I try to learn something new from each book. One of the trash novels I read had a marine biologist as the central character. He was on a golf course with a lovely young lady and she was complaining about being bitten by our infamous "no seeums." He informed her that they don't actually bite—instead they deposit a microscopic bit of acid on the skin which is why the bite burns at first. I researched this bit of information on the Internet and found it was true.

History of Zihuatanejo

Historians disagree on the origin of the word Zihuatanejo. A variety of versions on the naming exists. The following are slightly different but historically accurate versions.

One version is that the name was derived from the Aztec province of *Cihuátlan*, which means "land of women." Legend has it that a *Tarascan* king, *Caltzontzin*, frequented the bay with his many wives, their attendants, and a few guards to enjoy the sea, the sand, and the sun. The name "land of women" probably came about because the entourage of the king included many more females than males. He ordered the reef in front of *Playa Las Gatas* to be built to keep away the abundant exotic fauna that inhabits these waters so that the women would have a "safe pool" in which to enjoy the water. A more elaborate version of the same legend has it that the king would leave the females of his entourage near the principal beach while going on to *Playa Las Gatas* with only males and that this custom led to the naming of the settlement "place of women." It has been reported that the original *Náhuatl* name *Cihuátlan* was misspelled by *Hernán Cortés* in a report to King Richard III in 1534 and since then, through a series of other changes, refined to its present spelling. *Cortés* mentioned the town of Zihuatanejo and a close-by island known today as *Isla Grande* or Ixtapa Island. Furthermore, he remarked that the place seemed to be inhabited by women only. It is a good possibility that the natives saw the *Cortés* fleet heading for the bay and, as they were accustomed to do, they sent all their women to the island to keep them safe and away from the eyes of foreigners while the men hid in the bushes. That may be the reason the Spaniards saw only women and assumed that they were the only inhabitants, reconfirming the significance of the town's native name. Eventually the *ejo,* was added, which means of little importance—hence the emergence of Zihuatanejo—land of women of little importance. This name stuck and has been used for at least the past three centuries.

Another theory according to Dr. Cowan:

While not much supportive evidence exists, there is the possibility that in Post classic times, the status of women was high. If women were involved in weaving and in the cloth production system, this system may have been organized in ways that elevated some of them to positions of power and prestige. Even during the first decade of Spanish exploration and settlement in the region, tales persisted of a legendary land in the west where women ruled. An early letter sent by Cortés to Carlos I of Spain forwarded the report that Ixtapa Island, near Zihuatanejo was populated only by women.

While this report fueled rumors about a land of amazons, the cluster of women found on the island was probably misinterpreted. Ixtapa Island has been used even in the last century (during the Mexican Revolution) as a shelter for women during times of danger from assault by outsiders.

The discovery of *La Chole,* an archeological site outside the town of *Soledad de Maciel,* has unearthed pre-Colombian artifacts from a variety of groups including *Aztec, Toltec, Omec, Zapotec, Tarascan,* and *Mayan.* Many visitors and locals used to buy artifacts from this site from *Doña Justina* who walked *Playa La Ropa* every day in the 70's. I thought they were fake but amassed a goodly sized amount as did Anita Cowan and especially Anita Hahner. We were all very fond of the elderly lady and her granddaughter and wanted to help out financially as she had come all the way from Petatlán to sell her wares. I was most surprised when I eventually had them carbon dated at the University of Texas and found they are the real deal.

With the arrival of *Hernán Cortés* and the Spanish conquest of *Tenochtitlan* by 1521, the *Costa Grande* was beset by new social and political forces. *Cortés* dispatched troops to seek the *Mar del Sur* (Pacific Ocean) and to assess the mineral wealth of the western regions. After *Ferdinand Magellan* discovered the Philippine Islands in 1526, ships from Mexican ports, mainly Acapulco, embarked in search of trans-pacific routes. *Cortés* sent several Spaniard carpenters and their assistants to Zihuatanejo to build three ships using the fine wood found around the area (oak and red cedar) and the natives as helpers. *Playa La Madera* was the loading site for timber and debarkation point for the Orient after the ships were built. These ships baptized with the names of *La Florida, Espiritu Santo,* and *Santiago* left Zihuatanejo on October 31st, 1527 under the command of Captain *Alvaro Saavedra y Céron* for the Phillipines. They left behind a rustic wood pier and shipyard. Spices, fabrics, porcelains, and most important, the coconut palm, were returned here. Eventually Acapulco supplanted Zihuatanejo as the major port along this coast.

After the arrival of the Spanish, life changed for the native inhabitants. The area known as Ixtapa was given to the son of a conquistador as an *encomienda* (tribute). The haciendas and ranchos in the *Costa Grande* attracted the natives—providing work and security. Agricultural production increased including coconuts, cacao, cotton, sesame seeds, and some coffee.

The Manila Galleon was launched from Acapulco in 1565. For 250 years, the galleons linked the far flung interests of the Spanish empire. The ships carried cargos of coin and bullion mined and minted in New Spain which led to the arrival of pirates around 1575. Most famous among these pirates were Sir Francis Drake and Admiral George Anson. William Dampier arrived in 1704 with pirate ships and reported in his log the presence of 40 homes. A landing party of crewmen came upon more than 100 armed men on horseback who fled when the English began firing.

By the beginning of the 1800's Spanish intrusion in the area was vehemently resented. In 1810 *José Mária Morelos* arrived with 3,000 men and gained control of the region.

The goals of the Mexican revolution were formalized in *Chilpancingo*, present capital of *Guerrero*, in 1818. Spain was expelled in 1827. For those patriots large tracts of land were granted. One of our local families, the Galeanas, was awarded much of the land between Acapulco and *La Union*. During this time, Zihuatanejo was still a sleepy little village with most residents living in *Agua de Correa*.

Zihuatanejo began to develop as a village during the presidential tenure of *Porfirio Diaz* during the late 1800's and early 1900's. During this period, boats in the bay were loaded with agricultural products and shipped overseas.

The first families to settle Zihuatanejo lived principally along the *Playa Municipal* between the lagoon and the estuary—site of our canal. The residents living in *Zihua* fished, or helped with the export of lumber.

Not until 1920 did the first modern communication system arrive in the form of the telegraph. The Mexican revolution destroyed plans by a U.S. company to construct a Zihuatanejo-Acapulco railroad.

The tourist trade in Mexico began advancing during the 1920's due to the automobile and commercial air travel. Acapulco became a desired tourist destination and those few hardy souls that ventured outside known tourist areas found Zihuatanejo and liked what they saw. As a result of Acapulco's popularity, with the jet set following World War II, Zihuatanejo's reputation grew.

In 1923, Zihuatanejo was designated as a *Puerto de Altura* (a port with sufficient depth to allow large ships to dock). Shipping activities increased and the population grew. Cut timbers were brought to *Playa La Madera* and floated out to boats. A pier was constructed in 1925 at the present site of the archaeological museum but later moved to its present site after being destroyed by a hurricane.

This small community was amazed in 1932 when soldiers and equipment arrived and built an airstrip of sorts.

Aerolinea Zelandia began service in 1935 and most visitors stayed with local families as there were no available facilities. As locals saw the increase in tourism, many met the needs of tourists by building guesthouses. The first guesthouses were opened along the principal beach, the *Casa Eugena, Arcadia, Belmar,* and *Avila*. Few commercial eateries were available with most serving only fish, rice, and beans. Electricity was provided by a generator which was shut off at 10:00 p.m. and was used until electrical service became available in 1970.

The road between Acapulco and Zihuatanejo was made barely passable in 1945 and bus service by *Estrella de Oro* and *Flecha Roja* began and the trip took more than 15 hours and could be managed only during dry season.

A group of 5 investors from the U.S. and Mexico saw the need for tourist accommodations and built a hotel on *Playa La Ropa*. The hotel *Catalina* was opened in 1953 with 30 rooms. Many locals remember the time that Timothy Leary and his band of merry pranksters rented the entire hotel for several months and shocked everyone with drug experimentation and nudity. Needless to say, he was eventually asked to leave.

During this period, Zihuatanejo was still only a sleepy fishing village and had no church. A wealthy businessman from the U.S. donated $2,000 dollars for the building of the church *La Virgin Señora de Guadalupe* which was completed in 1954.

Not until the mid-sixties, when the Mexican government initiated studies to identify coastal sites for resort development, did Zihuatanejo emerge as a tourist resort. Limited tourism had little to no effect on the locals except to improve the economy slightly for those with the entrepreneurial spirit.

The Zihuatanejo–Acapulco highway was finally completed in the mid 70's and the airport that actually accommodates planes and has a concrete runway was finished around 1975 to provide airline service to the upcoming mega-resort Ixtapa.

Thousands of workers descended on the area to find employment in Ixtapa but Zihuatanejo remained a quaint little fishing village. Then, two unrelated events occurred, which were to drag Zihuatanejo into the 21st century. The information highway created by the Internet and used globally by the late 90's and the opening of the Zihuatanejo-Morelia highway which was complete in 2006 make information and access to the area easy—much to the dismay of the thousands of tourists that had been trying to keep *Zihua* a secret since the 60's. Bye, bye, quaint fishing village—hello big town with all the inherent problems—trash, noise, a scramble for the almighty dollar, etc. Some of the charm is gone but the beaches remain beautiful and the people friendly. I'm just so thankful I was able to enjoy the area before the fight for the tourist dollar began!

Orientation

Facing the bay, from the *zócalo* or town-square, the beach to the northeast, unseen from town, is called *Contra Mar*. The snorkeling is excellent and this beach is no longer accessible by road since the gated community *Monte Cristo* became a reality. From *Topes in Paradise:*

Topless Tourists

Back in 1971, when I arrived, Zihuatanejo was still just a sleepy little fishing village with a population of less than 4000. Money was scarce but life was good. The events affecting the rest of the world had little or no impact on the Indian and mestizo residents. Although access to the outside world had been available for years, the truth is, there were few that would endure the hardships of getting to Zihuatanejo. The road from Acapulco was dirt—little more than a widened donkey path and the bus schedule, which was sporadic at best, took almost nine hours. That is, if it wasn't rainy season which extends from mid-May until November. There were three rather large rivers to cross and if they were overflowing as was usual during the height of rainy season, the buses would have to stop, disembark the passengers, have them wade across the raging torrents of water, and then be picked up on the other side by another bus, if one were available. This process often took two days, which was a big deterrent to tourists.

Upon reaching this quaint pueblo, by bus or car, the road to the beaches was dirt and strewn with boulders the size of pregnant sows. The main road ended abruptly at the zócalo and the main beach, Playa Principal. Along this rather short beach were the main government offices at the south end and at the north end was the pier. There were three or four small one and two story hotels catering to the tourist or sports fisherman located on Playa Principal along with a few thatched open-air restaurants anchored in the sand. The bay curved north and south like the horns of a steer. To the north, a small rickety bridge, connected "downtown" Zihuatanejo with the portion of town known as La Noria, where most of the resident fishermen lived. A small estuary flowing under the bridge provided safe haven for the pangas used by the locals and ended perhaps 300 yards deep at the turtle factory. The beach in this area, unseen from town, is known as Contra Mar. Situated at the mouth of a dried-up riverbed, Contra Mar is often referred to as "pebble beach."

No one lived on this beach as it was very inaccessible from town. The path was treacherous and only for the adventurous. It was the perfect place for nude sunbathing and swimming, a very popular spot with the hippie crowd.

Three gorgeous, well endowed young ladies from Canada made the hazardous trip from Acapulco to Zihuatanejo and rented a bungalow at Milagro adjacent to mine. They wanted to see everything so we planned a day outing at Contra Mar. When we arrived, they immediately shed their bikini tops and jumped in the water. I decided to go exploring up to the mouth of the riverbed and told the young women I'd return in a short while.

The Mexican Navy, whose job it is to patrol the beaches, regularly descended upon Contra Mar, hoping to get a glimpse of females' au natural. I had been remiss in mentioning this to the women. When I got back I found three indignant and tearful young women tired of treading water. The soldiers had surprised them and picked up their swim tops. Using sign language, the soldiers had wanted, of course, the women to get out of the water and retrieve their tops. They adamantly refused. This went on for a while and finally the soldiers tired of the game and carried their swim tops to the highest point on the hill and hung them in a tree. They then moved a few yards away and were resting on some rocks. I ran up the hill and screamed all the obscenities I knew at the soldiers—all the while they were laughing hysterically but it did motivate them to get off their butts and retreat to town. I retrieved the swim tops for the young ladies and we trekked back to Zihuatanejo. The incident was not reported to the commandante and the girls didn't ask me to be their tour guide again.

The hillside community next to *Contra Mar* is comprised of homes from modest to luxurious and is known as **El Almacen**. House rentals in this area are usually reasonable and many foreigners have rented here for periods of time. There is a constant problem with water so if you expect all amenities all the time this is not an area for you. Remember to figure in the cost of water if desirous of renting in this area. A *pipa* of water, 10,000 liters, is a minimum of $40.00 U.S. and four a month is a conservative figure.

The neighborhood to the northwest over the bridge is known as **La Noria** or *Lázaro Cárdenas*, mainly populated by local fishermen. A fixed bridge (as opposed to our old funky wooden bridge) connects *La Noria* to *El Centro*. The neighborhood of **Emiliano Zapata** is located in the rugged terrain on the far side of *La Noria*. It is not a desirable tourist destination.

Vicente Guerrero located adjacent to *Emiliano Zapata* is a very modest neighborhood containing a large commercial zone situated along *Avenida Morelos*. The *centro social* (a large open air patio with room for dances and social events) is located here.

Playa Principal and *El Centro* extend from the canal to the municipal pier with the northern boundary *Avenida Morelos*. *El Centro* is the expression used to refer to the downtown area of any city or town. The *Playa Principal* is not the best beach because it is highly polluted but tourists and locals use it extensively.

Numerous restaurants and souvenir shops populate the *Paseo del Pescador* or boardwalk adjacent to the *Playa Principal*. At the canal end is the archaeological museum. The other end of the boardwalk culminates at the pier where the port captain's office is located. The ticket office for the purchase of tickets to *Playa Las Gatas* and Ixtapa Island can be found at the pier. Arrangements can be made here to rent sport fishing boats. Also located here is the cruise ship terminal containing a bar, fax machine, phones, and information service, which is open only when ships are in port which now means almost never.

Dominating the center area of the *paseo* is the *zócalo*. It is the focal point of the community where patriotic holiday ceremonies, celebrations, and public exhibits are held.

On the water side of the *zócalo* is the basketball court. There is always a game going and occasionally volleyball is played here. Most Sunday evenings, cultural events for the community are held here. One might view skateboard competitions, clowns, poetry readings, and lots of singing and dancing.

The high concentration of commercial buildings, retail stores, restaurants, and hotels of *El Centro* result in heavy pedestrian traffic from early morning until late at night.

Next to *El Centro* and behind the market is the neighborhood of **Las Manzanas**. Principally a middle-class neighborhood, numerous hotels and apartment buildings have been constructed since 1982. A few restaurants and service stores comprise the perimeter.

Playa La Madera consists of a hotel zone interspersed with residences. It is adjacent to the *Playa Principal.* A concrete path and bridge from town now connects the two. The concrete path along the water is in deplorable condition—it's not safe to walk at night as the lights have burned out or been stolen. Most of the hotels and bungalows located here have full cooking facilities and this is a favorite spot with long-time visitors.

On the south side of *Playa La Madera* is the community of **Darío Galeana**. Largely residential, it has expanded greatly in the past few years.

Adjacent to *Darío Galeana* and bordered by the canal is the *colonia* of **El Embalse**. This was a relocation area for squatters from other parts of town.

Across the canal between the *Kyoto Circle* and the major highway to Acapulco is located the *colonia* of **Super Manzanas**. Many lovely homes line the streets with a few apartment and condo projects built in recent years. Many Americans live in this area as it is considered safe and quite close to town.

Adjacent to *Super Manzanas* is the area of town known as **La Boquita**. The telephone office is located here as is the hospital. The perimeter is commercial in aspect, and includes car, soft drink, and beer distributorships. Most importantly, the huge *Comercial Mexicana* grocery store is located here.

Between *Playa La Madera* and *Playa La Ropa* are numerous restaurants, private homes, and some rental property.

Playa La Ropa is the largest beach in the bay and was developed on former *ejido* land. Many Americans and other foreigners have chosen to make this area their home, so many in fact, that the southeast end of *Playa La Ropa* is known as gringo gulch. There are numerous hotels, bungalows, and restaurants here. The name *Playa La Ropa* (meaning the clothes) is derived from a time when a Chinese galleon had problems in a storm and lost a load of clothes, which later washed up on the shore.

Beyond *Playa La Ropa* beach is **Playa Las Gatas**. *Las Gatas*, the cats, is named in honor of a small shark that has whiskers and no teeth. This *pez* looks like a cat in facial features and is very playful, now rarely seen.

There is a footpath of sorts between *Playa La Ropa* and *Playa Las Gatas*. It is not a particularly difficult walk but I recommend the water taxi service from the pier. It is supposed to run from 8:00 a.m. until 4:30 p.m. every fifteen minutes and costs less than four dollars for a round-trip ticket. It is a small price to pay to assure one's safety as from time to time there have been some muggings on the path. From *Topes in Paradise:*

Naked as Jaybirds

Robberies in Zihua seem to be cyclic in nature, a rash of many and then a lull. The fall of 1990 we were having a rash. There were robberies all over town and especially on the footpath between Playa La Ropa and Playa Las Gatas.

Sitting with Bill Fisch on the second story of Rossy's one afternoon I saw two Canadian men I had met the previous evening in town. They were walking on the beach and I yelled to them to join us. They declined saying they planned to walk over to Playa Las Gatas. I warned them about the robberies and suggested they take the shuttle from the pier, as it would be much safer. These were two large, muscular macho men, and they just laughed at me.

About an hour later, a young Mexican boy approached my table. "Linda," he said, "your friends are hiding in the bushes down by Tania's house and they need your help. They said you would give me some pesos to deliver the message." I had no idea what friends he was talking about and why they would be hiding in the bushes but naturally I decided to find out. I gave the young boy a few pesos and walked down to the end of Playa La Ropa and sure enough, squatting in the bushes on the side of Tania's house were the two Canadians—stark naked! On their walk to Playa Las Gatas, two men with guns jumped them and took everything including their skivvies.

When I was able to stop laughing, I went to the stick house and borrowed some shorts for them to wear and then delivered them back to their hotel. I was soooo good. I never said, I told you so.

A few families live on *Playa Las Gatas* and there are restaurants, dive shops, and Owen Lee lives at the far end of the beach. *Playa Las Gatas* is known for its point surfing and the clarity of the water. Definitely the most popular snorkeling spot and during peak season, especially on the weekends, the beach is packed.

A path behind *Playa Las Gatas* and a 45-minute walk uphill will take you to the lighthouse. One is rewarded with a breathtaking view of the bay and ocean. Another path leads to a small cove called **Playa Manzanilla**. A new road has been completed on the backside of *Playa Las Gatas* to access the new luxury development where lots start at over $100,000 U.S.

Two other neighborhoods of note to complete the orientation are **El Hujal** and **Agua de Correa**.

Leaving town, driving past the monument entitled *Fuente del Sol Naciente* (source of the rising sun) is a golden ball supported by three orange columns—to the south is Acapulco. The highway is lined with numerous restaurants and commercial establishments. The most important to my mind are the two *Pemex* stations (gas stations). Behind the central gas station is the neighborhood of *El Hujal* where numerous lovely homes are situated.Further along the highway one passes on the left the original settlement named **Agua De Correa**. It is largely residential and includes some of the oldest homes in the area. A dam constructed above the neighborhood holds back the stream that once carried water to the estuary of *La Boquita* in *Zihua*. The town cemetery is located here. *Agua de Correa* is populated mostly by Mexicans and many tourists never bother to explore this oldest and perhaps one of the most interesting parts of town.

I have purposely included some of the outlying neighborhoods in the orientation because some of the better bargains in food and lodgings are to be found in these areas.

The guidebooks extolling Mexico on $40.00 U.S. per day do not apply to *Zihua* and certainly not Ixtapa. Admittedly, there are a few hardy souls who can and do manage but the days of cheap holidays in *Zihua* have gone the same route as the burro—almost extinct. Good friend Rod Bishop keeps threatening to write a book on how to visit Mexico on $250.00 U.S. a day. Hotel prices have risen dramatically as have restaurant prices and the combination puts a strain on most wallets–along with the hefty airfares.

I have tried to be as accurate and fair as possible in the evaluation of everything in this book but I know my prejudicial nature surfaces from time to time. Truly, it is my sincere desire to provide accurate information and helpful tips to visitors and locals alike but the people who know me, know I'll tell it like it is.

This revision, I have identified places mostly by their general physical address as opposed to a number on a map. *Zihua* finally put up street signs with names in 2010. My friend Joy, who lives here full-time said she knew more street names in San Miguel de Allende than *Zihua*. Since most of the buildings downtown are homogenous or color co-ordinated, I feel it's time for people to learn the street names. The to assign a number. Most are the street name followed by s/n (*sin numero*). Following is another interesting article by Michel Janicot published in ADIP regarding street names. I took the liberty of editing "down" this article as it was extremely long.

Much has been written about the last emperor of the Aztecs, whose name in *Náhuatl* means "setting sun" or "falling eagle." book is being published as an e-book as well as a regular book and I've noticed that maps do not integrate well in the e-book format. Furthermore, to my knowledge, there are no really good maps of *Zihua* that could be tailored for the book format. Although *Zihua* has 130,000 plus residents, probably 80% of the town and surrounding neighborhoods do not have "physical numbers" in their address. I went over to town hall to find a number for my property. Firstly, they were amazed that anyone would want an assigned number and secondly, there are very few numbers–only lot numbers. People "arbitrarily" give their home or business a number–I numbered my house #4. Two doors down my neighbors have #36. Directly across the street is #1 and next door is #31. As I said, it's up to the individual Cuauhtémoc had been critical of Moctezuma for his policy of appeasement against Hérnan Cortés. He was captured and tortured by the Spanish and eventually tried for treason and hanged. Cuauhtémoc is highly venerated throughout Mexico and you can find a park, school, street, or public buildings named after him in almost all Mexican hamlets.

Juan Alvarez, a native of Atoyac, Guerrero, was a wealthy young man who chose to become a cowboy and joined Morelos—fighting heroically during the revolution. He fought against the Americans and the French.

Pedro Ascencio was a pure Indian miner born in Guerrero who also joined *Los Insurgentes* and fought with Morelos. He is remembered as a man of great valor and courage.

Another son of Guerrero, Indian Ignacio Altamirano didn't learn Spanish until the age of 14. However, he made up for lost time by attending college. He went on to become a deputado, mayor, magistrate, and president of the Supreme Court. He founded an influential literary organization and published numerous magazines and wrote several novels.

Hermenegildo Galeana was born in Coyuca, Guerrero. He fought valiantly with Morelos and as a result was named *mariscal*, the highest rank ever bestowed upon a military man.

The fifth most illustrious hero of the Mexican Independence movement born in Guerrero is Nicolás Bravo. Although from an affluent Creole family, he did not sympathize with the Spanish regime. He fought valiantly against the Spaniards but was eventually captured and imprisoned for a time. He served in many important offices and also fought against the Americans at Chapultepec.

Vicente Guerrero was another insurgent leader who allied with Juan Alvarez against Iturbide. It is unclear if the state of Guerrero is named after him or whether named after the word *guerrero*—a warrior. He suffered betrayal and kidnapping and was eventually executed by a firing squad.

Zihuatanejo honors two women who fought in the Independence movement, Antonia Nava de Catalán and Catalina Gonzalez. Nava was born in Guerrero and during the revolution was known as La Generala. During the fierce battle of Jaleaca, food became so scarce that the leaders decided to kill and eat captured soldiers. She said, "We want to be sacrificed in support of the Independence movement." Gonzales was also part of the battle but little is know about her.

Ejido (street) refers to land granted by the federal government to the community and held in common by its inhabitants. Famed revolutionary general Emiliano Zapata formulated the concept of Ejido with his slogan *"Tierra y Libertad."*

Recognizing the importance of music in the daily life of its residents, the city of Zihuatanejo named one of its streets in honor of one of Mexico's best known composers and guitarists, José Agustín Ramirez born in San Jeronimo. His songs remain as permanent as the flowers of the Guerrero coast.

The two small alleys connecting Nicolás Bravo and Juan Alvarez streets are named for two poets and writers, Carlos Pellicer and León Felipe.

All of the above downtown streets are encompassed by Benito Juárez to the east, José Morelos to the north and Cinco de Mayo to the west. Every city in Mexico has at least one of its streets named after one of these famous men or women of Mexican history.

Behind the municipal market lies an area whose streets are named for fruit bearing trees–delightful sensory names: *mandarinos, cerezos, ciruelos, palmas, palapas, aquacate, mangos, naranjos, cocos, guayabos, higo* and the omnipresent *limones*. Editor Victoria Priani has informed me that almost all trees are masculine and all the fruits are feminine.

The *Playa La Madera* area has three major streets: *Adelita, Valentina, y Eva Sámano de López Mateos*. As every student of Mexican history knows, the first two were famous mythical women who followed their men fighting on the front lines during the Revolution.

Atop the hill is Eva Sámano de López Mateos, named for the wife of Mexican president López Mateos. As the First Lady of Mexico, she devoted herself to raising funds for special projects, schools, hospitals, and the like. Zihuatanejo's high school is named after her.

Quite the diverse picks for naming of the streets—from war heroes to mythical entities.

Crime, Climate, and Cost of Living

These are the three most often asked questions of locals and need to be addressed somewhere in the guidebook. I think the following article borrowed from the *San Francisco Chronicle* addresses the crime issue best:

Quick—which national capital has the higher murder rate: Mexico City or Washington, D.C.?

If you answered Mexico City, you'd be in good company—after all; Mexico is a war zone, isn't it? But you would be wrong, on both counts.

Based on FBI crime statistics for 2010 and Mexican government data released early this year (2011), Mexico City's drug-related-homicide rate per 100,000 population was one-tenth of Washington's overall homicide rate - 2.2 deaths per 100,000 population compared with 22. (Drug violence accounts for most murders in Mexico, which historically does not have the gun culture that reigns in the United States).

And while parts of Mexico can be legitimately likened to a war zone, drug violence afflicts 80 of the country's 2,400 municipalities (equivalent to counties). Their locations have been well publicized: along the U.S. border in northern Baja California, Sonora, Chihuahua, Nuevo León and Tamaulipas states, and south to Sinaloa, Michoacán and parts of San Luis Potosí, Nayarít, Jalisco, Guerrero and Morelos states.

The flip side is that more than 95 percent of Mexico's municipalities are at least as safe as the average traveler's hometown. Yucatán state, for example, had 0.1 of a murder for every 100,000 people in 2010 - no U.S. tourist destination comes close to that. Most cities in central Mexico, outside of the scattered drug hot spots, have lower murder rates than Orlando.

It would seem fairly clear—fly, don't drive, across the border into the safe regions. Yet whenever people say they are going to Mexico, the invariable response is "Aren't you afraid?"

Media sensationalism accounts for much of the wariness. "Gangland violence in western Mexico" "Journalists under attack in Mexico" and "Mexico mass grave toll climbs" sound as if the entire country were a killing field. The story might name the state, but rarely the town and almost never the neighbourhood. And some reporters apparently are confused by the word "municipality"—some of the killings reported as being in Mazatlan, for example, actually happened in a town miles away from the city - akin to attributing East Palo Alto's slayings to San Francisco.

But the biggest factor may be that travellers looking for a carefree vacation simply find it easier to write the entire country off than to learn that areas to avoid.

The Mexico Tourism Board is working to change that. Efforts so far have concentrated on getting accurate information to travel agents, who funnel the lion's share of tourism to Mexico's popular destinations. Independent travellers' primary source of information is the State Department travel alerts (travel.state.gov), which are finally getting better at pinpointing the trouble spots.

To date, 283 U.S. citizens have been killed in Mexico since 2006 according to the U.S. State Department. Most of these people had Mexican surnames and close family ties in Mexico. There were 435 murders in Chicago in 2010. Perhaps not a fair comparison but I just can't figure out what all the fuss is about. It seems a little silly to me to live in fear all the time and personally I have refused to allow the *"narcotraficantes"* or other criminal elements to affect my life profoundly. I still drive alone "the highway of death" between Cuidad Victoria and Harlingen once a year. That's not gonna change! In over 40 years and more than 60 trips driving to and from the Texas border, I have never once had the slightest problem. However, I am travelling more cautiously these days—I put new tires on my SUV as a precautionary measure against getting caught on the side of the road. I also now have a cell phone to call for help should it be necessary. I also didn't recently buy a newer SUV because a "little old lady with a blind dog in an 18-year-old Ford Explorer" is not a target for druggies or thieves or so I tell myself and so far so good. Newer SUV's are thief magnets and I know several people that have had their vehicles stolen at gunpoint in the area. Travelling by bus these days requires certain precautions. Many buses have been robbed at gunpoint—even the *directos* because the drivers tend to "pick-up" extra passengers and pocket the money. I immediately inform the bus driver that I will report him and write down all pertinent information from his credentials—this has kept many a bus driver from stopping for extra passengers and kept the bus on time. It doesn't always work but intimidates most bus drivers. I try not to travel with much money and nowadays, if I have to have my passport and ID, I put them in the luggage hold of the bus. Most thieves don't have the luxury of searching checked luggage. Recently, I travelled by bus to Guatemala. I had been told the ATM machines were not safe to use as crooks had learned how to "clone" credit cards so I took American dollars with me. I spent an afternoon sewing the money into clothing. The bus ride was 40 hours and not a lot of fun but I didn't worry about my safety or the safety of my stuff.

Now that I've covered national and international crime, let's move on to the issue of local crime which affects tourists, Mexican nationals, and foreigners. The crime rate in Zihuatanejo is very high—when sifting through the tons of material regarding our lovely beach resort; I noticed that I had written more stories about being robbed than anything else. I've personally been robbed in *Zihua* a total of 14 times that I can recall. There's a reason all the homes in the more affluent neighbourhoods have rows of barbed wire or electrical fences surrounding the property along with bars and cross bars on all the windows. The homes lacking these features have not been immune from thieves—the owners just can't afford the investment. Even with the above and security lights on my third floor, thieves broke into my house for the fourth time in less than two years, Christmas of 2010. They built a ladder to clear the electric fence, then used a crowbar to open the sliding glass door of my neighbour's bedroom, grabbed spare sets of keys to both houses and took what they wanted. I feel like I'm living in a maximum security prison—obviously I have too much stuff and it's oh so tempting to the poor.

Speaking of poor, this may be a good place to interject a bit about the make-up of the general population—now placed at 130,000–up from 40,000 back in 1992 before the huge building mania began in the area and the dramatic increase in day laborers. According to the 2010 census, the average educational level of *Zihua* is a dismal 8.3 years—meaning very few inhabitants over the age of 15 have completed more than junior high school. The census bureau counted only 535 residents with a college degree, which includes many of the foreigners living here. It's no wonder that *Zihua* with a small population of affluent residents is a breeding ground for poor, uneducated thieves. From *Topes in Paradise:*

Munching Lunch

When I wrote my first guidebook I didn't have a computer. Anita Lapointe offered me the loan of hers so I was in the routine of going to her house every day to sweat in her hot little apartment, learn the basics of DOS, and work on my book for several hours.

We were living on Playa La Ropa at this time, directly below the scenic overlook. Entrance to the house was from the road, through a short gated fence and down some 82 steps literally carved out of the dirt. The other entrance was from the beach and up 30 traditional concrete steps.

As I was unlocking the gate at three in the afternoon one day, I had the perception that something was amiss. From my vantage point, high above the house, I noticed there was a large hole in the roof that hadn't been there that morning when I left.

Instead of immediately running to the Villa de la Roca for help, I freaked and ran down the dirt steps toward the house. All I could think about were Bambi and Thumper (my two cockers) locked in the house. I had neither expectations nor perceptions of what I would encounter.

In an instant, as I put my key in the lock to open the door, I noticed the remains of someone's lunch on my table along with several empty beer bottles.

As I turned the deadbolt and slung the door inward, a young man holding one of my Henkel butcher knives in his right hand greeted me. I don't know who was more startled, me or him. I only know I let out a bloodcurdling yell and peed my pants. He lunged for me with the knife on his way out of the house and I managed to trip him but couldn't get hold of him. Continuing to scream, I chased after him around the side of the house momentarily, knowing I couldn't catch up to a scared, physically fit teen-ager with my knife. As I turned back to the house to check on my dogs, another young man came bolting through the door with one of my beer bottles in his hand for a weapon. Out of the corner of my eye I could see Carlos and Martha from the Villa de la Roca racing up the beach steps to my rescue. The young man swung the bottle at me and I managed to dodge it, receiving only a glancing blow. I tackled him to the ground but his strength was too much and he scrambled to his feet and raced up the steps with Carlos hot on his heels.

I sat on the porch crying and sobbing hysterically with Martha patting me on the back until I calmed down. The dogs were sniffing round me not understanding what all the commotion was about. Martha went to call Tim and I went inside to assess the damage.

The kids had only taken jewelry valued at about two-thousand dollars. They had a pillowcase (these are handy if you don't bring your own duffels) and it was filled with the TV, VCR, several of my dresses, Tim's shoes and pants, and other assorted items. Carlos returned with a grim look on his face. He had recovered my knife but couldn't catch the kid. The incident was not reported to the police as we didn't have home-owners insurance and I stayed home the next day to repair the barrel tiles on the roof.

I don't know what made me angrier—the fact that I lost some very expensive jewelry or the fact that those two asshole children, before breaking in through the roof, sat at my kitchen table and ate peanut butter and jelly sandwiches and drank Tim's beer!

Climate:

It is easy to say that during high season (December until Easter) the weather is generally balmy and the temperature rarely gets above 95 degrees and during low season or more or less between May and the end of hurricane season the weather is hot and humid and temperatures can reach into the 100 degree plus range. These statements are generally the rule but it seems that so far in this decade the exception is the rule. From 2000-2006, Mexico was in drought conditions similar to conditions currently in Texas. There was very little rain and temperatures, especially in August and September, reached 100 degrees plus daily. Between 2006 and 2009, the weather was more true to norm but in 2010 and 2011, we had the heaviest rainy season I and old-time locals can remember with lots of tropical storms occurring in late May and June.

Some people don't understand the effects of humidity. Humidity equals sweat and mold and mildew. I have an *equipale* table and chairs. I have to clean them every three days as on day three they start turning green—yes, green. That's mold growing on the furniture. I have to keep a fan blowing in the closets because the clothes start to smell of mildew. The fingers and ankles of many tourists sometimes swell as there is so much salt in the heavy, humid air; it actually penetrates skin causing sodium retention just as if one had added lots of salt to their diet.

High season brings balmy weather and lower humidity. For the locals, our blood has thinned and we can get downright cold. I have pictures taken at one of the *Troncones* full-moon parties and everyone is wrapped in a tablecloth for warmth because the temperature was in the mid–sixties. A couple of years ago, friend Tania called really early in the morning to invite herself over for a cup of coffee. Since this is something she had never done before, I asked why? She said she was so cold; she needed to drive in her car so she could use her heater!

The area is also subject to numerous earthquakes every year. Most last less than one second and are not noticed by the general population. Others last several seconds and while a little scary, rarely do these result in any damage. The big one that struck Mexico City in 1985 had its epicenter located 25 miles off our coast and broke several windows but didn't do any major damage except to the Ford dealership whose roof collapsed.

I hope these examples of our climate will give you an idea of what to expect, depending on the season, during your vacation. From *Wash Gently:*

The Case of the Crying Porpoise

There aren't too many earthshaking events in our little town, so that when anything out of the ordinary happens, it attracts a lot of attention. Such was the case of a baby porpoise who swam dangerously close to our bay shoreline and cried pitifully.

Word of the strange-behaving porpoise spread rapidly and soon the beach was lined with the curious and concerned. The porpoise would skirt the shoreline and shriek at the people assembled there. No one did anything and the porpoise flung himself ashore and continued his pitiful wailings. Several people picked him up and carried him to deep water but each time he would repeat his beaching act.

One elderly man on the beach began to cry. He had made a pact with his recently deceased wife to communicate with her in some manner after she was dead. He was sure that the crying porpoise was the reincarnation of his wife. Another witness was sure that a ship or a swimmer was in trouble and that the porpoise was trying to lead someone out to help them. Speculation ran from one extreme to the other.

A Mexican Air Force colonel gathered the baby porpoise in his arms and put him aboard his small launch while others splashed sea water on the baby to protect him from the sun. They released the porpoise in the open sea beyond the mouth of the bay, but when they returned with the launch, the baby was also back and keeping up his crying. Again they gathered up the porpoise and took him out to sea and again he returned to the edge of the beach. The third trip proved the charm and the baby porpoise swam out to sea.

That night an earthquake hit us and did extensive damage for miles around. Now, although there are skeptics, we know what the thoughtful little crying porpoise was trying to tell us.

Personally, I keep a close eye on the bay because I believe that one of these days our baby will ease in close to the beach and squeak out. "You dummies, I tried to warn you.

Cost of Living

Living in Mexico is certainly much cheaper than living in the States and that's one major reason there are so many Americans and Canadians that are permanent residents of the country. *Zihua* is more expensive than other areas of Mexico because it is a tourist destination. High gas prices, almost $4.00 U.S. a gallon at this writing, certainly result in higher food prices in the market. It would be safe to say that a single person renting an apartment would need a minimum of $1,500 U.S. per month to live. That would exclude someone that drinks imported alcohol and eats out a lot. Personally, I spend less than $800.00 U.S. a month during low season and around $1,200 U.S. a month during high season but I own my own home, buy local produce in the market, and eat out an average of only a couple of times a week. The same quality of lifestyle in the U.S. would run me in excess of $3,000 U.S. a month.

Quaint Customs and Local Legends

In order to really understand the charm and beauty of Mexico, one must possess a smattering of knowledge of the vast differences, both cultural and psychological, between Mexico and its North American neighbors. The following is an attempt on my part to initiate you into some of the more glaring cultural differences and to introduce you, the reader, to some of the local legends that inhabit our fair city. I hope you'll find this section amusing as well as educational.

The most obvious difference between Mexico and most other countries is language. By all means, try out your Spanish. Mexicans by nature are very patient and proud of their language and heritage. They are pleased to find foreigners trying to speak their language, no matter how bungling your attempts might be. Unless it's a very complicated matter you're trying to convey, with sign language and patience you'll usually succeed.

Many English words are quite similar to Spanish but have an entirely different meaning. Two that come to mind; the first, *estúpido* can be dangerous and the second, *embarazada*, potentially embarrassing. *Estúpido* does mean stupid but never use this word in reference to a Mexican, as it is extremely offensive. If you must convey your displeasure over something or someone, please use the word *tonto*. Better yet, keep your mouth shut.

Embarazada, on the other hand, does not mean embarrassed, but pregnant. I've heard a lot of gringo men use this word and the response is usually hoots of laughter.

The Mexican language is fraught with innuendoes. If you're not clear about the meaning particularly in using curse words, be very careful.

A case in point: Locally, the word *cabrón* (defined in the Mexican dictionary as a cuckold husband) is used extensively among friends and even acquaintances here in *Zihua*. It's used so often in *Zihua* than when I originally moved here, I thought it was a term of endearment. Shortly after my arrival, I went to Oaxaca to check on my clothing export business and was invited to join a large table of gringos and Mexicans for a drink at one of the lovely outdoor cafes. One of the Mexicans finished telling a rather fanciful story about *brujas* (witches) and *hongos* (magic mushrooms). My response was *"Ay cabrón, no lo creo."* The Mexican sitting across from me grabbed the edge of the table and flung it in my direction. I think he was about to punch my lights out when the Americans forcibly restrained him. Obviously, the word *cabrón* is not a term of endearment in the Oaxaca region.

This might be a good place to point out Article #33 of the Mexican constitution. If you, as a foreigner, insult or demean a Mexican, in any way, it is considered just cause for deportation. This sounds ominous and is in fact no laughing matter.

I have been threatened with Article #33 on numerous occasions over the years but no one has yet filed against me. When I'm really angry at a Mexican, I try to use it as a mantra to calm down. Sometimes it even works! From *Topes:*

Got Milk?

My favorite example of misplaced syntax concerning the word cabrón occurred in my early days of living in Zihua. I was dating a Mexican at that time, as was one of my best friends. Neither of us spoke Spanish well but we tried. We were attending a party one evening with our boyfriends and, in those days, the men outnumbered the women about ten to one. The conversation turned to food and the men were discussing how much they liked barbecued goat (cabra). My girlfriend, wanting to participate in the conversation, said to the assembled guests, "Oh, me gusta mucho la leche de cabrón." An ensuing silence filled the room and her boyfriend turned beet red. After an embarrassingly long pause, the conversation resumed and she turned to me in her soft Texas drawl and said, "Did I say something wrong?" "Yes," I replied. "We were talking about how much we all enjoyed barbecued goat and you told them you enjoyed the act of fellatio." She paled to such an extent; it was as though she had been caught in the very act. She was attempting to tell the assembled guests that she enjoyed goat's milk.

Social and Psychological Differences
(Customs and Confusion)

Mañana syndrome: The *mañana* syndrome is not a symptom of laziness or inefficiency, but rather a philosophy of an entirely different concept of time. Remember, you are in Mexico and on Mexican time. If you invite Mexicans to a party or function and tell them 7:00 p.m. chances are they won't show up until eight or nine—if you're lucky. When trying to get a mixed group together, I have solved this problem by telling the Mexicans to come at six and the *gringos* to come at seven. This way everyone shows up about the same time, more or less.

A commonly used term referring to time is *al ratito*, literally meaning in a little while. This could be several minutes or several hours, usually the latter. When I have an appointment here, I always carry a book. Sometimes while waiting, I get to read a page, usually a chapter, and sometimes it feels like I will finish the book.

An important Mexican custom is the *abrazo* or hug. Handshaking, hugging, and cheek kissing are the customs of saying hello and goodbye, or when stopping on the street for a moment's recognition, and these are never hurried or ended abruptly. Sometimes, it can take me two hours to walk down *Cuauhtémoc*, there are so many people I know and must greet accordingly. My parents were visiting a while back and my father decided to accompany me on one of these morning walks. When we finally reached our destination, three blocks from our starting point and an hour later, he asked in all seriousness if I were planning to run for mayor.

Trying to explain or understand a Mexican's logic can be a futile exercise. A maid may leave a job for no reason other than *ganas*—she felt like it. My friend, Anita Hahner of the *Búngalos Pacíficos*, hired a plumber to fix a leak. He needed a part and she gave him three dollars to make the purchase. He never returned, leaving valuable tools at the job site. From *Wash Gently, Dry Slowly:*

Gregorrio's Restaurant

Gregorrio is a very handsome man of about 45 years. He has a mass of curly gray hair and a matching handlebar moustache. His expression is always filled with good humor and his eyes sparkle with enthusiasm. He is a master of animated conversation and it is seldom necessary to understand Spanish to understand Gregorrio. He is very well educated and has a degree in accounting.

For 14 years Gregorrio was employed as an accountant but when his company expanded and Gregorrio was forced to travel around Mexico by light aircraft, he quit. He didn't like the suit and tie business anyway.

He opened a small, 10 table restaurant on La Ropa Beach in Zihuatanejo and became a chef. I became his premier customer, for he was an excellent cook and soon became a good friend. When the tourists were on the beach, Gregorrio did a good business, but most of the time, only one of two customers were in the restaurant at the same time. I often wondered how he stayed in business but Gregorrio seemed happy and undisturbed.

Independence Day (Sept. 15-16) is an important holiday in Mexico, and during that time the beaches are filled with people celebrating. The hotels are filled and most restaurants are operating at full capacity. On that day, I made my way to

Gregorrio's for a very late breakfast, fully expecting to find the restaurant filled with people. Instead, there was a closed sign at the gate and Gregorrio was at his ease in a hammock.

"Why?" I asked Gregorrio. "All this business and you're closed?"

Gregorrio raised his brows and explained very simply.

"I like a neat, clean restaurant, and on these holidays too many people come in to eat, so to avoid the clutter, I just close the restaurant."

He went back to his ease in his hammock and I went to a cluttered restaurant for breakfast.

The idea of planning seems unnatural. Businessmen would rather gamble on large, quick profits than long-term capital gains. The idea of saving money is not appealing to Mexicans. The most frustrating evidence of Mexican logic is experienced when one wants to rent a house or an apartment. As to be expected, rents are much higher during the winter months. Many individuals are desirous of signing a year lease and offer the owner a sum that, over the course of a year, would be much higher than the rental he or she wound receive if the residence was only rented during high season. However, Mexicans will not budge on this. They would rather keep a home vacant eight months of the year and hope they can rent it for four months at big bucks, but effectively earning less than they would on a yearly rental.

Almost every foreigner that lives here has experienced this rental phenomenon and we spend endless hours trying to analyze it. Naturally, this makes no sense to me at all. To most *gringos*, some money is better than no money but to a Mexican, *Así es*—that's the way it is.

Alan Riding, in his book *Distant Neighbors*, comments, "the Mexican works to live." The image of success is more important than any concrete achievement. This is nowhere more evident than at the extravagant fiestas held by many of the poor Mexicans to celebrate coming out parties for three-year olds, graduation from nursery school, and *quince años* (girl's fifteenth birthday parties) or lavish weddings. Huge sums of money are spent on these affairs. Quite often, Mexicans will ask an unsuspecting *gringo* to be a *comadre* or *compadre* to their child. This equates to a godparent and entails participating financially in the child's entire landmark important events throughout their lives. Many foreigners are happy to do this, as they are able to participate in the Mexican community. Others feel taken advantage of as it does become very pricey. Be very careful before you take on this type of responsibility.

Status and appearances are crucial throughout society. The poor spend ostentatiously to hide the "shame" of their poverty, going into debt to pay for village fiestas, lavish weddings, birthday parties and funerals. Among the more affluent, similar symbols proliferate. An expensive present reflects the wealth of the donor as much as the importance of the recipient. Men wrestle for the privilege of picking up the check in a restaurant, while the American practice of "going Dutch" is considered offensive. From *Wash Gently, Dry Slowly*:

Dining Out

Mexico teaches the new resident many things, patience being one of the most valuable. This virtue is often best learned in small village restaurants where meals are prepared for each individual order rather than mass produced.

After the meal is completed, the diner is then obliged to check the bill. Each item is checked and then all addition is checked. After the total price is agreed upon, the bill is paid.

One evening in a restaurant in Zihuatanejo, after a 3-hour dinner, the bill of a companion and I was finally resolved. For some unremembered reason, I felt an obligation to pay and insisted that I pay. My Mexican companion, Jorge, was equally insistent that he put the charges on an account, or "tab" which he ran at this particular restaurant.

After a bit of discussion between Jorge and me, the owner of the restaurant came to our table and whispered to me.

"Let Jorge put it on his account, and don't be concerned because it makes no difference. Jorge never pays his bills."

Another unusual phenomenon is the space invasion issue. Most North Americans have what is known as a comfort zone and invasion of this space can cause distress. This is unknown in the Mexican community. People tend to get right in your face and touch and gesture with their hands constantly. They also travel in packs and live in, to me, very cramped quarters. I've found that if a woman leaves her husband and takes her children with her, the men find it impossible to live alone and go back to their mother's home for comfort. Mexicans simply can't believe that I live in a two-bedroom, two-bath house by myself. It's simply not done here.

Another issue is speed. North Americans find it incomprehensible that the Mexicans will spend hours over lunch or dinner, stand in line without complaint for more hours—but when a Mexican man gets behind the wheel of a car, he thinks he's Dale Earnhardt Jr. at the Daytona 500. My only fear, when I travel to the States in my sturdy little SUV, is that I will get rear–ended. I drive a steady 70 miles an hour on the divided highways and it's as if I am driving like a little old lady. I'm passed by cars really putting the pedal to the metal at over 100 plus miles an hour.

Hard to comprehend is the Mexican attitude toward animals—especially household pets. The situation has improved over the years—there was a time when children would cross the street to kick a burro, dog, or cat. An irrational fear of pets is ingrained from an early age and a lack of respect of animals is the accepted norm.

In April of 2005, I purchased another *cachorra* (or puppy) cocker spaniel. At 5 pounds and 10 weeks, she was hardly an intimidating puppy. Daily I took her to the *Villa del Sol Residencias* where guests with very small children would come to play with her. Without exception each small child wanted to hug and kiss her. However, if I walk her downtown for an evening on the *Paseo del Pescador*, the small Mexican children scream, cry, and run away. From *Wash Gently, Dry Slowly*:

The Saga of Inez Garcia

Once upon a time in the small fishing village called Zihuatanejo in the south of Mexico, lived a most unhappy, unloved and unnamed puppy. This sad little battered creature shared only the name of "street dog" or "beach dog" from the habits of the "no-home" dogs who roamed the streets and beaches in search of sustenance. This particular dog, much like many of her street brothers, had an ill-defined scheme of colors that could best be defined as similar to the stripes of the tiger, although somewhat duller tan and black. In structure she most resembled a whippet that had been rejected from that classy clan. Her heritage was unknown unless one chose to recognize "beach dog" as a classic breed of distinction.

As with many of life's ironies, the tough life for this little beach dog grew worse as she grew into maturity. She was brutally attacked by packs of grown and oversized male dogs and while still only a child-dog she became pregnant. She sought help; refuge and attention among the street people but was repulsed by rocks and sticks that were throw at her and by the kicks from those whom she approached. One brutal kick from the boot of a cruel man broke her pelvis and kicks reduced this frightened pathetic puppy to a quivering mass of pain and she was further abused by others who passed by her.

What thoughts about mankind must have coursed through the throbbing head of this lonesome and injured puppy and how confused she must have been. Her only crime is that she was not born of royalty and that she lived where man was busy scratching out an existence for himself and could not be further burdened with the support of a lowly, mongrel dog. She meant no harm and posed no threat to anyone, asking only for a bite to eat and a soft pat on the head. Instead she was beaten with sticks, stones, and the jackboot of man. She offered love and companionship and received only cruel abuse.

Then, a man who himself was afflicted with one of life's ironies and was confined to a wheel chair, came upon this battered puppy and his heart went out to her. He and his wife, for reasons known only to them, adopted this wounded puppy and named her Inez Garcia. They took her with them to Guadalajara where she was given medical treatment and all the necessary immunizations for taking her from Mexico to the United States. After arrival at their home in Bucks County, Pennsylvania, Inez was treated for all the many ailments from which she suffered. Cesarean section was performed to relieve her of the puppies she could not deliver because of a broken pelvis.

Inez prospered and although she walked a bit crooked because of her many injuries; she became a proud dog and a loved pet. When the owners returned to Zihuatanejo the following year they brought Inez along. Here, she was allowed to run free along the beaches during the daytime but was restrained at night. During one of her daytime romps she somehow aroused the ire of a man who chopped her across the shoulders and side with a razor sharp machete. Some children brought the bleeding Inez to her owners who thought that she was mortally wounded and should be put sleep. A veterinarian who was called to administer a sleep drug thought he could repair the terrible cuts and save Inezs life and after two weeks in intensive care she was on the road to recovery again!

After her recovery, Inez had more problems as her owners were changing their place of residence and could no longer keep her. Tom and Donna Hoopes, a couple of gentle persuasion, knew the owners and were very familiar with the story of Inez. They chose to adopt her. Tom and Donna live in Muscatine, Iowa, and Inez was delivered to them from Pennsylvania, arriving at their home as a passenger in a prestigious new Rolls Royce. Disney and his magicians could hardly invent such a scheme; this nondescript, abused dog, this scarred and abused survivor of tragedy, sitting as a pampered queen among the luxurious appointments of this exclusive car, a luxury afforded only a few humans.

An immediate love affair blossomed between Inez and the Hoopes four-year-old daughter; an affair that has become stronger as they have been companions for the past six years.

Inez, at two years old, was enrolled in a dog obedience class where she was the only dog without these snobbish papers of registration and breeding. There, disdaining her lack of documented heritage, she finished first in the class of more than 100 other dogs. Regardless of her excellent performance she couldn't be awarded a fancy ribbon because she didn't have the proper papers. It was a small matter that she didn't get a ribbon, for Inez doesn't need this type of trappings to show her class. She has the love of her people and a big velvet chair of her own. In return, she gives her love and undying devotion to those who love her and whom she loves.

Although the news is filled with stories of man's inhumanity to man and animal, every once in a while the soft and humane side of man surfaces in a story such as this of the Hoopes and Inez Garcia. All too bad that such things can't become universal and the bad ones the exception.

Salute to Tom and Donna and to the original rescuer of Inez, travelers and visitors with a heart as soft as a marshmallow and to Inez who had a will to survive as stout as granite. May they all enjoy each other for many years to come and may Inez some day pass on the message to other dogs that mankind is not all bad.

Many *gringos* have made the comment that there doesn't seem to be any prejudice in Mexico. This is incorrect. There exists in Mexico a very strong class system. Lightness of skin seems to be an important parameter. Generally, the more Spanish the blood, the higher the class. At the bottom of the system, one finds the Indians. Next are the *Mestizos* (mixed Indian and Mexican blood). When a scapegoat is needed those in power can and often do use the Indians. A case in point: Many years ago, the governor of the state of Guerrero held a conference inviting mayors and other important individuals to discuss the decline of tourism in the state and decide what action could be initiated to advance tourism. Traditionally, the Indians, who are the indigenous artisans, have produced and sold their wares on the beaches and in the streets of tourist resorts. The conference decided that the Indians were to blame for the decline of tourism because "they hassled the tourist" to buy their products. As a result, they were banned from selling on the beaches. Indian markets were erected to house these individuals and their wares. In defense of the conference, I must say that the vendors in Acapulco had gotten out of hand but here in *Zihua*, there was never a problem. In recent years, authorities have backed off on this particular cause and we do have vendors back on the beaches but alas, my *pan dulce* woman and peanut man have disappeared.

According to Alan Riding, Mexico still has between eight and ten million Indians divided into fifty-six recognized ethnic and language groups and speaking over a hundred different dialects. There are 1.5 million Indians who speak *Náhuatl* and fo| many of these Indians, Spanish is a second language and in *Zihua*, there are many of the older generation that still do not speak Spanish. Since the conquest, all have been waging a battle against assimilation and disappearance. Their very existence is a tribute to their determination.

Proud of its Indian past, Mexico seems ashamed of its Indian present. Government buildings are covered with murals and sculptures extolling the heroism of the Aztecs, while museums house the exquisite jewelry, pottery, and artifacts found in pre-Hispanic ruins. But the Indians themselves, the direct descendants of that "glorious past," remain a conquered race, victims of the worst poverty and discrimination to be found in Mexico today. They have lost most of their communal lands, their culture has been besieged and eroded by "civilization" and even their past has been stolen from them.

Yet the strength and resilience of their religious and cultural vision of the world have helped preserve a separate Indian identity. Our own Sailfest was started to help the *Náhuatl* Indian children learn to speak Spanish so they could attend school. Many of these original enrollees are gifted and are being helped by the foreign community in their educational endeavors.

Another strange custom in Mexico is the use of titles. Titles are enormously important to the class system. Anyone who has graduated from college or university is always addressed by a title. Titles of nobility were banished by the 1910 Revolution, but new ones appeared. Such titles as *Don* and *Doctor* commonly used in other Latin American countries are seldom encountered in Mexico. But at lower levels of the bureaucracy and in business, to be a *licenciado,* or university graduate, in itself implies a sphere of influence and requires the wearing of suit and tie (except of course in the tropics) as evidence of clout. Academic achievement is less important than social style, and not a few self-confident politicians assume the title *Licenciado* without possessing a degree. More subtly, the head of an office is referred to, not as *Licenciado* So-and-So, but as *El Licenciado*, as if no other existed. At more senior levels of power, the President or a minister is know simply as *El Señor*, a title which normally means Mr. but preceded by the definite article becomes "The Lord" in a manorial or religious sense and is the most deferential form of reference. The title *Maestro* has several functions. A plumber, painter or carpenter will expect his skills to be recognized in this way, but many senior officials consider it important to give classes at the university, if only to be addressed as *Maestro*—teacher—by both their students and their former students.

If one has not gone to a university but has reached a high level of success or are over 50 years of age, they are referred to as *Don* or *Doña* (in the rare case of female achievement). Failure on the part of a foreigner to acknowledge these titles is a social gaffe. To the *gringo* it seems a rather silly affectation but an important one to acknowledge. When I first moved to *Zihua*, most of the locals called me *chaparrita* (meaning loosely, cute little girl). Nowadays, I'm often addressed as *Doña* Linda—yes, I am 40 years older but I don't need to be reminded on a daily basis.

Alan Riding in *Distant Neighbors* explains that formal and obscure language is probably the Mexican's prime weapon of self-defense. Using seemingly meaningless words and phrases, he can protect his emotions; avoid the risk of committing himself, and even lavish praise without feeling servile. The concept is simple: language has a life of its own, almost as if words rather than people communicated with each other. Empty promises and outright lies come easily since the words have no intrinsic value of their own.

Excessive frankness or directness is considered rude, and every substantive discussion must be preceded by small talk about family or political gossip. Language serves as the neutral ground on which people can relate without danger of confrontation.

The excessive violence in the area has certainly curbed my frankness and directness. I no longer give "the finger" or scream obscenities at rude drivers–especially if the driver is a young male with a $40,000 dollar car–a **very** common site around town.

People often ask of me what I feel is the biggest change in *Zihua* since I arrived. My answer is always the same–when I arrived there were four vehicles in *Zihua* and one of them was mine. Currently there are some 20,000 cars and taxis registered in the area and most are much newer than my 18 year old SUV.

Local Legends or *Los Ancianos*

One of the most often asked questions from tourists is "How many foreigners reside in Zihuatanejo–Ixtapa and how do they earn a living?" On average anywhere from 2000 to 5000 foreigners live in *Zihua* depending on time of year. Zihuatanejo–Ixtapa has a large number of snowbirds that return yearly to spend three to seven months here; some have been returning for over forty years. There are many variables, suffice to say, if you ask ten different local *gringos* the question, you'll get ten different answers. I used to call this section "colorful characters" but since all, with a couple of exceptions, are well into their sixties or more, I decided a new name was in order. In the last few years, I've noticed that the local rag *Despertar de la Costa* has called even youngsters in their fifties *ancianos*. I started watching for this diligently and I have discovered that if the individual being written about is a local with family ties in the community or of some importance, they are referred to as *gente de la tercera edad*. If they are a no count or a drunk found lying in the street, they are referred to as *ancianos*. I don't think the local rag thinks much of the foreign population and if one of us was to receive unwanted attention from the newspaper, I imagine we would be referred to as *ancianos*.

Since *Zihua* is almost exclusively a tourist-based economy, job opportunities are few and regulated by Mexican law. The law stipulates that a foreigner cannot hold a position that could be filled by a Mexican. Doctors, lawyers, accountants, and stockbrokers are not welcome to practice here. Electricians, plumbers, waiters, waitresses, and bartenders are equally unwelcome to practice their trades. As with everything else in Mexico, there are exceptions to the rule. Large hotels can, and do, employ foreigners in a variety of positions. In order to gain employment in Mexico, one must first obtain a written offer of employment from a registered Mexican employer and then change one's tourist status to that of *visitante no inmigrante*—FM3. The process is now easy and the cost is negligible.

With the election of a new PRI President in the summer of 2012, new immigration laws will be going into effect at the end of October, 2012 Details have been announced but. are unclear as of publication date.

Generally speaking, there are only a few categories in which a foreigner can be gainfully employed. One can be a schoolteacher or give English classes, since the government views native English speakers for teaching purposes an asset. Another alternative, and by far the most lucrative and popular, is the selling of real estate, be it time-share or full ownership. The Mexican government is desirous of foreign investment. It is wise enough to realize that the North American is much more likely to part with money to a fellow countryman or woman than release funds to a Mexican.

Several foreigners own businesses here, located on property they either own through a bank trust or through a Mexican corporation—*sociedad anónima.*

Big conglomerates are allowed to hire a limited number of foreigners in certain capacities. Managers and chefs of the large hotels are sometimes foreign. There are a few foreign hostesses at restaurants and numerous musicians.

This leads to the next most often asked question, "What brought these foreigners to Zihuatanejo–Ixtapa and what kind of people are they?"

Until the mid-seventies, the foreign population of *Zihua* consisted of a few hippies, non-conformists, and people avoiding stateside confrontation with the law for one reason or another.

Today, the foreign community is composed of a diverse group of individuals. The only common denominator shared by many, but not all, is the English language. Some live in luxurious homes in Ixtapa while others live in modest adobe houses. Some like to party every night while others are never seen in town after dark. Spending quality beach time with friends is a necessity for some of us while others shun the beach. Very few are young and just starting a family while most have retired and are enjoying visits from their grandchildren.

Our peers in North America or elsewhere generally consider us non-conformist. That's a label and I don't like labels, but I guess, "When the shoe fits, wear it."

I'm most appreciative to the following individuals for sharing their particular *Zihua* stories with me. I hope you, the reader, will enjoy them as much as I enjoyed writing them.

Isabel Fortune

Isabel first heard of *Zihua* in 1967 from friend Gerald Shaw, but she was preparing to leave Boston with her family to live in Managua, Nicaragua. She and hubby Jim were able to visit in 1968 and fell in love with the pristine beauty of *Zihua* and vowed to return. This was accomplished in 1969 when they drove from New England to our Paradise bag and baggage with two of their four sons and set up housekeeping in a tiny home above *Playa La Ropa*. Son Marcos received home schooling from mom and spent most of his waking hours fishing, surfing, carrying firewood and water up the hill, feeding the burro (not a pet—a necessity) and studying. There was no electricity or water in their home. This is when Isabel formed a special bond with the other women living on *Playa La Ropa*—giving each other friendship and strength to raise their families and survive in a primitive environment.

In 1979 her wonderful Wampanoag husband Jim died. Isabel was devastated and moved to the Greek Isles to start her life over again. However, the umbilical cord of her life was firmly rooted in the soil of Z so she returned in 1982 and started making cakes for Coconuts a few days a week. Helmet Leins of the *Villa del Sol* has always known a good thing when he sees it and snagged Isabel off the street and made her his private secretary.

She returned to Coconuts in 1983 and became the "**hostess with the mostest**" and also started teaching school at Institute Lizardi.

Seeing the potential for explosive growth in *Zihua*, Isabel built a *ranchito* in the countryside of Zihuatanejo that gives her loads of privacy, lots of room, and bunches of fruit trees.

Isabel is truly a treasured "Fortune" for those of us that know and love her.

Esthela Buenaventura

In *Náhuatl*, Zihuatanejo means place of women, and in keeping with that name, women have historically played an important role in this community.

One such woman is Esthela Buenaventura who is originally from the San Francisco Bay area. Esthela first came to *Zihua* as a tourist in 1970 and rented a one-room palapa without electricity and water on *Playa La Ropa* for the extravagant sum of twenty dollars a month.

It was there on *Playa La Ropa* that Esthela became friends with other women of similar ilk who between the years of 1969 and 1973 had moved to *Zihua* from various places in the United States. The "sisterhood" to whom this book is dedicated refers to the women of *Playa La Ropa*, all are still here, and each is a vital member of the community. Back in the early 70's, Esthela was already displaying her talent as an organizer. She became the unofficial "runner" for the group and would make the long trek into town and back by foot twice a day for supplies, mail, gossip, etc. She finally obtained a burro to help with her burden.

As *Zihua's* popularity increased and more English speakers chose *Zihua* as their vacation destination, the need for bilingual speakers and menus, etc. became more apparent. Esthela's first job was assisting some of the local restaurateurs in translation and renovating menus to accommodate the growing numbers of tourists. Pepe Solórzano, of the *Posada Caracol* hired Esthela to head public relations at the hotel and she also began classes in English for the staff.

New opportunities arose for her talents and energies with the creation of the resort area of Ixtapa in 1974.

Esthela worked several years in Ixtapa as a travel agent and public relations director for various hotels. She is the only American to serve as a director of the Hotel Owners' Association.

With a Mexican partner, she owned and operated her own travel agency for two years. She worked tirelessly in Ixtapa promoting tourism to the area for many years. She now is retired and happily enjoying her free time.

One might say she has dedicated her life to tourism in *Zihua* and it's quite true to say that very few foreigners have been as dedicated or hard working in their efforts here.

Judith Whitehead

Judith first came to *Zihua* in 1969 for a vacation. She was in love with a man and "fell in love" with the place. The love affair with the man died but the affair with the place is still alive and strong. She returned for a year in 1973 to stay with her children who were living here at the time. Judith continued her career in the legal profession until 1987 when she reached a point in her life where she was free to pursue her own goals of happiness. Judith returned to *Zihua* and now has her own real estate company, Paradise Properties. Judith considers *Zihua* a magical place. Most, if not all, the permanent residents share this view.

Joe Wells

Joe is an excellent example of the human spirit's ability to adapt to a foreign environment and thrive.

Joe arrived in *Zihua* in 1972 with his mother Trisha. Since the *gringo* community numbered only about 10, Joey, being the only teenager, had little choice but to learn Spanish if he wanted to enjoy the friendship of his Mexican peers. He took to the task tenaciously, true to his colorful character, and soon mastered the language with all of its color and expressiveness. The family eventually returned to California but Joey couldn't stay away, returning often to enjoy his passions for surfing, playing basketball, and to see his sweetheart, Pepina, daughter of long time resident, Helena Krebs. Eventually Pepina moved to California to be with Joey. They were married there in 1977. They remained in California for a time until the allure of *Zihua* became too great and they ultimately returned to open a restaurant in 1984.

Their restaurant, **Café Marina,** located next to the basketball court in the *Casa Marina* complex, has been written up in numerous publications and is famous for its delicious pizzas and reasonable prices. It houses one of the local book exchanges which make it a popular spot with the foreign residents.

Nicole Dugal

Nicole first came to *Zihua* almost fifty years ago. Enchanted with this small fishing village, she vowed to return one day and make it her home. She spent many years living in Mexico City, Paris, and Cuernavaca. When her two lovely daughters were grown and finishing college, she was able to realize her dream of living on the beach. Nicole returned and negotiated a lease on a small 6-room hotel, which she eventually sold. Nicole's special flair for style and charm brought her to the attention of the owners of *La Casa Que Canta* where she helped design the rooms and manage. Her creativity can, if you're lucky, be seen in the design and interiors of many of the magnificent homes built in *Zihua* and *Troncones* in the last few years.

Jan Hardy

Jan is a retired speech therapist from Denver, Colorado. Jan first arrived in *Zihua* in 1980 on a vacation special offered by "Ports of Call"—a travel club operating out of Denver. It was love at first sight. Working for the school system, she had lots of vacation opportunities and returned frequently. Opting for early retirement in 1988, she returned to *Zihua* and bought two pieces of property. Jan taught English for years and loves to play Scrabble. She is very involved in the Mexican community, constantly on the go attending birthday parties, *brindis*, and social affairs. She actively promotes local artists. Jan loves living here because as she puts it, "I wake up every morning and have not the slightest idea what the day will bring. Every day is an adventure."

Jan has the best of both worlds, spending her winters in *Zihua*, and summers living in the Black Hills or traveling

Dewey McMillin

Dewey is the proprietor of *Casa de la Tortuga,* a seven-bedroom bed and breakfast located on *Playa Troncones.* Dewey was a commercial fisherman in the Pacific Northwest and began vacationing in *Zihua* when *Playa La Ropa* was considered strictly a hippie hangout. After being on three vessels that sank (on the last occasion, he spent four frigid hours in a lifeboat before rescue), he decided to change his lifestyle. Karolyn McCall, his long-time girlfriend, after spending a stressful and depressing eight years with the animal shelter in Seattle, decided a change was in order also. They sold their home, cashed out their retirement fund and in Karolyn's words "spent all the money here." Their first purchase was a 1965 retired school bus in which they loaded all their possessions and drove to *Zihua.* The *Casa de la Tortuga* had been a vacation home owned by Dewey and several buddies. He made arrangements to buy out the others and after a lot of hard work and much expense; it is now a thriving business enterprise. Karolyn and Dewey are no longer together but she is still part of the *Troncones* community. She has never lost her love of animals and has spent several years raising money for an animal preserve.

Dewey, a few years ago, reconnected with an old girlfriend from Seattle, and he and Jill got married in 2003.

Dewey, not one to rest on his laurels, has almost single-handedly developed the beach of *Troncones*, becoming a real estate tycoon. They live in their lovely home in Troncones and enjoy the good beach life.

Robin Bashbush

Robin first "discovered" *Zihua* in 1975. She had met a young man from Mexico City and moved there to be with him. Through him, she obtained employment with the American Benevolent Society where she worked for eight years.

They vacationed in *Zihua* every chance they could and she fell in love with this tropical paradise.

When Robin returned to the States, she was determined to obtain a job that would allow her travel to Mexico; hence, she became a flight attendant and proceeded to spend all her free time in *Zihua.*

On one of her many visits, she met Victor Bashbush, longtime resident, originally from Puebla. They were married in 1987 and Robin enjoys her "dual" lifestyle of working for weeks for the airline, then spending two weeks and sometimes more at home in Ixtapa with hubby and friends.

Tania Scales

In the very early 70"s, there arrived in *Zihua* a small group of women. This was not a planned union, as they came from all parts of the United States and none knew each other previously. They were in search of an alternative lifestyle and seeking a special place in the universe.

Remember, *Zihua* means land of women. Some individuals believe that in the entire world there is one special person for them. Along those lines, many believe also there is one special place.

Zihuatanejo is that special place for this group of women. All of them are still here and would never consider leaving. One such special woman is Tania.

Tania grew up in Ohio. In 1972 she was contemplating a trip to *Oaxaca* when a friend, recently back from *Zihua*, showed her a painting of a beautiful beach with an inscription written across the bottom, "Nothing is real unless it is now."

The painting touched her soul and she became determined to visit Zihuatanejo during her Mexico trip. When she arrived, she fell in love with this tropical paradise and, although she spent a lot of time in Oaxaca, she decided to make *Zihua* her home.

She eventually met and married Dan, an affluent Texan who had fallen in love with *Zihua* and with Tania. They commenced building a home high on the mountain of *Playa La Ropa*.

I personally considered Tania a little eccentric at this time of her life. She wanted a bathroom with a sunken tub and marble tile. I found it a little strange to watch the donkeys trudge up the mountainside hauling marble slabs. You see, there was no water or electrical service to the area at that time.

Mountaintop living lost its appeal when they had to share the neighborhood and their bed with scorpions, spiders, snakes, and other creatures. They eventually moved closer to the beach into what is affectionately known as the "long house."

The mothering instinct followed the nest building and Tania and Dan produced three beautiful daughters, all of whom were born at home in *Zihua*. Their names are *Sirena* (the mermaid), *Maya*, and *Ana Isabel* (who was named in honor of Isabel Fortune, one of the original group of women to settle here).

Tania spent the next several years rearing her beautiful family. However, with the girls occupied in school, Tania had a lot of free time on her hands and decided to indulge in her passion for Mexican folk art

She opened her own store, the **Galería Maya**, and stocked it with original, lovingly made, folk art items from all over Mexico and Guatemala. Her love of Mexico and the indigenous craftsmen of the country were reflected in the great success of her gallery. She knew personally all the artists whose crafts she displayed and many of the "starving artists" she had known have become master craftsmen with their works being shown all over the world. Unfortunately, Tania decided to close her store when the worldwide economic crisis worsened. Tanya remains a huge fan of indigenous craftsmen and has a marvelous collection of "goddesses" and women carved in wood. Please visit www.templomaya.com

Tania is one the *Zihua* success stories. She has a beautiful home and a beautiful family.

Michel Janicot

Michel was born in France in 1938. He received his B.A. and M.S. degrees from San José State University, and taught in Africa with the Peace Corps. He has written extensively on a variety of California historical subjects and decided to make *Zihua* his winter home in 1992. Michel prefers the simple life and speaks softly with a charming French accent. He has been a major contributor of extensive research material and articles for *Another Day in Paradise* magazine which is no longer published. He is a true authority on many of the historical aspects of our fair city and I love picking his brain.

When in residence, he likes to hang out on *Playa La Madera* during the day and can occasionally be found at Coconuts restaurant in the early evening enjoying a glass of red wine. I'm especially grateful to Michel for allowing me to use some of his research material in this book.

Victoria Priani

Victoria is another Texas gal who became disillusioned with the state of affairs in the States. She was living in Washington in the early 80's and decided to give herself a 30th birthday present in 1982 and visit *Zihua*. Over the course of a year, she returned four times and decided to stay. Like many of us in the beginning, we had some wild and crazy times. (Mexican men can be so much more romantic than their counterparts in the states). José Antonio Priani Piña (Pepe to his friends), much older and an esteemed and highly respected architect, met Victoria shortly after her arrival. He knew immediately that he would one day make her his bride but wisely put off pursuing Victoria until she had a year to settle down.

Pepe offered Victoria stability and a culturally diverse union that would immerse Victoria into Mexican culture and where she would learn to speak **perfect** Spanish. Because she is acquainted with Mexicans in all walks of life, she is capable of putting the right nuance and words to translations and/or work as an interpreter.

Pepe and Victoria shared a wonderful life together until his death in 2004.

Victoria is also an awesome Scrabble player and has a green thumb extraordinaire. She was my neighbor for five years and I miss her gardening abilities.

Victoria, like most of the women living here, couldn't imagine a life outside of *Zihua*.

Linda Fox

My love affair with Mexico began when I was five years old and has never diminished. My parents took me to *Laredo* and it was love at first sight. When friends in college were going on ski vacations during spring break, I would sneak off to Acapulco to visit friends.

After college graduation, I made a serious attempt to fit into the mainstream of life. I married my high school sweetheart, got a job as a social worker, picked up a mutt at the pound and rented a cute duplex in the Montrose area of Houston.

My husband, Mike, discovered the wonders of marijuana shortly after our marriage in 1968 and went from straight to strange. He quit his job at a bank, grew his hair long, and decided we should open a "hippie clothing store."

Deciding it would be best to indulge him in what hopefully would be a passing phase in his life, I acquiesced.

Mexican clothing was a hot ticket item in 1971 and we couldn't keep enough items in our clothing store to satisfy our customers. Our partner agreed Mike and I should move to Mexico and ship clothing back to sell.

Our first stop was Oaxaca where we made marvelous purchases and arranged to have a supply of clothing shipped to our store on a regular basis.

We loved Oaxaca but decided we preferred the beach. So, after taking care of business, we headed for Acapulco. I didn't like living in Acapulco so friend Al suggested I visit Zihuatanejo, a small fishing village about 150 kilometers north. He said it was quaint, quiet, and a tropical paradise and he had a good friend, Owen Lee, that lived there. I packed up the car, the dog, the doggie downers, and some stuff and took off at the crack of dawn.

Al failed to mention a couple of important items concerning this trip. Most importantly, he failed to mention the asphalt road dead-ended about ten miles north of Acapulco. Fortunately the month was March and rainy season had yet to begin.

There were few bridges but numerous rivers between Acapulco and Zihuatanejo so I had to detour from the dirt road and drive through the boulder strewn riverbeds. The trip took nine hours and I was a basket case by the time I finally arrived in Zihuatanejo.

Entering town, the narrow rutted dirt road passed by the *Zafari* motel and the old airport. *Cuauhtémoc*, at that time, had a dozen or so one-story houses and shops. It dead-ended at the *Zócolo* or town square.

It was the middle of the afternoon, and with the exception of one small restaurant, the town appeared to be deserted. The shops were shuttered up tight against the mid-day sun and I saw neither cars nor pedestrians. It was really ugly.

Weary with fatigue, Dude and I got out of the car. By this time Dude's doggie downers had worn off and he started howling.

Squatting on the steps of the restaurant, I also started to cry. This was the tropical paradise Al had described. I felt like I had descended into a scene from the Twilight Zone.

I knew I didn't have the energy to return to Acapulco that afternoon and necessity dictated I find accommodations as soon as possible.

As I wearily got to my feet, I noticed a man crossing the *Zócolo*. Immediately I knew he was a foreigner. Whether tourist or local didn't matter at that moment—I needed contact with a fellow human being that spoke English.

I launched myself at this unsuspecting soul. Fortunately, it was Owen Lee. Owen calmed me down and the next day, introduced me to the beginnings of "the sisterhood"—Margo, Grace and Esthela. As they say, the rest is history.

As one can see, the individuals living here come from all different walks of life and backgrounds. They share mostly the English language and a love of Mexico, especially Zihuatanejo. Living in a foreign environment can be difficult and everyone experiences minor, and sometimes major, difficulties that would never be encountered in a more civilized culture. Seven-Eleven's and big Mac's might eventually make it to the area but part of the fun of living in a foreign environment is learning to roll with the punches. The Mexican version of the Quick-Stop, *OXXO*, arrived in 2010 and the area is now home to at least a dozen, putting many mom and pop operations out of business. Regarding foreigners, there has been more growth in the community in the past ten years than in the last fifty. I have actually started dividing the foreign community into what I call pre and post CM (*Comercial Mexicana*), which opened on July 6th, 2000. Around that time, plans were on the drawing board to have stoplights. Most city streets were paved, Prodigy finally started working fairly well, and the banks, telephone, and electric companies went on-line and bills could be paid quicker and more efficiently. Also "chain" stores started buying and refurbishing downtown buildings, which have diminished the quaint fishing village look. Traffic increased exponentially and tour buses became a routine sight at the beaches. It's as if *Zihua* jumped from the mid-twentieth century to the 21st century overnight. The newcomers complain about how "tough it is to live here" but I refuse to listen because they have no idea what tough living means to those of us that have been here a long time. With the above in mind, in my humble opinion, Jimmy Buffet sums it up best.

**CHANGES IN LATITUDE, CHANGES IN ATTITUDE
NOTHING REMAINS QUITE THE SAME
ALL OF THE RUNNING AND ALL OF THE CUNNING
IF WE COULDN'T LAUGH, WE'D ALL GO INSANE**

What's That??

As with most places, *Zihua* has its own little unusual sights, customs, and peculiarities. This section is dedicated to an explanation of our weirdness, so to speak. You'll be an expert of the local scene without ever having to leave your hammock.

The Parthenon: High on the mountain above the *Playa La Ropa* road.

The following is an excerpt from an article written by our own Michel Janicot for publication in *Another Day in Paradise*. It was considered too radical for that publication but not mine.

The Partenón

Overlooking Zihua bay on the road to Playa La Ropa is a singular stone structure known as El Partenón. Access to the faux temple is by a cobblestone driveway that leads to the hilltop. Whereas the original Parthenon in Athens was built to honor the goddess virgin Athena, Zihua's Doric style replica was a monument built to satisfy the colossal ego of its owner, Arturo Durazo Morena.

Nicknamed El Negro, Durazo owed his political destiny to his childhood friend, José López Portillo, Mexico president from 1976 to 1982. The short, swarthy (thus the nickname El Negro) Durazo, "poverty-stricken and of uncertain parentage," was an apathetic student, a brawler and member of a juvenile street gang. As a bodyguard, Durazo shielded his friend from the tougher elements at the Benito Juárez School where they both studied and chaperoned Portillo's sisters to dance halls. Later Durazo became a bodyguard and chauffeur for Manuel Prieto, one of Mexico City's most notorious gangsters. Portillo appointed him Chief of Police for the Federal District after El Negro provided the president with security forces during the presidential election campaign. The appointment "briefly outraged the public" because Durazo was already under a grand jury indictment in the US on drug trafficking charges.

During his tenure as police chief, El Negro built up a huge racketeering empire, based on corruption, arms dealing and extortion. On a relatively modest annual salary of $18,000, Durazo somehow acquired 2 luxurious mansions, one near Mexico City and El Partenón. In 1978, appropriating titles to municipal ejido lands, Durazo embarked on the construction of the temple using various sources of revenue, including drug trafficking and the employment of police officers paid by the city, who built the mansion. (In a television interview, he declared that he and his wife had built the house in their spare time during weekends in Zihuatenjo).

El Partenón was built of marble imported from the famed quarries of

Carrara, Italy, luxuriously appointed with Hellenistic statues, paintings and murals, bronze sculptures and chandeliers, mirrored ceiling and walls, nine bathrooms and a Jacuzzi. The grounds had an artificial cascade and lake, a swimming pool, a private menagerie of exotic birds, wild felines and crocodiles, and let's not forget the disco. An underground tunnel led to Playa La Ropa. Portions of the tunnel are still visible at a point along the road to the beach.

The Durazo case came to light in 1982 after he and his protector, Portillo, lost their jobs—"and the scale of his embezzlement astonished even the Mexicans." Durazo's corruption "effectively cancelled two years worth of Mexico's tourist earnings," put officially at $1.1 billion in 1978.

With a new administration arriving in 1982, Durazo fled the country and was arrested by US authorities in San Juan, Puerto Rico, in July 1984. Reporters ask him how he had accumulated so much wealth and he replied with a straight face, "I'm a very astute investor."

Sentenced to 11 years and three months, he obtained an early release in March of 1992, after serving seven years and eight months. He died in Acapulco on August 5, 2000, of colon cancer at 77.

The federal government confiscated El Partenón when Durazo was sentenced to prison. In August of 1989, the state of Guerrero appropriated the property. Also, the family heirs started contesting the property as belonging to them.

The mayor of Zihua at one time was put in charge of selling El Partenón at auction but "nobody wanted it." The city petitioned the state to release the property to the municipal authorities "in payment of diverse debts incurred by El Negro," and would repair it and use it as a vista point, a convention center, or casa de cultura."

In November 2011, the villa was donated to the school of tourism here in Zihua; however, there was a question of who would pay for the restoration and for what purpose would it be used. In March of 2012, the heirs to the estate have filed yet another lawsuit claiming the property once again and nothing but litigation will happen for the forseeable future.

Buses parked all over town with motor running and no one inside:

Again, the Morelia highway has opened up our area to 40 million nationals—all considered potential tourists by city fathers. These buses bring folks from all over Mexico to spend a day or perhaps a day and a night in our fair city. Round trip from almost anywhere in Mexico is ridiculously inexpensive. For the most part, the people visiting are economically challenged and the local newspaper has dubbed them *los atuneros* or the tuna fishers. These individuals travel with their own provisions and traipse down the beach with coolers filled with food, soft drinks, booze, chairs, and everything imaginable they need to make their holiday complete without putting any money into the economy. The only thing they leave behind is their trash. The city fathers welcome these tourists *con brazos abiertos,* but are not willing to provide any infrastructure to accommodate them. Until 2010 there were no garbage receptacles anywhere in town, including the beaches. The homeowners association of *Playa La Ropa* put up $1100 U.S. before Easter 2010 to buy trash cans for the beach. I was at a meeting between city fathers and the association and heard the *registro* for garbage pick-up guarantee there would be three pick-ups per day during the very busy Easter season. Walking the beach daily I noticed the same garbage from the day before—except more of it and took pictures to prove it. However, so did the newspaper and they made a big deal of it (not that it made any difference at all).

The city provides only four pay restrooms costing five pesos/person and only one of these is close to *Playa Principal.* There are none on *Playa La Madera* or *Playa La Ropa.* When the city refurbished the street behind the museum, they didn't replace the restrooms located by the parking area for the *atunero* buses. I talked to the man that was in charge of the restrooms and he said they didn't replace them because they weren't used! I've heard it said that these people see our bay as their toilet and our beaches as their garbage can. Unfortunately, I have to agree with this statement.

***Capricho Del Rey*:** Where the *Playa La Ropa* dirt road dead ends.

As one sits facing the sea on *Playa La Ropa,* one can visualize (the jungle has almost completely repossessed the site) a fabulous hotel-restaurant complex climbing up the side of the hill to the left. This complex is the *Capricho del Rey* or whim of Kings. This complex got under way in 1968 when two outrageous Americans in concert with a Mexican partner decided to build a resort. Many talented artists were initially involved in the project but lack of money halted their endeavor in 1972. The Mexican partner was unfortunately killed in 1975 and the distraught widow decided to lease the project to a wealthy Mexican for a paltry sum of money. Later, realizing she had made a grave error, the widow and family began trying to regain control of the project. The legal battle was fought for more than a decade and the family finally gave up the property and now it still sits, abandoned and neglected, in all its glory; a true whim of kings.

Clusters of Really Ugly Buildings with Satellite Dishes on Road to Ixtapa:

These buildings are low-cost government housing, which contain over 19,000 units: a drop in the bucket compared to the true needs of the community but a valiant, if ugly effort.

A Man with a Steam Cart Blowing a Whistle:

This vendor is selling either hot dogs or *camotes*—sweet potatoes. You can purchase a white or yellow *camote*. My preference leans toward the yellow. The other whistle blower is sharpening knives—he'll get them really sharp but I am told his methods wreak havoc with the knives.

Creatures of the Day and Night:

Besides the assortment of look-alike dogs, cats, burros, and pigs, there are some indigenous critters that may not be familiar to a foreigner.

Zihua is home to a variety of iguanas or *garrobos* in all colors and sizes. They look like throwbacks to prehistoric dinosaurs but are not carnivorous, nor dangerous. They used to be sold in the market but are now considered an endangered species. You won't find them on restaurant menus, as it's now illegal to sell them for human consumption. After they are doused in chili salsa, it is hard to tell what they taste like. They do have sweetness like rabbit.

Most iguanas are small, ranging from one to two feet, but there are varieties that can reach six feet or more. They can be found in common (as on roofs or in back yards) or uncommon abodes. From *Topes in Paradise:*

Ladies, Look Before You Leak!

On the way home from the beach, I realized I should have used the bathroom at Rossy's before I left. By the time I pulled in the drive, I was in "distress." I opened the door and raced for the toilet. As I relieved myself, something scratched my behind—naturally I flew off the seat and landed on the bathroom floor with my *underwear around my ankles. It was a bit of a shock to say the least. Cautiously peering into the bowl I spied a **huge** iguana. Instead of leaving it alone, I took a pair of tongs from the kitchen to try and retrieve it and all I managed was to pull off its tail. I requested help from neighbor Victoria Priani and she calmly tried to extract it using towels and gloves—also to no avail. I then thought a man's input might be of help so I called neighbor Paul and told him I had an iguana in the toilet. Being a gentleman, he agreed to come over and assist in the efforts to remove the critter. When he arrived I opened the previously closed bathroom door and Paul said, "Where's the iguana? I thought you said it was in the bathroom." I replied— "in the toilet bowl."*

"Whoa, whoa, whoa—I don't do toilets," said Paul as he quickly made his exit.

I continued various extraction methods until it became dark. I decided to close the lid, put a rock on it, close the bathroom door, and wait until morning. It was gone. A once in a lifetime occurrence or so I thought.

In May of 2005, I was playing ball with my new cocker spaniel, Chuleta. We were in the hallway and I bounced the ball very hard and saw it could bounce into the toilet but instead bounced off the head of another iguana, which, this time was perched on the rim of the bowl! I panicked, having a new puppy in the house and rushed over to Victoria's once again. With plastic bag in hand, Victoria returned to my house and calmly picked up the iguana (still sitting on the toilet bowl) and deposited it in a tree. The lesson to be learned here—never sit on a toilet seat without looking first!

The *coatimundi* or *tejón* in Spanish looks like a raccoon with an anteater's snout. They make excellent pets if you are a night owl as they are nocturnal creatures. They are curious and cuddly and can wreak havoc in a home in the blink of an eye.

Geckos or *cuijas* are small, almost transparent lizards that should be part of every household in Mexico. The more geckos I see in my house, the happier I am. Cockroaches are their Beef Wellington and scorpions their double-fudge chocolate cake for dessert. They tend to leave small-pellet-sized calling cards but I'll take a little lizard poop any day to a scorpion bite. How do geckos manage to walk up walls and across ceilings? It turns out the little critters use atomic energy—not the kind that makes things go boom but the force of mutual attraction between molecules. The lizards have millions of microscopic hairs protruding from their feet. These tiny setae latch on through surfaces so tightly that they bond through molecular force. Most other creatures that like to stick closely to surfaces use friction, suction, glue, or wet adhesion. From *Wash Gently, Dry Slowly:*

The Gecko

One of my neighbors who live in the hills behind my house makes and sell her own special brand of granola. Before the transparent plastic bags invaded the village, the granola was packaged in a piece of newspaper and twisted closed at each end. The granola is excellent and I always accepted the news-wrapped package without question.

Now we have plastic bags that can be bought in town, so the granola maker packages her product in these see-through miracles of modern chemistry. The first batch of plastic packaged granola which I bought contained a live gecko. The gecko is a small, almost transparent, soft lizard with delicate, band-like markings. The gecko is harmless and really beneficial, for its diet consists mostly of insects. The gecko, when alarmed squeaks. I pointed out the very alive gecko that was included in my bag of granola. With almost total disinterest, the señora looked at the packaged lizard.

"It is free," she told me as she turned away to hide the twinkle of her eyes.

Then a giggled" Adios," and the gecko and I were dismissed.

Scorpions, or *alacranes*, are part of the downside of living in a tropical paradise. There are two varieties common in Zihuatanejo. The first is the large black scorpion, which can reach several inches in length and can scare the hell out of you. Actually its venom is not extremely potent and it is not considered very dangerous.

The smaller (usually one inch or under) are golden scorpions and the ones to be very wary of. Their sting can be fatal to children, pets, and even to adults should you have an allergic reaction to the venom.

Scorpions are nocturnal but I've seen them at all hours of the day and night. They prefer humid, warm, and dark lodgings; i.e., toes of shoes, under pillowcases and sponges, and in the creases of a damp towel. Being bitten in the morning is much better than later in the day. Their poison has less punch then as they feed at night. The head of the local hospital gave me this information. If you should be so unlucky as to encounter one and be stung, the best course of action is to immediately go to a doctor, clinic, or hospital. Hospital staffs are very experienced in dealing with the scorpion stings. The usual procedure is to administer an injection to counteract the venom, then, keep the patient under observation for a few hours. From *Topes in Paradise:*

Shoo, Shoe

The funky little beach house Tim and I moved into the spring of 1991 was perched above Playa La Ropa on about 2 hectares of overgrown vegetation. We were inundated with scorpions, madre de alacranes, tarantulas, killer bees, snakes, and ants. It was a small price to pay for a free beachside residence. It took twice weekly visits from the pest control folks but eventually I could venture to the bathroom in the middle of the night without turning on every light in the house and checking for critters.

I was part of a bridge game group and we often rotated between houses. On this particular evening, I was hosting the weekly game. Anita LaPointe and Dorothy Synodis didn't much like coming to my house at night as there were 82 dirt steps from the street down to the house and of course the inverse when returning. Drinking heavily was not an option as the stairs were very dangerous.

We were sitting around the bridge table and I happened to be the "dummy" (a bridge term which means not participating in the hand) when I noticed my cocker puppy Bambi across the room under the hammock with her hackles up and staring rigidly at the floor. I got up and went over to investigate. Within two inches of her cute little button nose was a "golden scorpion" with its tail curled in a striking position. In a very quite voice, I turned and called to the table, "shoe, shoe." Dorothy said, "Whaaaaaaaat do you want?" Again, "shoe, shoe—there's a scorpion under the hammock."

"Are you frigging nuts Linda—you can't shoo away a scorpion," Dorothy once again said.

"I'm barefoot—throw me a damn shoe Dorothy so I can kill the sucker," I screamed.

"Don't get all bent out of shape—why didn't you just say you wanted a shoe," as she tossed me one of my shoes from the floor and that was the end of the potentially deadly critter.

When I returned to the table, I tried to discuss what had happened with Dorothy but she insisted I was looking at the scorpion and saying shoo instead of shoe. Dorothy and I always did have our differences.

Zihua is also home to a variety of snakes, not often seen up North—notably coral snakes and boa constrictors—although with all the development going on, I think most of the snakes have left for calmer pastures. From *Wash Gently, Dry Slowly*:

Chelan

Chelan is a beautiful little 6-year old girl who lives in a palapa high on a hill above my house. She is as knowledgeable in her environment as most adults and much more so than many. She knows all of the trees by name and knows the native fruits that are edible. She is bilingual and is at ease speaking either Spanish or English..

Chelan and I were going to a beach picnic one Sunday and she was to meet with me at my house where some friends from town were to pick us up to take us to the picnic. The appointed hour came and Chelan didn't show up. The car from town arrived and we all waited for Chelan. The day was very hot and no one wanted to walk up the steep hill to Chelan's house, so we just waited.

Chelan finally came nonchalantly tripping down the path, bright, cheery, and ready to go.

"Why are you so late?" I asked.

"I had to wait for a snake," she answered.

All of those waiting perked up at the word snake.

"What do you mean you had to wait for a snake?" I asked Chelan.

"A big boa snake about 4 meters long was across the path and I had to wait," she answered simply.

"Wait for what?" I pressed.

"Wait for the snake to pass so that I could pass," was her logical explanation.

Like it has been said, "And a little child shall lead us."

Lastly, *Zihua* is home to tarantulas and a variety of small land crabs. From *Wash Gently, Dry Slowly:*

Land Crab versus Expatriate

In this section of Mexico there is a land crab that flaunts the red, white, and blue colors of America. This crab lives in lagoons, swamps, sewage dumps and other low-rent districts. He/she survives on waste. When this type of crab reaches the age of consent and exercises that privilege, they go to the beach and lay their eggs. Thousands of baby crabs, slightly larger than Texas houseflies, are born and they run for their lives to the nearest lagoon or swamp to grow up. Once matured, they then repeat the process of their mothers. The mother crabs, having laid their eggs, crawl out into the open sea to die.

It seems that these crabs, with their flamboyant Evel Knieval, red, white and blue exteriors, would share a mutual compassionate respect for resident Americans who fly those same red, white and blue colors. I have found that such is not the case and have instead discovered that these crabs have souls as black as the inside of a coal miner's sock.

A giant crab of this species, of about six inches across the back, and pincers with a reach just short of that of Muhammad Ali, has established his (or perhaps her) fortress within my bathroom commode. I know that this crab is aware that I am a gringo, for I still drink bottled water and listen to Dolly Parton music. Still, he lurks within these murky waters and continues to better me in the gun battle which has been raging between us for many weeks.

Being without conscience and not bound by the terms of Geneva, I started my offensive with poison. Terrible things, such as 190-proof tequila, mescal of unknown parenthood and Mexican hot sauce (with and without chiles), were poured into the lair of the crab. All I got for this effort was a more belligerent crab and the removal of all porcelain from the interior of the commode. Chiles here are rated (for their degree of "hotness") on a scale of 0 to 108, so I tried some of the 108 variety, and got a mad crab who could blow smoke rings.

Next I tried a surprise attack using both the Commode Lid Up (CLU) and the Commode Lid Down (CLD) tactics. (Any operation involving the military mind must be fraught with acronyms and abbreviations). These attacks involved a wooden spear of local guerilla manufacture made of hardwood and with a very sharp point. Commode Lid Up (CLU) tactic involved sitting on the tank top waiting for the enemy to appear and then dropping the spear quickly. With skill bred of the intensive training of three wars I would drop the poised spear only to see my unscathed adversary withdraw at supersonic speed. The Commode Lid Down (CLD) tactic was much the same except a rope around the lid was used to stealthily raise the lid and the spear was then plunged in immediately. Negative results.

Both the CLU and the CLD methods were used with weapons variations. In lieu of the spear, I used heavy, black volcanic rocks, gathered from the non-tourist end of a beach. The results of these attacks were as with those of the spear except the fallout of splashed water about the battlefield created an unpleasant environment, and destroyed resident face and toilet tissues.

I now use the compulsive, random, non-scheduled attack much like that which the 8th Air Force used for saturation bombing in World War II. This involves the CLU approach with thrusts of startling suddenness of the spear, followed immediately by a shower of selected volcanic rocks. These, too the evasive crab has repulsed with alarming dexterity. A copy of my survival books is missing and I suspect that I am guilty of giving comfort to mine own enemy.

As a variation to the continuing battle, I tried a 50 foot plumber's snake, a real live boa snake, and a small explosion using a flotilla of cherry bombs. All to no avail.

The battle rages on and there appears to be no end in sight. Although I am sure that the infernal crab has a drastically different point of view from my offensive viewpoint, I feel that I can at least contain him. With the CLD procedure I hope to confine the battlefield to the commode interior. Still, when of those necessities born of human needs and demands, I open the commode lid, old Red, White, and Blue, with his ridiculously protruding eyes, is always there. He extends the gigantic claw upward, always in threat, never in friendship, and the skirmish begins.

Because of his continual threat and not wanting to be suspect as a part of his deplorable behavior, any guests needing to "powder their noses" are forced to use the outdoor facilities.

I feel that before this battle is ended I will be found to have a soprano-like, high-pitched voice because sooner or later that damned crab is going to catch me with an exposed, unprotected flank.

The Worm in the Bottle of Booze:

This is the golden worm of the mescal cactus, guaranteeing you are drinking the real thing. It is very *macho* to be the one to drink the worm.

Take a bottle home with you. It's guaranteed to be an instant party icebreaker.

Beef Hanging on a Clothesline in the Market:

This is *cecina* or dried, salted beef, which is very popular with the locals that don't have refrigeration. It is a very distant cousin to beef jerky. My German shepherd, Bello, used to enjoy going to the market with me. He normally was very well behaved. One day I was chatting with a friend and walking out of the market and not paying attention to the dog. I heard an old woman screaming "*Señora, señora!*" I glanced over my shoulder and there was Bello dragging a four-foot piece of *cecina* on the dirty floor. I apologized profusely to the woman and offered to pay for the beef. She said there was no harm done and threw it back over the clothesline!

A Chapel set in a Lake on the way to the Airport:

This is the temple of the *Virgin of Guadalupe* built by neighboring townsfolk some fifty years ago. It is a small chapel set in the center of a small lake filled with floating lily pads. It is open to the public for viewing during the day. Residents often visit to pray for ailing relatives and an occasional wedding or baptism is held here. Should you like to visit, heading towards the airport, on the old road, take a left on the dirt road in front of the stand selling *miel* or honey. Take the next left off the dirt road, park your car, and follow the footpath over the pond. If you drive over the *Puente Coacoyul*, you've gone too far. By the way, the honey sold here is exceptionally delicious.

Clusters of new stores in the downtown area with a sign *Casa de Empeño*:

These stores are the Mexican equivalent of pawn shops, a sad testimonial to the plight of the poorer Mexican people. There's also been a huge increase in the number of pharmacies in town—when people are depressed, they get sick more often.

Milagros:

Mexico is a predominantly Catholic country with a long history of religious tradition born from the merging of Catholicism and pre-Hispanic beliefs. Mexican Catholics place their saints in very high regard and have very personal relationships with them. They believe in miracles and divine intervention, and believe their patron saints are watching over them daily. When they have bad fortune they seek assistance and when they have good fortune they think there's someone to thank. These solicitations and offerings are placed in churches and their simple and sincere beauty has spawned modern art forms, based on these traditions.

Miracles or *milagros* are small gold, silver, copper, or brass charms, depicting symbolic woes; they are placed in shrines, churches, or pinned to walls during prayers to ask for assistance. An ear of corn to ask for good crops, a leg, an arm, a pair of eyes, if medical problems with those areas are present or a heart for heart disease (or love), there are *milagros* for every conceivable affliction. They are often sold individually as collectibles or found in religious stores or stalls near churches. A folk art has arisen from this tradition and you can find them in *Fruity Keiko's*.

Packed Restaurants on Thursday Night:

On any Thursday night in downtown *Zihua*, all the *"típico"* restaurants are packed with people, seated elbow to elbow at long tables covered with oilcloth. It's *pozole* night—a ritual for eating this regional dish. *Pozole* is a thick rich soup made from pork or chicken and hominy, and is both delicious and cheap. The locals only eat it on

Thursday but no one can remember why. And no one would dream of ordering in on any other day either, even though it's on the menus.

With several varieties of *pozole* to choose from there is something for every taste. The base is made from chicken or pork and puffy white pieces of corn called hominy. Hominy, when prepared from scratch, requires prolonged soaking of the dried whole kernels of corn in a lime and saltwater solution to transform then into an edible consistency. Now it comes in cans, vacuum packed, or frozen at most grocery stores.

The choices of *pozole* are red, green, or white—the colors of the Mexican flag: Red (made from various chiles), green (from *pepitas* or pumpkin seeds), or white (from the unadulterated meat stock).

Pozole is intentionally bland and requires considerable doctoring up—personalizing it to your own taste from the assortment of condiments that fill the center of the table: Small bowls of oregano, paprika, chopped onion, sliced avocado, diced *chiles, totopos,* or fried corn chips, piles of *chicharrón* or fried pork skins to be crumbled on top of the *pozole,* as well as heaps of sliced limes. Traditionally a small shot glass of *mescal* is served to wash down the *pozole.*

Why is Everything Closed?

Festivals, Celebrations, and Special Events

New Year's Day	January 1
Three Kings Day. (Epiphany) ★	January 6
Sailfest ★	Feb.6-10 (2013)
Constitution Day	Feb. 5
Flag Day	Feb. 24
Birthday of Benito Juárez	March 21
Guitarfest ★	First week of March
Easter	March 31, 2013
International Fishing Tournament	May(1st week)
Labor Day	May 1
Holy Cross Day. Mason's and Builder's Day	May 3
Battle of *Puebla*—Victory over French in 1862	May 5
Mother's Day	May 7,2013
Teacher's Day	May 15
Naval Day	June 1
Father's Day	June1, 2013
Father Hidalgo's Death	July 30
Day of the Assumption celebration	August 15
State of the Nation Address	Sept. 1
Heroic Children's Day ★	Sept. 13
Independence Day Celebrations	Sept. 15-16
San Jeronimito River Regatta	Late October
Feast of San Francisco	October 9
Columbus Day	October 12
Halloween ★	October 31
All Saint's Day ★	November 1
All Soul's Day (Day of the Dead) ★	November 2
Celebration of the Revolution of 1910	Nov. 20
Rio Balsa international speedboat race ★	Early Nov.
Feast of Immaculate Conception	December 8
Feast of Virgin of Guadalupe	December 12
Posadas	Dec. 16-24
Christmas	December 25
New Year's Eve ★	December 31

★ (Further explanation)

December 31st: New Year's Eve. Nationwide. Mexico rings in the New Year with celebrations featuring music, dance, food and fireworks. Streets are filled with revelers, and friends and families congregate for parties that often last till dawn. There is lots of gunfire in certain areas of *Zihua*. One tradition celebrated here calls for eating twelve grapes, one with each stroke of the chiming bell at midnight, for luck during the next 12 months.

January 6: Three King's Day (*Día de los Santos Reyes*). The Feast of the Epiphany recalls the arrival in Bethlehem of the three wise men, *reyes magos*, bearing gifts for baby Jesus. This is the day of traditional gift giving for children in the central and southern regions of Mexico. *Rosca de Reyes*, a crown-shaped sweet bread decorated with candied fruits with a small doll baked inside, is served on this day. Whoever is lucky enough to find the figure in his slice of bread must host a party on February 2, Candlemas Day, offering *tamales* and *atole* to the guests.

Feb 7–12, 2012: 11th Annual *Zihua* Sailfest. *Zihua* has in the past been home during high season to as many as 120 yachts. Rick's Bar catered to the yachting community and in 2000, numerous yachties" approached Rick about giving something back to the community for all the good deeds the community had performed for them and in 2001, Sailfest was born. It was decided that a five-day festival of fun, games, yachting events, and parties would serve as a fund-raiser for the very poor *escuela Netzahualcóyotl*. More about the school in Clubs and Organizations.

March 7–11, 2012: 8th Annual Guitar Festival. A week of live music. Mexican and international musicians come to *Zihua* to play in various venues around town, with bar shows and gala dinner shows throughout the week in a wide variety of genres: jazz, classical, blues, traditional Mexican and more.

September 13th: Heroic Children's Day. The date has no relevance to *Zihua* but the story behind this holiday is interesting in illustrating how Mexico honors defeat and death. From *Distant Neighbors*:

The U.S. Congress admitted Texas into the Union in 1845 and Washington was increasingly covetous of the unpopulated Mexican lands to the west. Some Mexican generals decided that Texas' incorporation into the United States was a cause for war, and in 1846 they sent troops north of the Rio Grande. The United States, on the other hand, immediately saw the challenge as the excuse it needed for invasion. First, U.S. forces secured Texas and occupied Los Angeles and Sante Fe, then, led by General Zachery Taylor, they marched south, defeating an army commanded by Santa Anna in February 1847. Meanwhile, General Winfield Scott landed troops at Veracruz and began advancing toward the capital, also defeating Santa Anna in the process.

Scott finally took Mexico City in September of that year, and the American flag was raised above the National Palace. The last Mexican resistance came from young cadets at Chapultepec Castle, some of whom, according to legend, wrapped themselves in the Mexican flag and jumped off the ramparts to their deaths rather than surrender. On February 2, 1848, in exchange for $15 million, the Mexican government signed the Treaty of Guadalupe Hidalgo and surrendered half its territory—890,000 square miles, which included California, Arizona and New Mexico as well as Texas –to the United States. Soon afterwards, American troops withdrew, leaving a mutilated nation in danger of even greater disintegration.

October 31: Halloween. In *Zihua*, children don't go door to door trick or treating. They put on costumes and with parents in tow, come to town to trick or treat in the bars and restaurants. They make out like little bandits as most tourists in town are not prepared for children in costumes so the children receive lots of candy and money from the tourist. From *Topes in Paradise:*

Trick or Treat

A custom in Mexico for centuries is the celebration of the Day of the Dead or All Soul's Day. The two-day celebration is observed by paying homage to deceased family members. The graves are cleaned and celebrations are held at the gravesites. Flowers, particularly Cempasuchiles or marigolds, festoon the cemetery and tiny candied skulls and skeletons are sold in all the marketplaces to add to the feast in honor of the deceased. This time-honored celebration coincides with the American Halloween celebration. Since the early seventies, when American television first came to Mexico, many of our Southern neighbors have begun to adopt their northern counterpart's holidays—albeit sometimes with a twist.

In 1989, a group of locals were sitting at Coconuts in the bar area a couple of days before Halloween. Suddenly, three children burst through the door and approached their table. These impish little kids had utilized charcoal, ash, and chalk to make their faces appear ghoulish. They had put black plastic garbage bags over their slender frames and used chalk to make the body appear skeletal. They each carried a large paper bag for their goodies. However, instead of screaming "Trick or Treat," they chanted in unison, "Give us money, give us money," in English while bobbing up and down to their chant. The locals were so astonished and amused they dug into their pockets for change. Mario, the manager, was so delighted with their ingenuity that he permitted them to solicit the diners—something that is never allowed at Coconuts. Word of their coup spread rapidly and, while no other urchins were allowed to solicit inside the restaurant, the tradition of Halloween, American-style was born in Zihuatanejo.

November 1st and 2nd-*Dia de los Muertos:* Gabriela Brana, chef and co-owner of the fabulous *El Cilantro* restaurant in Ixtapa, wrote the following article which appeared in the November 2001 issue of *Another Day in Paradise* magazine.

The festivities of All Soul's Day and the Day of the Dead "Todos Santos y Los Fieles Difuntos" are among the most spectacular in Mexico.

In some places there is a distinction made among those who died by murder (October 28th), those who died when they were children (November 1st), adults (November 2nd), and even the souls who are in limbo, those children who died before being baptized (October 30th).

Some historians like Friar Diego Durán explain that Miccailhuitoutli or "the feast of the small dead ones" was celebrated on the ninth month of Tlaxochimaco (August) while the older dead ones were remembered on Xocotlhuitzín (September).

These festivities are the result of the syncretism of pre-Hispanic and Catholic religions. When the Spaniards arrived in Mexico their beliefs were merged with the practices that had been carried out by the Aztecs for several centuries, establishing a tradition that has been handed down by generations up to the present.

The cult to the dead ones is one of the basic elements of the religion of ancient Mexicans. This practice dates back to 1,800 B.C. during the period known as Late Pre-Classic. Aztecs celebrated the dead during July, August and September in worship of goddess Mictlecacihuatl, queen of Chignamictlan, or the ninth level of Hell. They believed that life and death constitute a unity, death does not mean the end of existence, and it is a transient road towards a better life.

Due to the firm conviction that the dead return every year, the people set up altars in their homes to remember their beloved dead ones.

These altars are decorated with "Cempasuchil" flowers, candles, silk-paper ornaments, fruits and the departed one's favorite dishes along with his or her favorite drinks, tequila, hot chocolate, beer, coffee. Incense fills the air as the photograph of the deceased occupies the most important place, surrounded by sugar skulls with the names of relatives and friends (dead or alive). There is also "pan de muerto" a special kind of bread, rounded and with small bones on top of it, baked for the occasion and covered with sugar, "calabaza en tacha" a rich compote of pumpkin in a syrup made with piloncillo (a kind of molasses), there are tamales, mole, diverse skeletons made of clay, paper mache or sugar and, of course the brand of cigarettes favored by the deceased.

The dead are expected to pay their visit on November 1st and 2nd and eat and drink from their offering. The following day, family and friends gather to remember the departed ones and to share the food and drinks prepared for them. It is also customary to write "calaveras" (literally skulls) which are poems that talk about important people, be it the president, famous actors and actresses, sports figures, celebrities, one's boss, friends and relatives. They describe in a humorous way how they were taken by the "calaca", (the skinny one, the bald one, the bony one) dancing, playing or singing, to the other world. Mexicans joke about death, dance with it, flirt with it, and smile at it, not out of disrespect but due to the deep understanding that it is this life which is transitory.

Then it is time to go to the cemetery and visit the graves, decorate them with flowers, candles and ornaments. Some cemeteries are famous for the colorful rituals that take place in them. People spend the night in them amongst thousands of candles and flowers, incense and religious fervor.

Some of the most beautiful are in Mixquic, near Mexico City, Pátzcuaro, in the State of Michoacán and the ones in Puebla, Oaxaca, and Morelos.

Late November: *Rio Balsas* **Nautical Marathon—Bay of** *Zihua.* Considered the most important jet boat marathon in Mexico and one of the most important events of its kind in the Americas, the *Rio Balsas* Marathon covers almost 500 miles in six consecutive days and welcomes international participants from all over the world.

Housing and Real Estate

The tangled history of land development in the Zihuatanejo area is instructive. Dr. Cowan on the subject:

To understand land acquisition and distribution, one must go back to 1937 when the first ejidos (lands to be held in common by a designated group of local farmers) were formed. The ejido de Zihuatanejo was to include 3800 hectares of land, which would be distributed among the heads of 76 families. The land was expropriated by the government from the Inguaran Hacienda (75%) and from a few powerful families. The expropriation was not entirely successful, nor peaceful.

Later, when Ixtapa-Zihuatanejo was to become a model resort complex, the government again expropriated lands from the ejidos to complete the project. For the purpose of national development, the government is allowed to expropriate land. Thirty-three per-cent of the land needed for Ixtapa was in the hands of two landowners. Negotiations were completed in 1969, not without bitterness and a fight on the part of one landholder.

In Zihuatanejo, each of the 320 members within these ejidos that had land expropriated was to receive two centrally located and urbanized lots of 600 square meters each and a cash settlement in compensation for his land needed in the Ixtapa-Zihuatanejo development. Payments actually received varied from $1,600 to $10,000 dollars. Twenty percent of the money to be paid to members was to be invested in ejido projects, the largest of which was the Hotel Calpulli, located on La Ropa beach and opened in 1973. This hotel was purchased from the ejido in 1995 and razed.

President Luis Echeverría Alvarez (1970-1976) led an administration that gave unprecedented attention to the growth of tourism and industry. Under Echeverría, a federal government institution known as a fideicomisario (a local arm of a national trust) was put into place with emphasis on coastal sites. The fideicomisario assumed jurisdiction over expropriated lands, arranging transfer to private or lease ownerships. Foreign investment, which had been prohibited in the constitution of 1917, was partially reopened with the Federal investment Law of 1973.

FIBAZI was instituted in 1974, as Dr. Cowan points out, to oversee Zihuatanejo development and supervise the regularization of land. (A process by which the Mexican government grants clear title to all properties held in Zihuatanejo). To obtain clear title, landholders are required to pay a fee per square meter, which includes the "purchase price" and cost of urbanization.

Initially fees were set at $3.75 to $7.00 per square meter. Payment could be made in installments at 13% interest.

71

Due to inflation, these original fees escalated greatly. One of my friends on *Playa La Ropa* completed her regularization in 1990 at a cost of $18.00 per square meter. By 1992, the price had escalated to almost $70.00 per square meter. If I'm not mistaken, all lands along the beaches in the area have now been regularized.

But then, as Dr. Cowan details, there have always been lots of difficulties:

Many parcels were held by families who had lived on the land for decades—on properties, which had been obtained through a range of transactions, which were illegal, semi-legal and legitimate.

FIBAZI, under pressure from the locally formed residents' association tried to respect the rights of residents to stay where they already lived but this was not always the case owing to the overall needs of the community for public services.

Hostilities came to a head in 1981 over a parcel of land leading to Ixtapa settled by paracaidistas (squatters) who had settled on land not yet regulated and legally the property of FIBAZI. Understaffed, efforts to dissuade the settlement were ignored and finally on March 12, 1981, federal troops were brought in to knock down and burn these houses. The outraged residents of this area stormed the FIBAZI office (causing the director to barricade himself inside and call frantically for reinforcements).

This went on for three days and food was smuggled to the director in a briefcase by the owner of the Captain's Table restaurant. No more troops arrived and the director wisely agreed to resettle these people elsewhere.

As a result of regularization and urbanization, new zoning laws had to be enacted. No longer do we see the donkeys, pigs, and chickens meandering down the streets of town. Some residents keep pigs and chickens, and an occasional burro may be seen but most are gone in the name of progress.

FIBAZI, hoping to curtail urban sprawl and prevent another Acapulco, enacted a law to block random settlement in the hills around *Zihua* by limiting service to no more than 70 meters above sea level. Beyond this level, land has been classified as national park land.

However, as one looks away from the ocean to the vista of the surrounding mountains, it's obvious even to the untrained eye that this plan has not worked. The hills are populated by squatters and "partially" legitimized by various political groups with promises of regularization in exchange for their votes. These squatters have the best views in town and *Zihua* now has a reputation as a "squatter's paradise."

Real Estate Investment in Mexico

Before you invest, remember to take all those precautions you normally would follow in connection with an investment in North America or elsewhere in the world. Also be aware that in a foreign country, with unfamiliar customs and laws, and where you must communicate in a foreign language, the problems you may encounter can be further complicated.

The Mexican Constitution prohibits foreigners from owning land for a distance of 100 kilometers from the borders and 50 kilometers from the coast. These areas are called *Zonas Restringidas* or "Restricted Zones."

There are two basic ways around this; the first, and most common, being the use of a *fideicomiso* or bank trust. Under the trust agreement, a bank is the trustee, or actual titleholder of the property. The foreign buyer is the beneficiary of the trust having all rights to use, enjoy and sell the property, but is not the legal owner of record and his exercise of his trust agreement rights depend on the specific wording of the trust agreement from which he benefits. The bank can hold the title of the property in trust for a period of fifty years. All trusts must have the approval of the Secretariat of Foreign Investment before the final documentation can be delivered to the beneficiary. They must act within 45 days to deny the application presented by the trustee or the trust is approved automatically.

The second option for foreigners wanting to own property in Mexico is the formation of a Mexican corporation or *sociedad anónima*. The constitution of a Mexican corporation, i.e., the intentions or uses to which it will be put to use, vary greatly and this will determine the percentage of foreign ownership allowable. In some cases, as few as two shareholders are necessary and they can both be foreigners. In others, a number of Mexican shareholders and a higher percentage of Mexican ownership will be a requirement.

The Pros and Cons: Trust vs. Corporation:

In general, a trust will be more expensive to set up (currently somewhere between $5000 and $6000 U.S. for a lot and home) and will have an annual maintenance fee of something like $500 to $600 U.S. A corporation will only cost about $3,000 U.S. to set up but will entail ongoing fiscal obligations that will cost a minimum of $2,000 U.S. yearly. Foreigners who wish to own homes here for their own use or even for a vacation rental business are well advised to stay in a trust. The trust document will allow you to run a B & B or engage in the rental market and the fiscal obligations will be much less severe than those for a corporation. The concept of a "holding company" is unheard of in Mexico. *Hacienda*, the Mexican IRS, will assume that a corporation has been created for the purpose of making money and will demand that tax declarations be filed on a monthly basis, regardless of the fact that there may be no financial activity. The attendant accounting fees will certainly run to at least $2,000 U.S. yearly.

The Pitfalls:

The purchase of property in Mexico is far more complicated for foreigners than a similar purchase elsewhere. The first difficulty is determining true ownership. The law requires property registration, but in practice, this is not always done in a timely fashion; therefore, the person in possession of the property may not be the registered owner and may not have the right to transfer title to the property. As there is no formal title search in Mexico, the buyer has little recourse, except through the criminal courts, in the event the transaction proves fraudulent. For this reason, the services of a reputable notary are a must for your own protection.

Property sales in Mexico are taxable, with the burden falling on the vendor. Naturally, the vendor may request the purchase price as stated in the contract to be much lower than the actual sales price. It works to the advantage of the purchaser also, as taxes are assessed on property valuation. However, if there are problems, the purchaser will only be able to recoup the official price stated in the contract.

The only legally binding contracts in Mexico are those written in the Spanish language. A contract written in English is worthless. The purchase price should be stated in *pesos*, not dollars. The services of a translator *(perito traductor)* are important to protect your interest should you not be fluent in the language.

All property transactions in Mexico must be processed through the offices of a government appointed notary. In Mexico, notaries are educated as much as U.S. lawyers. A regular attorney cannot be substituted to do the job.

In resume, having made a decision on what to buy, you will now want a competent translator, unless you are fluent in Spanish and also understand the Napoleonic Code system of law, and a Notary. Your notary will ensure that your bank trust or corporation is set up correctly, the proper permits and registrations done, and will provide you with originals of the documents. Always remember that over and above what you pay for your new property, you'll have legal fees as mentioned above, annual property taxes, and annual fees related to either a trust or a corporation.

If looking for condo property, be aware that real estate developers in Mexico are not required to invest any of their own funds, nor are they required to capitalize the development prior to offering it for sale. What this generally means to an investor is that the funds obtained from unit sales will go directly to construction costs, or in some cases such as *Cascada*, directly into the pocket of the developer. Clearly, with even the most reliable and responsible developer, such financing practices carry great risks. Variables such as exchange rate fluctuation, increases in material or labor costs, and natural disasters, which would not be fatal to a properly capitalized development in North America, can result in the project running over budget or even going bankrupt. In the hands of a disreputable developer, such practices provide a "license to steal."

When discussing real estate with tourists that are interested in buying a home in Mexico, I usually suggest they consider a condo rather than a house if they don't plan to live here year round. With a condo, you have the necessary monthly maintenance fees but the cost of maintaining an "absentee owner" home can be very expensive. Homes cannot be left unattended which means the expense of live-in year-round staff with also bills for water, electricity, etc. You must rely on good luck when hiring live-ins or arrange for a reliable property management firm to take care of all attendant problems. On site management at a condo provides the security and maintenance necessary on the owner's behalf without the attendant hassles of live-in help. You may hire a couple to take care of your home and when you return to visit, find that the couple now has their children and grandchildren living on your property. If you don't care to share your million dollar home with a dozen Mexicans and decide to fire the couple, you will probably end up in court paying huge fines and wasting much of your vacation time.

There are numerous condominium complexes available in both *Zihua* and Ixtapa. Before signing anything, check out the reputation of the firm!

For information about your developer, call your Embassy in Mexico City. Ask for the property attaché, and inquire as to whether or not there have been any complaints filed with them regarding the company in question.

If, after making inquires about the company, you are satisfied that your investment will be sound, make sure of the following:

If you are shown a model condo and told, "Your condo will be identical" get it in writing—in Spanish. If the model has big-ticket items such as stove, refrigerator, air conditioners, washer-dryers, and fans, make sure your contract contains a list of these items in Spanish. Do not take anything for granted.

Make sure your contract stipulates exactly how much your maintenance fee will be each month. Don't allow them to give you a guesstimate. As a parameter, the going rate is from about $200.00 to $600.00 per month depending on the size of the unit.

If the development company offers you a rental program (if you are to be an absentee owner), find out what percentage you will receive. Some companies charge as much as 50%.

If you are buying in the pre-construction phase of a project, again, get it in writing—in Spanish—the promised date of completion of the project. This will allow you to estimate how soon you can get your *fideicomiso*. Make sure any agreement you sign is properly notarized and witnessed.

If you are buying into a completed project, insist on seeing the condo rules and regulations. Ask for their tax documentation, proof of ownership, and find out what bank has handled trusts for other owners. If the company cannot provide you with the above, run, don't walk, away.

I know some of this sounds pessimistic but I want my readers to be aware of some of the problems and pitfalls involved in buying property in Mexico.

In 1989 I bought a condo at *Cascada*. The ordeal was a nightmare. The developer had never paid for the property from *FIBAZI* so at one point they wanted to repossess. The developer also stole my air conditioners saying that they were not part of the written inventory; therefore they had the right to remove them. The owners had to pay astronomical maintenance fees because the developer sold many condos to people and gave them free maintenance as a condition to buying. The owners had to pay for the condo rules and regulations because the developer couldn't afford to pay for them—$15,000 U.S. dollars.

You can't get title to a condo without the above. The developer pocketed money from buyers instead of paying the bank mortgage and the owners had to instigate several lawsuits to keep the bank from foreclosing on their condos. These are just a few of the things that happened. When I went to sell in 1996, even though I sold my condo for the same price I paid for it, the Mexican government said I had to pay capital gains in the amount of $12,000 dollars. Basically I paid $150,000 pesos and sold it for $350,000 pesos (this was because the pesos devalued). They wanted capital gains on the difference without taking into consideration the devaluation. My ex-husband was able to squash this stupidity and I finally rid myself of the pink elephant. Also the cost of administering the trust had escalated five times the original agreement.

This is probably a good place to mention one other type of Mexican investment, time-share. We are fortunate in that the time-share developments in Ixtapa have very fine reputations. This is not always the case in other resort towns. As time-share resorts have aged, many have been sold by their original owners or have changed management companies. The new owners/managers have not always lived up to the original contractual obligations. They have been uncooperative in exchanging periods of use or type of accommodation, although the investors' contracts had provided for such exchanges. Many new owners/managers have failed to accept the validity of the original contracted time. Some have allowed the level of service and the conditions of the accommodations to decline. There is little that can be done should any of the above happen beyond filing a complaint with the Mexican Consumer Protection Agency, *PROFECO*, which is already over-burdened with these cases.

Again, Ixtapa offers many fine time-share resorts with lots of happy customers. I know one individual at *Pacífica* that, over a period of a few years, has bought eight weeks.

For my readers really interested in real estate investment, I strongly recommend you peruse on-line the back issues of *Another Day in Paradise.* Beginning in November of 2003, the magazine began including articles by prominent attorneys regarding real estate investment and one should definitely take the time to read these informative and well-written articles. The magazine is no longer published but the website remains intact.

www.anotherdayinparadise.com

Casas Y Camas (Accommodations)

For the months December through April, accommodations are sometimes difficult to find unless sought well in advance. Rental properties, apartments, and hotels are filled and charge premium prices at these times. Prices are greatly reduced off-season. However, unless arriving at Christmas or Easter, you should be able to find something, as there are at least 3000 rooms in *Zihua* alone. With the economic crisis in the U.S. and the purported drug cartel violence in the area, there are a lot more vacancies these days than in prior years.

Renting: All sizes, from efficiency apartments to luxurious villas, can be found for rent here year round. Rental by the day, week, month, or year is available. The most desirable months are December through April, considered high season. For high season, read big bucks. May, June, September, October, and November, are bargain months. The Mexicans vacation in July and August since the children are out of school and most places won't bargain during this time period. It is best to make arrangements at least six months in advance if wanting accommodations during high season. If you plan to stay a lengthy period of time, try to get a contract in Spanish with the price stated in *pesos*—not dollars.

Inexpensive places to rent can generally be found only by word of mouth. We have only a couple of bulletin boards at restaurants with listings or local papers with rental sections. There are a few listings in *Despertar de la Costa,* but Mexicans are not accustomed to advertising in newspapers. Signs often appear in many storefront windows around town. Realtors can be of assistance if you're looking for a monthly rental in the $1,500 dollar plus range. Mexicans have told me they don't want to put for rent signs on homes as it is a notification to thieves that the house is empty. Local thieves enter these homes and steal toilets, all the copper pipes and anything that is not set in concrete.

Renting in town can be noisy, with traffic and pedestrian sounds. However, you're within easy walking distance of the market, most beaches, and the nightlife. Renting on *Playa La Ropa* can be noisy in a different way. The braying of donkeys and squawking of chickens can keep you awake all night. Most foreigners are not familiar with these sounds and find them most annoying.

Again, locals are a good source of information. Find them at *Café Marina* for breakfast, *Rossy's, La Perla,* or *Paty's* on *Playa La Ropa* during the afternoon, and The Flophouse or *Casa Arcadia* during the evening.

There are now several websites to check out real estate and everything else you want to know about the area. Most of the real estate listings have their own websites or links through the following complete with photos.

www.zihrena@zihua-ixtapa.com
www.ay-zihuatanejo.com
www.zihua.net
www.zihuatanejo.net
www.ixtapa-zihuatanejo.com

Rental and Real Estates Agents:

CENTURY 21/ALPHA 2000: ☎ 553-0017. ✉

www.century21ixtapa.com.mx Location is backside of the Ixtapa shopping plaza, across the parking lot from *Bancomer*. The staff here gives the same quality of service found in the States.

Costa Grande: ☎ 554-1999 or 📱 (755)100-7100/120-2533. *Nicolás Bravo* #62. Visit www.costagranderealestate.com or ✉douglas@mexicomail.com Douglas Hudson speaks fluent Spanish and has real estate listings for almost all pocketbooks. Completely bi-lingual and very knowledgeable.

Don Francisco Properties: ☎ 554-4924. Fax: 554-9377 or 📱 557-0149. Francisco of *La Perla* fame has many properties on the beach for sale and for rent including a family owned hotel at the end of *Playa La Ropa*.

Visit www.donfranciscoproperties.com or ✉ laperla4@lycos.com

Estrella: *Nicolás Bravo* #39. ☎ 553-8183, fax 554-1454 or 📱 (755) 558-4203. This is a Mexican company that generally specializes in lower-end properties for rent or sale. They found a niche and are doing well. Visit www.estrellabienesraices.com.mx

Mexico Beach Property: *Playa La Ropa* road across from entrance to *Residencias Villa del Sol.* ☎ 554-6448 or 📱 (755)120-2637. John Murphy is a long-time local and with his fluent Spanish and many years in *Zihua*, he is enormously popular. John knows all those "off the beaten path" places for sale as well as the regular local market. Visit www.mexicobeachproperty.com or ✉john@mexicobeachproperty.com

Ocean Front Property: ☎ 554-4506 or 📱 (755)558-4696. Judy Diyanni has been in *Zihua* for over 30 years and is fluent in Spanish. She is specializing in raw land rather than houses for sale but has a vast knowledge of both. ✉ judiyanni@yahoo.com

Paradise Properties: Office by Dolphins on *Playa La Ropa* . ☎ 554-6226 or 📱 (755)557-0078. Judith Whitehead goes the extra mile to make her customers happy. Visit www.paradise-properties.com.mx. ✉ jude@prodigy.net.mx

TICARSA/Tim Sullivan: ☎553-3218, fax 553-3219, or 📱 (755)108-5071. Tim's my ex-husband and has been selling real estate for over 20 years. He is very well qualified to assist foreigners to purchase or rent a home. He doesn't just sell you a home—he will take care of the paperwork involved once you have purchased a place. Visit www.ixtaparealestate.com ✉ ticarsa@prodigy.net.mx

Valle Properties: ☎ 554-4154. Luis Valle has some lovely rental properties available in *Zihua* and near *Playa La Ropa*. ✉ luisvall@prodigy.net.mx

ZihuaBello: ☎ 544-8585. www.ZihuaBello.com

Buying Real Estate: The days of buying a home on the beach with a view for $100,000 dollars have gone the same path as the burro—almost extinct. A home in *Zihua* or Ixtapa now costs the equivalent of a home in the U.S. and with the current economy perhaps more expensive than U.S. prices. The Americanization of *Playa La Ropa* is a reality. High construction costs, land speculation and the influx of many foreigners with large pocketbooks contribute to the high cost of owning one's own vacation or retirement home. "The sky is the limit" with homes and condos in the area usually ranging from $100,000 to $10,000,000 dollars (yes, that's ten million dollars). Generally when you buy, it's 100% cash up front. Since 1990, there has been limited financing, although the interest rates are much higher here than in the States.

Definitely, with the above in mind, deal only with reputable real estate brokers.

Construction: Many foreigners come to *Zihua* for a vacation, fall in love with the area, and decide to build their dream/retirement home. My advice to those wishing to build rather than buy is that one must be totally dedicated to the project and be possessed of unlimited patience.

Time means *mañana*. *Mañana* doesn't necessarily mean tomorrow. Therefore build only by contract. The contract should state the exact time and peso figure for the finished work. If not finished on time or within the contract amount, there should be a penalty clause. The inverse is true also. If the construction is finished on time and within budget, there should be a bonus clause. The agreed upon amount should incorporate building permits and social security—which covers injury for workers and is a must.

Set up a payment system and have all money accounted for by receipts. Keep your own set of records. If you're not fluent in Spanish, hire an on-site bilingual supervisor to oversee the project.

Plumbing and electrical work can be very important. Proper grounding, heavy gauge wire and sufficient circuit breakers and outlets must be insisted upon. Remember, foreigners have more electrical needs than most Mexicans.

The high cost of building materials more than offsets the relatively cheap labor costs. Construction costs vary widely depending on the building site and design.

Before investing, it is wise to consult locals who have built a home themselves. It could turn out to be your worst nightmare or a dream come true.

El Centro Hotels

The following is a listing of hotels and *búngalos* available in and around the downtown area. There is no longer more than a handful of what I consider really inexpensive lodgings. Prices in recent years have soared—mainly attributable to the high demand for air conditioning which most hotels have installed by necessity. Unless otherwise specified, all rooms have ceiling or floor fans and private baths. Most have hot water. Don't take it for granted—check out the room and turn on the tap before placing your plastic or pesos on the table. Also, check out the beds and pillows. You can buy a mattress for $400 pesos—and you get what you pay for. A lumpy mattress with a pillow as hard as a rock can make your stay miserable. Most of the really inexpensive places do not accept plastic so be sure and ask about credit card policy before running up a bill.

There are now so many rooms for rent that I simply couldn't list them all. The listings I have compiled are places I personally know or others have recommended. If the place you are looking for isn't listed, it doesn't mean I don't like it and refuse to give it a recommendation— it's because most hotels can be found on the Internet and "a picture is worth a thousand words." I don't want this little guidebook to expand like my waistline has and become 500-1000 pages long.

With the Morelia highway now complete, we have become inundated with thousands of Mexican tourists every weekend complete with huge buses clogging the streets and taxing the local public facilities. As a result, literally hundreds of locals have signs up to rent rooms. A lot, not all, of these smaller establishments are not legal, i.e., they are not registered with the Mexican IRS or the *Secretaría de Tourismo* and don't' have the proper licenses issued by the city. If you should have a problem at one of these "hotels" or guesthouses, there is no legal recourse. If staying at a "legitimate lodging" you can file a complaint with the consumer protection bureau (*Profeco*) and they actually investigate to resolve whatever the issue might be.

Rates are generally double occupancy. Expect about a 30% discount during low season. Rates are in U.S. dollars. The following is based on high season rates per day.

Inexpensive: ★ $35.00 or less.
Moderate: ★ ★ $35.00 to $75.00.
Moderately expensive: ★ ★ ★ $75.00 to $150.00.

Expensive: ★ ★ ★ ★ $150.00 to $2,000.00 plus.

A more detailed description of most of the following lodgings, complete with pictures, can be found on the Internet sites listed on a page 79. Also, with the exception of the very inexpensive hotels, all have Wi-Fi. It doesn't always work, but the hotels have paid for the service. One last item of note—many of these hotel phone numbers are actually cell phones but they haven't been listed as such on the websites. I e-mailed a lot of these places and mentioned this error but with the exception of one hotel, no one corrected their websites. Since most visitors can't speak Spanish and almost no one at any of the hotels can speak English, I left the phone numbers the way the owners listed them on their websites just because…Also don't forget, if calling a cell phone from a landline you must first dial 044 plus area code (755) and then the number.

Adrianita's Hostel: ★ *Calle Mangos #25.* ☏ 112-1023. Located behind the market, this is a very popular hotel/hostel catering to the budget minded. Featuring 6 private rooms with bath for $20.00 U.S. per night or dorm room with 6 beds and shared bath for $10.00 U.S. per night. Visit www.angelashostel.mx or ✉: angelashostel@hotmail.com

Bugambillas: ★ *Las Mangos #28.* ☏ 554-5815. This simply furnished small hotel behind the market offers a good bargain for the budget minded.

Casa Aurora: ★ *Nicolás Bravo #42.* ☏ 554-3046. Clean, neat, little hotel for the budget-minded.

Casa Elvira: ★ *Paseo del Pescado.* ☏ 554-2061. An institution for over 50 years. This ten-room guesthouse is right in front of the beach. Guests share a bathroom-shower arrangement. Very clean but sparse. Ideal for the really budget-minded.

Citlali: ★ ★ *Calle Vicente Guerrero.* ☏ 554-2043. Across the street from Coconuts, this is a small charming hotel that keeps guests coming back year after year.

Hotel Adelita: ★ *Juan Alvarez #34.* ☏ 554-2028. Small hotel with 10 rooms—a few with air conditioning. E-mail: adelita@yahoo.com

Hotel Avila: ★★*Juan Alvarez* #2. ☎ 554-2010. This 27-room hotel with air conditioning, telephone service, and satellite TV was one of the first in *Zihua*. Extensive renovation has made it one of the nicest and most popular downtown spots with many rooms overlooking the bay. They now have lovely apartments (without a bay view) across the street from the hotel for long-term rentals.

Hotel Casa Bravo: ★ *Nicolás Bravo.* ☎ 554-2528. Small 7-room hotel is a very popular place with the snowbirds that come down every winter. They offer discounted weekly and monthly rates. There is a lovely apartment on the top floor, which may be available.

Hotel Gaby Inn: ★★*Calle Palapa* #135. ☎ 554-7808. Air conditioning, hot water, mini-kitchen, and living room make this hotel in the market area a good bargain for the price.

Hotel Hi-Sol: ★★ *Cinco de Mayo* end of *Calle Gonzalez.* ☎ 554-0595. Hotel in the heart of *centro* with 21 junior suites. All rooms are air conditioned with balcony, ceiling fans, hot water, living room, cable television and parking. Immaculately maintained.

Hotel Idalia: ★ *Vicente* Guerrero(close to *Ejido*). ☎ 554-2062/554-3199. My favorite very inexpensive hotel in *centro* but very basic. A real favorite of budget-minded snowbirds. Hot water and fans. Several rooms have refrigerators.

Hotel Imelda: ★★ *Calle Gonzalez.* ☎ 554-7662. Fax. 554-3199. A 78-room hotel close to the market area with good-sized rooms. Now offering air conditioning, cable television, room telephones, and two pools. Restaurant on the premises and off the street parking. ✉ hotelimelda@prodigy.net.mx

Hotel Zihua Inn: ★★*Calle Las Palapas.* ☎ 554-3868/554-3921. Fax. 554-7430. This hotel has 48 large rooms—most with air conditioning. Pool and parking available.

Hotel Suzi: ★★ *Esq. Juan Alvarez y Vicente Guerrero.* ☎ 554-2339. This 18 room hotel, some with air conditioning, is quite popular and a good value. The owners are extremely nice and quite helpful.

Posada Michel :★ *Nicolás Bravo.* ☎ 554-7423. Each of the rooms, overlooking a courtyard of sorts, has a ceiling fan and private bath.

Raúl 3 Mariás: ★★*Juan Alvarez*. ☎ 554-2977. Same family as *Tres Marías*—less stringent guest rules. Good bargain for the price but if you're a night owl, you might not enjoy the navy band, which starts up every morning right behind the hotel at sunrise. Not all the 20 rooms are the same, so check out a few before making a decision.

Zihua Centro: ★★★ *Augustín Ramirez* #2. ☎ 554-5330/5340. In each of the 74 air conditioned rooms and 6 suites, you'll find a ceiling fan, satellite TV, and telephone. They also offer a restaurant, bar, swimming pool, garage parking and laundry service. Visit www.zihuacentro.com or ✉ reserve@zihuacentro.com

These are a very few of the *centro* hotels—there are dozens more—even a youth hostel on *Avenida Las Salinas* #50—*Rincon del Viajero*. The following are "in town" but not "downtown."

Casa de Fantasía: ★★★★ Located in *Almacen*—across the bridge and up the road to the left. ☎ U.S. 1(323)656-6910 or Fax. 1(323)650-3060. A two story home with two separate apartments of 2/2 or rented as a 4-bedroom villa. ✉ HugoSalas@aol.com

Cielo Mar: *Paseo de los Hujes* #5. ☎ 112-1383. A therapeutic recovery house located in *El Hujal*. Visit www.drostrov.com or ✉ eostrov@aol.com (I couldn't allocate a price range because it would of course depend on what medical treatments would be necessary).

Hotel Rubi: ★★ *Calle Rubi* #71. ☎ 554-8985 or ☎ (755)724-9476. Off the beaten path but still close to town. Well maintained small hotel with pool.

Hotel Solimar Inn Suites: ★★ *Higos* #4. ☎ 554-3692/0662. Very popular with the snowbirds looking for long-term rental. They have 12 complete suites for rent. Visit www.solimarinn.com or ✉solimarinn@ixtapa-zihuatanejo.com

El Tradicional: ★ *Av. Morelos* #165. ☎ 554-2920 or fax 554-8515. Older hotel on the outskirts of *centro* designed with families in mind. There are 45 rooms and a pool. Visit www.ixtapa-zihuatanejo.net/eltradicional or ✉ eltradicionalzih@hotmail.com

The manager and part of the family that owns the hotel, Eloisa, has some lovely long term rental apartments for rent close to the market and *Playa La Madera*. ☎ 554-2714.

The Boat House: ★ ★ Located in *Almacen*. Mike and Dee have a lovely small house for rent close to the pier. ☎ 1(410)777-5780 or ✉ zihuadee@yahoo.com Captain Mike is a strong advocate of catch and release fishing.

Tres Marías: ★ Located in *Almacen*. Over the bridge and to the right. ☎ 554-2191. *Tres Marías* has long been a favorite of many visitors. If you're a party animal or a night owl, this is not the place for you. Guest rules are very stringent. Partying, although not prohibited, is not encouraged. Their 25 rooms have wonderful balconies with a terrific bay view and the price is right and security excellent.

Villas El Morro: ★ ★ ★ *Paseo El Morro*, Lot 4 (next to *Villa Vera* Hotel). ☎ 557-1544/554-9013. Located high above *Almacen*, this hotel features 7 unique suites with breathtaking views and a pool. Visit www.zihuatanejo-villaselmorro.com or ✉ reservaciones@zihuatanejo-villaselmorro.com

Playa La Madera and Vicinity

Playa La Madera, located between town and *Playa La Ropa*, is a favorite choice of international travelers. Although not the prettiest beach, accommodations are within a five-to-ten-minute walk from town—located far enough away to avoid the traffic and pedestrian noises. Most accommodations have kitchenettes. The burglary rate here is much higher than in other parts of town. Be vigilant.

Playa La Madera basically consists of two street—the mostly level bottom street which is *Calle Adelita* or the street up the steep hill *Eva Sámano de López Mateos*. With few exception and I do mean few—a beach view is going to entail a taxi ride or a walk or climb up a steep hill.

Arena Suites: ★ ★ ★ ☎ 554-4087. New owners of older hotel on *Playa La Madera* right on the beach. www.zihuatanejoarenasuites.com ✉ bungalowsley@prodigy.net.mx ✉ arenasuites@hotmail.com

Bahía Suites: ★ ★ ★ ★ *Eva Sámano López Mateos*—to the right. ☎ 554-3225/7655. These are private condos rented out for the day, week, or month. There are 21 units from studios to luxurious penthouses. A/C, TV, Jacuzzis, pool. Stunning views.

Búngalos Allec: ★★ *Eva Sámano López Mateos.* ☎ 554-2002. There are 6 small and 6 large bungalows located literally steps from the beach. All have kitchenettes. The decor can best be described as "I Love Lucy"-style 50's. Visit www.Búngalosallec.com or ✉ reservar@bungalosallec.com

Búngalos Pacíficos: ★★★ *Eva Sámano López Mateos* #34—to the right. ☎ 554-2112. These 6 bungalows are a fixture in *Zihua*. All bungalows have three beds and a small kitchen area. The balconies are huge, providing shade and sun areas. Owner, Anita Hahner, speaks fluent English, German, Spanish, and French. She is a great hostess and extremely knowledgeable about the area. Visit www.bungalospacificos.com or ✉ bungpaci@prodigy.net.mx

Búngalos Sotelo: ★★★ *Eva Sámano López Mateos* #1. ☎ 554-6307 or 544-6345. These very nice bungalows cascade down the hill directly to the beach. They are all air conditioned and some have very large terraces. Very nice. ✉ reservar@bungalossoltelo.com

Casa Adriana: ★★ *Eva Sámano López Mateos*—to the right. ☎ 554-2601. There are several one-bedroom units with refrigerators and balconies. There is also a large two-bedroom suite. Visit www.casaadriana.com.mx or ✉ casa_adriana@yahoo.com

Casa Azul: ★★★ *Eva Sámano López Mateos*—to the right. A tropical complex with 3 apartments. One week reservation a requirement. Visit www.casaazul-zihuatanejo.com or ✉ info@casaazul-zihuatanejo.com

Casa de los Sueños: ★ *Calle Adelita* #1. ☎ 554-5984. Small and rustic *Búngalos* for rent. No view.Visit www.casadelossuenos.com or ✉ lucilamairen@yahoo.com.mx

Casa Lagartija: ★★★ *Eva Sámano López Mateos*—to the right. ☎ 554-9391. A very old home on *Playa La Madera* completely restored and converted to wonderful bungalows. ✉nj.rubaloff@g.mail.com or visit www.casa-lagartija.com

Casa Loma Bonita: ★★ *Calle Adelita.* ☎ 554-5896 or 📱 (755)105-3369. Three nicely appointed suites with ocean view. Visit www.vaccaciones.com

Casa Sun and Moon: ★★ *Calle Adelita* #10. ☎ 554-5216. This small hotel complete with lovely gardens and pool perches on a cliff above *Playa La Madera*. There are single rooms and suites with shared cooking facilities and balconies with stunning bay views. Visit www.sunandmoon.com.mx
or ✉ reservations@sunandmoon.com.mx

El Milagro: ★★★ Road to *Playa La Ropa*. ☎ 554-3045. One of the oldest complexes in town. A favorite of German snowbirds that return yearly. 17 suites with all amenities.
Visit www.ixtapa-zihuatanejo.net/elmilagro or klausbuhrer@hotmail.com

Hotel Brisas del Mar: ★★★ *Eva Sámano López Mateos*—to the left. ☎ 554-2142/8382. This hotel complex on *Playa La Madera* cascades down the hillside, and most rooms have a balcony with bay view. There is a large pool and restaurant on the beach. Visit www.hotelbrisasdelmar.com or ✉ info@hotelbrisasdelmar.com

Hotel Irma: ★★ *Calle Adelita*. ☎ 554-8472 and Fax 554-3738. There are 75 air conditioned rooms arranged on several levels around the pool. One of the first hotels to open in *Zihua*. It is still a first-class establishment. Visit www.hotelirma.com.mx
or ✉ vtasmexhotels@prodigy.net.mx

Hotel Palacios: ★★ *Calle Adelita* #24. ☎ 554-2055. There are 28 rooms here and prices vary. Some of the rooms are dark and small while five have an ocean view and are quite comfortable. A pool and restaurant are on the premises. Make sure you look at your room before renting. Weekends tend to be noisy.
Visit www.zihuatanejo.net/hotelpalacios or
✉ hotelpalacios@zihuatanejo.net

Hotel Vic-Mar: ★ *Paseo La Boquita*—two blocks past *Kyoto Circle*. ☎ 554-3821. Old and tired but cheap!

Mi Casita: ★★ ☎ 554-4510. *Escénico a Playa La Ropa s/n*. Next to *Kau Kan*. There are 6 cute rooms here with a lovely ocean view. (I couldn't find a website).

La Ceiba Suites: ★★★ *Calle Remedios—Playa La Madera*. ☎ 554-7826. These are beautiful one to three bedroom condos individually owned but many are rented during the year No bay view.

Visit www.ceiba.com.mx or ✉ rental@ceiba.com.mx The rental units start at about $150.00 U.S. per day and if you can live without a beach view, this is an excellent value.The huge number of robberies has been reduced—all that was necessary was firing an employee.

La Quinta de Don Andrés: ★ ★ ★ *Calle Adelita.* ☎ 554-3794. Now containing 12 luxurious villas and a small house separate from the property. Renovated completely in 2010. Most villas have full kitchen. Visit www.laquintadedonadres.com or
✉ reservations@laquintadedonandres.com

Los Arcos del Noé: ★ *Eva Sámano López Mateos*—to the right. A quaint 16-room hotel with kitchen facilities for most of the rooms.

Villa Cruz del Mar: ★ ★ *Calle Adelita.* ☎ 554-3619. A lovely nine-room complex surrounding a pool and gardens. Very quiet. Different layouts with most containing cooking facilities.
✉ vepaozg@prodigy.net.mx

Villas Mercedes: ★ ★ *Calle Adelita.* ✆ (755)108-5054. Seven rooms with pool and all amenities. Prices same for low and high season. However, the hotel sits on a corner and one street has a sign saying rates are $45.00 U.S. and the other street has a sign with $55.00 U.S. and then the board behind the registration desk says $400 pesos. Visit www.hotelvillamercedes.com or ✉ elmo01@prodigy.net.mx

Villas Miramar: ★ ★ ★ *Calle Adelita.* ☎ 554-2106 or Fax 554-3359. These villas, containing 18 air conditioned suites are some of the nicest in the area. The grounds are beautifully maintained and the rooms large and nicely decorated in the Mexican motif. The suites consist of two buildings, one on either side of the street. Each one has its own pool.

Villas Naomi: ★ ★ ★ *Ade*litas 114. ☎544-7303. Newest hotel on *Playa La Madera.* Visit www.villasnaomi.com

Villa Polinesia: ★ ★ *Paseo de la Boquita.* ☎ 101-9823 or 110-0500. A fully equipped 5-room complex close to the beach. Modestly priced and a good value for the money. Visit www.villapolinesia.com or
✉ juanluisdelagarza@gmail.com

ZihuaCaracol: ★ ★ *Calle Adelita #10.* ☎ 554-9519 or from U.S. or Canada 1(800)570-8178. One of the oldest hotels in town but completely renovated. The rooms are rather plain.
Visit www.hotelzihuacaracol.com or ✉ reservas@hotmail.com

Playa La Ropa Accommodations

Playa La Ropa has some beautiful accommodations and most have pretty good security but don't be lax about guarding your valuables and never leave your door unlocked.

Amuleto: ★ ★ ★ ★ *Calle Escenica* #9. ☎ 544-6222. Magnificent small boutique hotel high above the bay. Only 5 rooms. No children under 16, no dogs, no smoking, no TV, and no radio.
Visit www.amuleto.net or ✉ reservations@amuleto.net .
Búngalos Tucanes: ★ ★ (Map LR 2). ☎ 554-3392 or Fax 554-8546. Secluded garden compound off the beach offering one and two bedroom attractive bungalows. ✉ casa-tucanes@hotmail.com
Búngalos Vepao: ★ ★ (Map LR 3). ☎ 554-3619 or Fax 554-5003. This is a well maintained, fifteen bungalow complex right on the beach. All units contain kitchen facilities. Visit www.bungalosvepao.com or ✉ vepao@yahoo.com
Casa Buenaventura: ★ ★ ★ ★ (Map LR 47). ☎ 554-4924 or ☎ (755)557-0149. Six-room hotel with all amenities located a scant two blocks from the beach. Visit www.casabuenaventura.net or ✉ donfranciscoproperties@g.mail.com
Casa Cuitlateca: ★ ★ ★ ★ (Map LR 4). ☎ From US and Canada 1(877)541-1234. This is a magnificent small B&B above *Playa La Ropa* containing 4 different guestroom/suites. Children are not allowed unless the entire villa is booked.
Visit www.casacuitlateca.com or ✉ marathon24@prodigy.net.com
Casa de las Piedras/Casa de Bambú: ★ ★ (Map LR 5) ☎ 554-3095. This is a charming home for rent above *Playa La Ropa*. It is outdoor living at its best and receives rave reviews year after year. *Casa de Bambu* and Hummingbird Treehouse are also available and are very unique accommodations especially if you like the outdoors. Visit www.casadelaspierdras or ✉ zihuacasa@hotmail.com
Casa del Arbol: ★ ★ ★ ★ (Map LR 22). ☎ 1(877)232-7265. This is **the** most fabulous home in all Zihuatanejo. It is also the highest and you can look down on the para-sailors! There are four luxurious bedrooms, an open-air living-dining area, television room, infinity pool, and much, much more. Visit www.casadelarbol.com or ✉ info@casadelarbol.com

Casa Heidi: ★★★*Carretera Escenica la Ropa* #114. ☎124-7153. A charming 6 room small hotel with all amenities.
Visit www.casaheidi.com or ⊠casaheidi@gmail.com

Casa Iguana: ★★★★*Paseo del Delfin* #3. ☎ or fax. 544-6922. Six very nicely appointed suites in the vicinity of *Playa La Ropa.*
Visit www.casaiguana.com or ⊠ casa_iguana@zihuatanejo.net

Casa Larga: ★★★ (Map LR 29). ☎ 554-6089. This charming home, just steps from the beach, can be rented in its entirety or as individual suites. ⊠ zcasalarga@yahoo.com

Casa Luna and Búngalo Azul: ★★★(Map LR 8). ☎ 1(310) 854-0096 or fax 1 (310) 657-5779. *Casa Luna* and the separate bungalow are located within a block of *Playa La Ropa* inside a gated tropical compound with pool, Jacuzzi, Wi-Fi—all the amenities. The *Búngalo Azul* consist of 3 very reasonably priced suites across the street. Visit www.villa-casa-luna.com or ⊠ parkec123@gmail.com

Casa del Mar: ★★★ (Map LR 17). ☎ or Fax 554-3873. The rooms are simple but the grounds are very nicely manicured right next to the estuary with sunning crocodiles on the property. Good lounge chairs, attentive service, and pretty good food. A very popular spot steps from the beach. Visit www.zihua-casadelmar.com or ⊠ reserv@zihua-casadelmar.com

Club Intrawest ★★★★ (Map LR 35). ☎ 555-0350 or in the U.S. 1(800)649-8816. Club Intrawest is the private resort club of Intrawest Corporation, a billion-dollar development corporation who owns and or manages 12 resorts worldwide. Opened in December 2004, it now offers its vacation home suites to existing members and as hotel rooms to the public. Frankly, it's fabulous. A visual conglomeration of Mexico combined with all the North American conveniences of a first rate hotel. Visit www.clubintrawest.com or ⊠ resorts@clubintrawest.com

El Tamarindo de la Zihngaras: ★★ (Map LR 12). *Paseo de La Ropa* #124. ☎ 553-8967. This is a private home a short walk from the beach. There are 4 complete suites—each unique and charming. There is a minimum five night stay and the owner prefers long-term rentals. ⊠ tamarindo@zhiua-ixtapa.com

Gloria María Búngalos: ★★★(Map LR 14). ☎ 554-6954. Right on the beach, these *búngalos* have quickly become very sought after. ⊠ reservations@zihuatanejo.cc

Hotel Casa Blanca: ★★ (Map LR 1). ☎ 554-3415. Four beautifully appointed rooms located at the very end of the road to *Playa La Ropa*. Steps from the beach.

✉ hotel_casa_blanca@hotmail.com

Hotel Catalina: ★★★ (Map LR 10). ☎ 554-2137 or 554-9321/25. The oldest hotel in town built in 1956 by five American businessmen, the **Sotavento-Catalina** complex is now two separate entities. The *Sotavento* is now full-time condo ownership. Visit www.catalina-beach-resort.com or ✉ info@catalina-beach-resort.com

La Casa Que Canta Hotel: ★★★★ (Map LR 15). From U.S. 1(888)5235050. ☎ 554-2722, 554-2782 or Fax 554-2006. Built on a cliff between the beaches of *Playa La Ropa* and *Playa La Madera*. The individual decor of its suites, each one with a salon and terrace, is a tribute to the different regions of the Mexican Republic. Two pools are offered—a fresh-water one on the main terrace and an ocean-filled one at the foot of the cliff. The complex contains Jacuzzis and massage rooms. An exquisite restaurant with impeccable service is on the premises. This resort is for the discriminating and wealthy. www.lacasaquecanta.com or ✉ guestservice@casaquecanta.com

La Villa: ★★★★ (Map LR 13) ☎ 112-1834 or call owners direct 1(408) 997-2214. Located a few steps from the Dolphins on *Playa La Ropa*, this extremely charming small boutique hotel offers all the amenities one would expect at a luxurious resort. Has received rave reviews. Visit www.lavillazihuatanejo.com or ✉ lavillaz@aol.com

Las Urracas: ★★ (Map LR 16). ☎ 554-2053/2049. These 17 rustic bungalows with kitchens are a favorite of many long-time visitors. It's conveniently located adjacent to the *La Perla* restaurant.

Los Arcos: ★★★ (Map LR 26). ☎ 554-5409. Three beautifully appointed suites and two apartments located near the end of *Playa La Ropa* adjacent to a private home owned by Nancy Lewis—a lovely lady full of information and lots of fun. Lovely grounds and pool area—a short walk to the beach. The entire home can be rented also. Visit www.losarcoszihuatanejo.com or ✉ info@losarcoszihuatanejo.gmail.com

Los Azucenas ★ ★ ★ *Calle* 1. (Toward the beach from the Dolphins). ☎ 544-6593. ☎ (755)100264 or 120-7710. This hotel is the latest edition on *Playa La Ropa* and has at this writing 12 suites. They are building additional rooms and condos on their very large lot next to *Paty's Mar y Mar.* The rooms are very spacious and lovely. Visit www.hotellasazucenas.com or ✉las_azucenas@hotmail.com

Pacífica Grand Resort & Spa: ★ ★ ★ ★ *Escénica a La Ropa.* ☎103-6022/3. Very luxurious resort time-share arrangement offering rooms to the public for around $300.00 U.S. per night low season. Their restaurant **Suspiro** is purported to be five stars—I have yet to meet anyone who has eaten there but the view is fabulous. Visit www.Pacificagrand.com.mx or ✉ paciserv@pacificagrand.com.mx

Quinta Troppo: ★ ★ ★ ★ (Map LR 18). *Playa La Ropa s/n.* ☎ 554-3423/7340. This is a beautiful 8 suite B & B overlooking *Playa La Ropa.* One of the best. Visit www.laquintatroppo.com or ✉ troppo@prodigy.net.mx

Rossy's Hotel: ★ ★ (Map LR19). ☎ 554-5034/4004. There are 29 double rooms just one short block from the beach. Visit www.hotelrossy.com or ✉ hotelrestaurantrossy@hotmail.com

Suites La Ropa: ★ ★ (Map LR 21). ☎ 554-8433. Located behind *El Pirata* restaurant, these small but very nice rooms are one of the best bargains on the beach. Visit www.zihuatanejo.net/suiteslaropa/ or ✉ suiteslaropa@yahoo.com.mx

Viceroy ★ ★ ★ ★ (Map LR 24). ☎ 555-5500 or Fax 554-2758. Reservation ☎ 1(866)905-9560. Helmet Leins, the former owner of *Villa del Sol* in 1969 helped define luxury in this part of the world. He started with six rooms which have grown to 35 rooms and 35 suites. He sold to the Tides in 2009 and in 2011 **The Tides** was purchased by a group of miners from Peru. When it became the Tides, they allowed children during high season and their patrons consisted of lots families with small children. During their first year of operation, I saw the very worst boob jobs than I've ever seen in my life. Visit www.viceroyzihuatanejo.com or✉info@viceroyzihuatanejo.com

Villa Carolina: ★★★★ (Map LR 27). ☎ 554-5612 or Fax 554-5615. There are four garden and two master suites in this gorgeous complex close to the beach. ✉ villacarolina@zihuatanejo.net.mx

Villas Ema: ★★ (Map LR 39). ☎ 554-2043. Located steps from the beach, these air conditioned rooms with kitchenettes and 2 villas are perfect for those not wanting to climb hills or a lot of steps. Owned by the same folks as *Citlali* with the same phone number, be sure and stipulate you want reservations at *Villas Ema.*
✉ villasema@zihuatanejo.com.mx

Villas Guadalupe: ★★★★(Map LR 6). ☎ 544-8383. Seven room boutique hotel with beautiful bay view. Home of *Tentaciones* restaurant. Visit www.hotelvillaguadalupe.com
or ✉ canjunso@yahoo.com

Villas del Palmar: ★★★ (Map LR 56). ☎ 544-7838/9663. There are 4 lovely *villas* and 2 studios. A very short walk to the beach. Visit www.villasdelpalmar.com or ✉ villasdelpalmar@hotmail.com

Villas Encanta y Bahía: ★★★★ *Escénica a Las Gatas s/n.* These two villas sit high above the beach with spectacular views. Very private and secluded. ✉ encahi2@aol.com

Villa Mexicana: ★★★ (Map LR 28), ☎ 554-8472/7888 or Fax 554-3738. *Villa Mexicana* stands as one of *Zihua's* finest, moderately priced, beachfront hotels. Each of its 64 rooms offers air conditioning and satellite TV. There is a restaurant, bar and swimming pool. Guest parking. Visit www.hotelvillamexicana.com

Villas Palmera: ★★★★ (Map LR 25). ☎ and Fax 554-3095. A six-apartment complex located at the end of *Playa La Ropa.*
✉ villapalmera@hotmail.com

Villa San Sebastian: ★★★ *Escénica a La Ropa s/n.* (Next to LR 47). ☎ 554-4154. These 9 guest suites are just a block off the beach and they command wonderful views of the bay. Also available is *Villa La Ropa*, a lovely home for rent close by.
✉ luisvall@prodigy.net.mx

Zanzíbar: ★★★★ (Map LR 30). A beautiful home for rent overlooking *Playa La Ropa*. Lois and David are gracious hosts and rave reviews are the norm. Visit www.zihuatanejo.net/zanzibar or ✉ vzanzibar@hotmail.com

Playa Las Gatas Accommodations

Playa Las Gatas Beach Club: ★ ★ ★   📱 (755)102-7111. Owen Lee has been renting out eco-friendly bungalows for over 30 years at the end of *Playa Las Gatas.* A true tropical beach getaway.

Condominiums on *Playa La Ropa*

Renting a luxurious condo on one of the beaches can be more economical than renting a hotel room. I've noticed that many of the local real estate agents have extensive listings for condos. Before the economic fallout in the U.S. lots of folks built or bought condos here as investment properties. I would imagine these rents would be very negotiable as the number of tourists has diminished in recent years. It's not a bad idea to visit VBRO—they seem to have extensive listings of condos and homes in the whole area.

Cascada: (Map LR 31). There are twelve gorgeous condos, some for rent in this project. The view is spectacular and there is a small guest pool. Each individual owner has their own listing agent.

La Casa Que Ve Al Mar: (Map LR 32). ☎ 553-2415. Part of the original *Cascada* project, these condos are absolutely gorgeous but if you didn't have a vehicle, it's quite the climb. There is no official website but if you plug the name into a search engine, **lots** of the individual condos pop up. Many owners list with VBRO.

La Cieba: ☎ 755-554-9534. Condo complex with huge pool located at the end of *Playa La Ropa,* adjacent to *Los Arcos.* No hills to climb and no bayview. Just steps from beach entrance. Judith Whitehead handles some of the rental properties. Noemi Serna Najera can also be quite helpful as she is the administrator. ✉ ceibaropa@hotmail.com

Los Mangos: Very nice complex on the road to *La Perla.* No view but again, no hills to climb and a minute to the beach. They have no administrator but one of the tenants, Linda Leonard (☎ 103-6032) is happy to help owners "gratis" find rentors and vice versa.

Preciosa: Next door to *Cascada.* There are 8 suites and 2 penthouses. They have great bay views and the condos are very well appointed and the finish work is some of the best in town. The parking situation is awful. There is no website but some owners are listing with VBRO.

Punta Peñasca: (Map LR 34). This 14-condominium complex is among my favorites in the area. Each condo offers a magnificent bay view with lots of glass and open areas. The interior craftsmanship is superb with lots of attention to detail. Prices and floor plans vary. Rentals through various real estate agents.

Punta Marina: (Map LR 33). ☎ 554-3995 or ▌ (755)557-3399. Stunning condos at the end of *Playa La Ropa.*
Visit www.puntamarinazihua.com
✉ puntamarina@msn.com

Residencias Villa Del Sol: (Map LR 24). ☎ 554-2239 or Fax 554-2758. Blending in with the hotel Viceroy, these condos are meticulously maintained and occasionally one comes on the market but not often as they are highly prized.

Sotovento Residencias: (Map LR 20). Not completed as of summer 2012..
Playa La Ropa s/n. ☎1(877)976-8283 or 554-7145.

Villas de la Palma: (Map LR 36). ☎ 553-0305. Twelve deluxe villas containing 2 bedrooms/2 baths and all amenities. Sometimes for rent—look for signs in the windows or check with a real estate agent.
The reader will notice I gave no prices for the above condos. Sale prices range from about $60,000 U.S. to around $1,000,000 U.S.

Villas Zitlala: *Paseo de Playa La Ropa* #116. This is the humongous ugly hole in the mountain across from the entrance to *Residencias Villa del Sol.* Jeff See, formerly of Coconuts, put together this project which halted due to the finances. It's been abandoned for a long time and is a reminder to what can happen if buying in the pre-construction phase of a project.

I would be remiss if I didn't mention **Monte Cristo** and **Cerro de Vigia.** *Monte Cristo* consists of 200 acres of pristine coastline located on the north side of town within the city limits. The homes being built in this gated community start in the millions—dollars not pesos. Food and Wine magazine had a three day event in *Zihua* in 2011and 2012 and locals were able to pay $25.00 U.S. and view three of these homes—truly spectacular. If you count yourself as "obscenely rich" or just want to see how the other half lives visit www.montecristomexico.com or call 1(800)421-7005.

Cerro de Vigía, located on the south side of town covering the mountain and ocean side of *Playa Las Gatas*, is our other gated community for the wealthy. I've been in several of the homes and they are lovely. Visit www.cerrodevigia.com or ☎ 553-3006/09 or ✉ Paradise-sales@cerrodevigia.com

Comidas y Cantinas

(Food and Drink)

Zihua has some very fine restaurants. compared to the 4 when I arrived in 1971, there is a huge variety in choice of venue and menu, I don't recommend food selections. With 100 restaurants today, just in the downtown area, Most food is safe to eat. For new arrivals vendors on the streets or market eateries. Restaurants use purified ice.

Note: If preparing food for you in your rental unit, a handy product to use for purifying is *Microdyn*—drops sold in most pharmacies. Soak vegetables or fruit to be eaten unpeeled or uncooked for 15-20 minutes in water containing one drop of Microdyn per liter of water.

There really are health inspectors in *Zihua* and kitchen personnel must have a health certificate and blood test before handling food. Cleanliness requirements, although not up to American standards, are enforced. If you have your doubts about the place, peek into the kitchen. Restaurants in Zihuatanejo have one thing in common— inconsistency.

Again, word of mouth is the best way to judge a restaurant's status quo. Sometimes the restaurateurs forget that without the locals support, they won't be local restaurants for long. There are 5,000 full and part-time residents in high season. If each of us talks to only one tourist couple a day—we have influenced 10,000 tourists! Do the math. Some of the owners tend to forget who butters their bread. Moreover, about 2,000 of those locals are here year-round.

Everyone wants to know why food costs in restaurants are so high, especially with an ocean bounty of fish and shellfish. The answer is simple. Local fishermen belong to a union co-operative. They set the price for sea life and this price is passed on to the consumer. Over the years, they bay has been stripped of our "famous red clams", oysters, and lobsters. Fishermen are forced to go further and dive deeper for these delicacies each year—driving the price up.

Lobsters, female and undersized, are regularly sold at the market, making them less available each year. The fact that foreigners like *huachinango* (red snapper) and it is thus much in demand, has driven up the price for this fish to much higher than the "catch of the day" or other offerings on the menu. A large variety of tasty fish are caught in the area including *pargo, sierra,* marlin, *corbita,* tuna, *dorado* or mahi-mahi, and most menus offer a "catch of the day" at considerably savings.

The Mexican government sets prices of meat products but their regulatory agency is so understaffed that very few of the meat vendors comply with the law. Most meat, whether it is hamburger or pork chops, runs about $3.50/lb. *Lomo,* or tenderloin of pork or beef is slightly higher. The finer restaurants order their meats from northern Mexico and may pay up to $10.00 per pound.

You can now buy beef tenderloin in the market or at *Comercial Mexicana* for about $9.00 per pound. I buy a kilo of beef tenderloin at *Tres Hermanos* on the backside of the market for $120 pesos a kilo making my filet mignon cost less than $10 pesos each.

Chickens are expensive on menus because they cost about $85 pesos each in the market (claws, head, and all). They are not mass-produced and high feed costs and the mortality-rate contributes to the very high price.

Another item of note: In North American restaurants, owners generally operate on a one to three mark-up: cost of food times three equals price. Many restaurants here use a one to five equation to arrive at price. Then again, many owners seem to pull a figure out of thin air—more popular items such as *guacamole* or *nachos* mean higher prices.

In all fairness, I must say restaurants pay an enormous amount in taxes. In the early 80's, the Mexican government initiated *IVA.* This is a value-added tax on all restaurant bills, hotels, goods and services. Originally this tax was added to the final bill. Many foreigners thought this was a service charge and therefore left no tip. Waiters in restaurants were outraged and in 1984 the government allowed IVA to be included in the bill as a "hidden" cost. This is now 16%. Hotels pay an additional 2% tax.

In addition to the value-added tax, restaurants must pay social security for workers (40% of the salary), state and municipal taxes, and income tax. These all add up and must be passed on to the consumer.

Unless you are one of those fortunate individuals able to say, "money is no object", beware of ordering imports such as Scotch, Bombay, or aperitifs. You'll pay between $8.00 and $12.00 a drink. Imported liquors are heavily taxed.

Remember, Thursday in Mexico is *pozole* day and Sunday's are traditionally *barbacoa de chivo* (goat).

Tipping

When calculating a tip on a restaurant or bar bill, the normal American or Canadian standard of 10% to 20% is applicable. Though it's true that restaurant and bar bills will include a 16% value-added tax, this money is remitted to the government and does not go to the service staff. Remember the person serving you earns approximately $4.00 to $5.00 U.S. per day in salary, so, needless to say, tips are their "daily bread."

You will also want to tip maids, bellboys, etc. according to the guidelines customary elsewhere.

There are, however, some differences in tipping policies in Mexico. For instance, it is customary to tip the attendant at the gas station but not taxi drivers. The locals know these "rules" and because we do, sometimes the taxi drivers won't pick us up because they know we don't tip. And yes, the taxi drivers recognize the locals. A long time ago, I had a taxi driver really cross the line one evening. I had him arrested and thrown in jail for three days. As a result, I couldn't get taxis to stop for me for about three years. That's when I had to buy a car.

Comidas y Cantinas
Centro

The restaurants have been coded as follows (not including drinks or tip):

🍽 Inexpensive—$50.00 pesos or less.
🍽🍽Moderate—$150.00 pesos or less.
🍽🍽🍽 Expensive—$200.00 to $250.00 pesos.
🍽🍽🍽🍽 Very expensive—$250.00 pesos or more.

In trying to determine what category to place the following restaurants, I looked at the menus and in whatever price range the majority of the entrees fell, that's where I put them. Many restaurants serve breakfast, lunch, and dinner and a determination as to category was then a personal call.

Most of the finer restaurants accept plastic. If in doubt, ask first; do not assume everyone takes credit cards. American Express is very unpopular in Mexico—try to use Visa or MasterCard instead.

Unless otherwise stated, reservations are not necessary. Most restaurants are closed one day a week. I have tried to make note of their particular closure dates but it is difficult as they change often.

When classifying as very expensive—as a chef, I can tell you almost exactly what the food costs on a plate. When I see $30.00 pesos on my plate and pay $200.00 pesos or more for the plate, I consider these restaurants very expensive.

Lastly, in the spring of 2011, I was bored one weekend and did a restaurant count. The total was around 170 (including the market). Fall of 2011, the five block downtown area had 99 and the market 32. Fall 2012, downtown area was up to 104 and the same 32 in the market. Many new places have a hand-written piece of posterboard for their menu and name—not even a small investment in a *lona* (plastic billboard costing about twenty dollars). Extortion is the new big deal here and many folks are closing their doors rather than pay money to the gangs—their families are threatened with kidnapping and their livlihood threatened by arson. It's tough doing business in Mexico these days so you may find many of the businesses listed in the following pages closed due to the economic hardships or the criminal elements.

Andy's Live Music and Bar: ❢❢ *Vicente Guerrero.* Next door to *Coconut's.* Fall 2012 being renovated so no details but it's looking good.

Agave: ❢❢❢ *Nicolas Bravo #49.* Great people watching spot on the second floor. Atmosphere is lovely and food is international.

Bandido's: ❢❢❢ *Cinco de Mayo*—across from native market. ☎ 553-8072. Live music Tuesday through Saturday during high season. Menu varied and food very popular. Open daily during high season and closed on Sunday during low season.

Barracruda: ❢❢❢ *Cuauhtémoc.* Rick's old locale. Live music. Opened November 1st 2011 and this new local is doing very well.

Café Marina: ❢❢❢ *Paseo de Pescador #9.* ☎ 554-2462. Open in 1984 by American Joe Wells, this is a small but excellent restaurant on the waterfront. Great nightly specials. He has a very loyal following and for good reason. His food is very good and reasonably priced. I can't say that about many places, unfortunately. Joe maintains a book exchange that is patronized by locals and tourists. Closed Sunday. Open 7:00 a.m. until 9:00 p.m. during high season.

Cafeteria El Sabor: ❢❢*A. Ramirez.* Coffe shop in Coconut's alley.

Casa Arcadia: ❢❢❢*Paseo del Pescador*—right on beach at museum end of beach. ☎ 554-8507. This is a great place to people watch and view the sunset. Two for one drinks all the time and they make really good daiquiris. Open daily 8 a.m. until people stop drinking.

Casa Elvira: ⟋●⟍●⟋ *Paseo del Pescador.* ☎ 554-2061. An institution in *Zihua* since 1956. The menu, specializing in Mexican seafood, has something for everyone. A "best value" in *Zihua.* However, it's hard to eat and have a conversation with all the vendors crowding the tables and singing musicians passing through. Under new management. Open for breakfast, lunch, and dinner daily.

Chilolo's: ⟋●⟍●⟋ *Calle Armada* #25. Cute very Mexican style restaurant off the beaten path with some terrific prices on seafood. Now open in the morning until early evening..

Chula Vista: ⟋●⟍●⟋Upstairs directly across from basketball court. Now serving food, this is a great spot to have a drink on Sunday evening and watch the entertainment at the court. Everyone used to get a fantastic hamburger or hotdog from the vendor in the middle of the street and bring them upstairs but now that this restaurant serves food, they don't appreciate this anymore.

Chuleto's: ⟋●⟍●⟋●⟋ *Paseo del Pescador s/n.* ☎554-6639. Closed Tuesday and only open for dinner. Paul's restaurant with the same heart, the same menu, and the same staff is one of the finest in town. Paul died in April of 2003 leaving everyone wondering what would become of "the best food around." The staff found a new locale and decided to re-open the restaurant that they had lovingly helped build and wanted to keep going in Paul's memory. The ambience is lacking but the food is still wonderful and there is a bay view. I always want to taste everything on the menu so try to go with a crowd.

Coconuts: ⟋●⟍●⟋●⟋●⟋ *Augustín Ramirez s/n.* ☎ 554-2518. The site of an old weigh-station and warehouse for exported timber built in the 20's. For many years, it was the private party home of one of the more prominent figures in *Zihua.* Bought in the late 70's by a group of investors from New York, Coconuts became an immediate success. The owners put in a circular bar with indirect lighting and placed tables in the patio area for dining under the stars. Small, twinkling Christmas lights strategically intertwined in the foliage add to the effect.

This restaurant changed hands in 2009 and was completely renovated and some locals feel "sterilized."

The menu is a wonderful read and the new menu prices have been adjusted to a more moderate level. Service here is the best in town and waiters speak English. Open for dinner daily in high season—reservations no longer necessary. (Closed May—October).

Daniel's: 🍴🍴 *Paseo del Pescador s/n.* ☎ 554-2010. Located on the beach side of *Hotel Avila*. Popular local hangout. Great place to have happy hour, as drinks are two for the price of one between 5:00 and 7:00 p.m. Quite often live music during high season. Open daily for breakfast, lunch. and dinner.

Don Memo: 🍴🍴 *Esq. Augustín Ramirez y Pedro Ascencio*. Relocated to alley across from Coconut's. Popular with tourists and locals. Good food at reasonable prices.

Doña Licha: 🍴 Corner of *Ejido and Benito Juárez*. Take out grilled chicken with all the trimmings. Sit down location on *Calle Cocos*—behind the big market.

El Mango: 🍴🍴 *Nicolás Bravo*—close to market street. ☎ 554-2421, This family-owned and operated restaurant is situated in their front yard. Service is friendly, portions large, and the price is right.

El Mediterraneo: 🍴🍴🍴 *Cinco de Mayo #4.* ☎ 553-8042 or 📱 (755)557-8576. A favorite of the locals. Good ambiance and the pasta is cooked perfectly. Closed Monday.

El Murmullo: 🍴🍴 *Pedro Ascencio*. In pedestrian walkway between main street and Memo's. Pretty good Thai dishes.

El Pueblita: 🍴🍴 *Av. Morelos #157.* ☎ 544-6851 or 📱 (755)105-0336. This is a lovely restaurant around an inner courtyard. The food is generally very good and both Sailfest and Guitarfest use this restaurant for venues. Thursdays José Luis Cobo plays the guitar from 3:00-5:00 p.m. Only place in town to serve liver and onions I think!

El Sabor: 🍴 *Agustin Ramirez*. Next to Fruity Keiko's. New trend in town to open coffee shops. This one serves good coffee and nice sandwiches and is open very early in the morning.

Fishing Hole: *Esquina Nicolas Bravo y Vicente Guerrero*. No food—just cheap cold beer and beverages with terrific local "barmaids". Locals hang here so great information gathering spot.

Frapioccas Zihuatanejo: 🍴 *Pedro Ascencio*. Another n"new" coffee shop in town. There are now five where there was only one a year ago.

Galeana: 🍴🍴 *Paseo del Pescador.* Next to museum. New location. My experience here was disappointing as they are stingy with their ice. Food is just so-so.

Garrobos: 🍴🍴 *Juan Alvarez #52.* ☎ 554-2977. Offering an extensive

menu with several unusual items such as *paella*. Their homemade soups and salads are excellent and the *flan* (Mexican caramel custard) is the best in town. Many restaurants offer *flan* on their menus but it's often packaged—a distant cousin to the real thing. To know if the *flan* is homemade or not, take a spoonful and turn it upside-down. The real McCoy will stick to the spoon. Packaged goop slides right off. Open for lunch and dinner. Owner Gregorio Lara Guzmán also does very nice catering. ☎ 554-6706.
Visit **www.garrobos.net** or ✉ **cater@prodigy.net.mx** or **garrobos_catering@hotmail.com**

Jacaranda: ℐ *Juan Alvarez s/n.* This five-stool eatery by the *Tres Marías* hotel offers very good, very cheap *tortas*. I've been eating their sandwiches for 30 years and thankfully some things never change. They are great. They also make delicious homemade yogurt. A best bargain for small budgets.

Lety's: ℐℐ Across the bridge by the pier and straight ahead. New location as of January 2012. Closed Tuesday and opens early afternoon. Lety serves really tasty seafood and probably the best coconut shrimp in town. Unfortunately, she's been "discovered" and her prices almost doubled so I can't frequent her place often.

Las Papas de la Abuela: ℐℐ *Augustin Ramirez.* New place in the Coconut's alleyway trying to cash in on the popular *Papas Locas*. Nice thing about this new restaurant is that it opens at 7:00 a.m. and closes around dusk. A baked potato can be had at anytime and you don't have to sit in a parking lot sucking up car and truck fumes.

Los Braseros: ℐℐ *Calle Ejido.* Long-time favorite of locals and tourists alike. Their speciality is tacos in all their variations. Great *frijoles borrachos*. Opens early daily.

Mandarina: ℐℐ *Av. Cinco de Mayo.* Across from church. Lovely small restaurant serving crepes and other goodies.

Mi Cafecito: ℐ *Paseo del Pescador.* Yummy frappachinos and coffee.

Mi Chayito: ℐℐ *Vicente Guerrero*—next to commercial laundry. ☎ 554-5799. Menu is a mix of Chinese and Mexican foods. One of the best restaurants in town. Almost all the entrées are under 80 pesos and they are all excellent. Service all day—closed Sunday.

Páccolo: ℐℐ *Nicolás Bravo.* During high season, live entertainment most evenings. Sports bar with extensive menu located in the back patio area. Serving breakfast also.

Papa Loca: ‍ *Colegio Militar*—close to car wash and *Super Cacahuate* store. Have great stuffed potatoes but not open until 6:00 p.m.

Piazza D'Angelo: ‍ *Esq. Nicolás Bravo y Galeana.* ☎ 125-2570 Closed Monday. Angelo, with his unique personality, cooks up some wonderful Italian cuisine. Unfortunately, this location, for some strange reason is cursed. Every restaurant that has been here over the past 40 years has been doomed to failure. Florien's *El Castillo*, Heiko's *La Cascada*, Kim's *Che Juan*, Gondwana with great Indian food, *Jarocho's*, and *Tango* (which has relocated to *Playa La Madera*—site of old Bay Club).

Pizzas Locas: ‍ *Vicente Guerrero* #10. ☎ 554-3569. This delightful restaurant has a varied menu with good pizzas and ribs and lots of other stuff. Part of the *Playa La Ropa "La Perla"* family, they do know how to cook and the bartender pours very generously. Home delivery.

Pollo Feliz: ‍ *Benito Juárez* (market street). I have to mention this place. It is Mexico's answer to Kentucky Fried but they only have grilled chicken and it is really good! When I'm too tired to cook or go out to eat, I head to *Pollo Feliz* where they fix you up with tortillas, marinated onions and salsa too. They now have *frijoles borrachos*. On *Avenida Morelos* as you come into Zihuatanejo and Benito Juárez—close to market.

Porte de Mare: ‍ *Paseo del Pescador*—right across from fish market on beach. ☎ 554-5902. Lovely restaurant with extensive menu and good ocean view. Daniel of same name restaurant on the beachfront has taken over the lease for this place and intends to keep it the same. Grand opening October 25, 2012.

Puntarenas: ‍ This restaurant was located in *Almacen*. It was one of the first really good places to go in *Zihuatanejo* beginning in the late 70's. I've left the name in because the following story about the place is so cute. From *Wash Gently, Dry Slowly:*

Manna From Above

The absolute best restaurant in Zihuatanejo is a small patio-type called The Puntarenas. It is operated by a rather dead-panned lady who treats one as their individual actions dictate as to how they should be treated. She welcomes those who behave and have manners and she treats them with her excellent food and good service. Those, such as loud-mouthed drunks and complaining tourists, she treats with her own subtle brand of justice. These she barely notices when they arrive and she delays giving them a menu for at least half of an hour. Everything that these folks order she is always "just out" although the kitchen is overflowing with the type of food ordered. Finally she takes their order, usually after their fourth choice but it takes a couple of hours for the orders to be delivered. Usually, the rowdy customers get the message and don't return or learn to behave as ladies and gentlemen if they do choose to return.

Breakfast in this little restaurant is so good that it must be from a heavenly cook book. The señora serves a fruit salad with mango, strawberries, melon, papaya, coconut and banana—with a gentle touch of lime. Then the fresh and hot bollilos with fresh butter and jam. Eggs and bacon with a pat of nut-flavored refried beans make up the entrée, one that few will ever forget after having enjoyed such a breakfast.

One morning I was fortunate enough to accompany KLM airline stewardess, Inge Bal, to breakfast to this temple of excellent food and it was always delightful, made even more so by the lovely companion. After we had finished breakfast we had a cup of hot cinnamon-flavored coffee while we lingered in the beauty of the awakening village. While I gazed at Miss Bal a big, fat mango fell from a tree above our table and landed smack in the middle of my coffee. The cup and saucer shattered and coffee splattered all over the place. While Inge and I went to the washroom to clean up, the señora cleaned the mess at the table and served cups of fresh coffee. The intruding mango was still in place on the table as a sort of centerpiece and as we were leaving Inge took it with her. As I was paying the bill I playfully asked the señora if there was an extra charge for the post-breakfast dessert mango.

She barely smiled and said that there would be no extra charge. "Compliments of the house, as you say, Señor."

RicoMar: ❢❢ *Nicolás Bravo y Carlos Pellicer.* One of the very best and absolute cheapest eateries in town outside of the market. Great *pozole* every day and green and red on Thursday, along with *tacos, chalupas,* fried chicken, and *enchiladas.*

Senor Pinto's: ❢❢❢ *Avenida Morelos y Presa de Amistad.* American owned and operated since 1994, they have a good menu selection and now have *Zumba* classes.

Sirena Gorda: ❢❢❢ *Paseo del Pescador.* ☏ 554-2687. Located near the pier, this cute, outdoor restaurant specializes in seafood tacos. Favored by the boating crowd and locals alike, it's a great place to people-watch. If you don't like people, you can watch satellite TV. Luis Muñoz, the very charming and articulate owner has created a very versatile breakfast menu. They have a "special logo" which is sold on T-shirts and aprons. Serving breakfast, lunch, and dinner. Closed Wednesday.

Tamales y Atole Any: ⏹ *Esq. Vicente Guerrero y Ejido* #18. Offering a huge selection of tamales, this restaurant is very popular. The decor is cute but one feels like a school child sitting on the little painted chairs. Open breakfast, lunch, and dinner.

TATA'S: ⏹⏹ *Paseo del Pescador.* Waterside of the Hotel *Avila.* It's a pretty good watering hole—lots of the locals hang here, at Daniel's, or at *Casa Arcadia.*

Teosintle: ⏹⏹ *Carr. Acapulco—Zihuatanejo* before the road divides. This is **the** *pozole* restaurant in *Zihua.* They serve *pozole* on Thursday and you will see the "movers and shakers" of town here. They are now open for breakfast and lunch daily. Live entertainment often and lots of fun. It's quite the walk from *El Centro* and all the taxi drivers know exactly where it is located.

Teppan Roll: ⏹⏹*Calle Ejido* #24. ☎ 554-9800. Very popular spot with locals—both Mexican and foreign. Pretty good food at pretty fair prices. Home delivery. There is now a new Teppan Roll located at Kyoto Circle with seating for over 200. It is open for breakfast, lunch, and dinner. They are trying to have special events and recently hosted a male stripper show. Since it didn't start until 10:00 p.m. I wasn't present and none of my friends attended so don't know what they turnout was like. There are a lot of complaints of traffic noise and bus fumes due to the location.

The Beachcomber Bar: ⏹ *Esquina Nicolas Bravo y H. Galeana.* Old bar with new name and ownership. Lots of locals hang here especially the younger crowd. (Well, young for Zihuatanejo).

The Flophouse Bar: ⏹ *Calle Ejido.* Reasonably priced drinks and the watering hole for locals, especially on Tuesday–live music night.

Zen Wishes Cafeteria: ⏹*Esq. Nicolas Bravo y Cuauhtemoc.* Very good.

Zihua Pancake House: Corner of *Av. Ejido and Galeana.* Closed Monday. Serving breakfast and lunch. They have an excellent menu and really good eggs Benedict—in my opinion.

Zorro Sports Bar: ⏹⏹ *Esq. Pedro Ascencio y Galeana.* Very popular with the tourists and locals.

Naturally, there are dozens more eateries in *Zihua*—the market alone has over thirty. There are terrific bargains to be found and good food in many of these places.

Comida y Cantinas
Playa La Madera and Vicinity

Bistro Del Mar: ❯❮❯❮❯❮ Right on the beach. Food and service are excellent.

Café Patio Mexica and Rufo's: ❯❮❯❮Calle *Adelita*. From 8:00 a.m. until 2:00 p.m. breakfast is served and Monica, one of the owner's, has a cooking school twice a week. However, during the evening, the restaurant becomes *Rufo's* and he puts out really excellent grilled entrée's and often has live music during high season. Usually very busy.

Country Fried Chicken: ❯❮❯❮ *Paseo La Boquita*. Very tiny restaurant serving pretty good fried chicken, coleslaw, and not so good mashed potatoes. Open 7 days a week and they deliver. ❯ (755)557-3561.

Doña Licha: ❯❮ *Calle Cocos*. Some of the cheapest and best food in town. They have a daily *comida corrida* for thirty-five pesos usually with a choice of eight entrees. Served with homemade *tortillas,* beans and rice. Open for breakfast (which is also great) and lunch.

Hamburguesas Mr. Cheef: ❯❮ *Ave. Jupiter*—across from *Comerical Mexicana.* Technically not in *Playa La Madera* area but shouldn't be left out. He serves really good burgers for sit-down or take out and has added fries to his menu of grilled burgers. Also on the next corner, within spitting distance of his place is another burger and hot dog stand selling my personal favorite burgers with all the trimmings for $25.00 pesos.

Kau Kan: ❯❮❯❮❯❮❯❮ (Map LR 52). *Escénico a Playa La Ropa*. ☎ 554-5731. Bon Appetit Magazine wrote up this charming restaurant as the "finest in Zihua" some years ago. It overlooks the ocean and the service and ambiance are excellent. Dinner only and reservations suggested.

La Casa Vieja: ❯❮❯❮ *Calle Josefa Ortiz de Dominguez #7. Playa La Madera*. ☎554-9770 or ❯ (755) 557-0837. Very nice older establishment with some of the very best food in town. They have the traditional barbecue on Sunday and their *cochinita pibil* is one of my favorites as is their quail and their *camerones y champinones al gratin* appetizer is the best I've ever had.

La Gula: ❯❮❯❮❯❮ *Calle Adelita.* ☎ 554-8396 or 112-1274. Rooftop dining at its best. Charming owner/chef José Luis Noriega and his lovely wife Rosalba García could not be more gracious. What they are

lacking in a bay view is compensated by great food at reasonable prices. Closed Sunday. Visit
www.restaurantelagula.com.mx
or ✉**lagula@zihuatanejo.com.mx**
La Mordida: ⬤⬤ *Avenida La Boquita.* ☎ 554-8216/2311. This restaurant serves inexpensive Mexican food and is very popular with locals and tourists. During high season, they offer grilled ribs, steaks, etc. and have prompt home delivery service.
Margarita's: ⬤⬤ *Calle Josefa Ortiz de Dominguez.* Formerly next door to Coconuts. Currently only open for breakfast—where the movers and shakers start their day.
Mariscos Chendo's: ⬤⬤ Located at town end of *Calle Adelita*, this restaurant has been famous for its coconut shrimp for years.
Nardo's: ⬤⬤ *Calle Adelita.* Very interesting menu but lacking ambience. Usually a pretty good crowd during high season.
Tentaciones: ⬤⬤⬤⬤ (Map LR6). *Escénico Playa La Ropa.* ☎5448383/84. Reservations accepted online:
canjunso@yahoo.com Gourmet dining at its best. They advertise as fusion Latin. The dinners are fixed price and reservations are strongly suggested, especially during high season. I personally am enchanted with *Tentaciones*—food and view are marvelous. I really need to sell lots of guide books because I really enjoy eating here!
Valeria's II: ⬤⬤ Beach restaurant on *Playa La Madera*. Also *centro* location next to museum.

Comidas y Cantinas, Playa La Ropa
Amuleto: ⬤⬤⬤⬤ (Map LR9).☎544-6222. Fabulous restaurant/hotel complex high above the bay. A view to die for and very expensive. During high season, reservations a must. Open daily
Cocodrilo Café: ⬤⬤ (Map LR 17). *Playa La Ropa.* The menu is simple but varied and they have a good house salad. Great lounge chairs (now a charge of $100 pesos to use them) and attentive service. Open breakfast, lunch, and closes at sunset.
Doña Prudencia: ⬤⬤ (Map LR 28). *Playa La Ropa.* Part of the *Villas Mexicana*, this ocean-side restaurant is a very popular breakfast eatery.
El Manglar: ⬤⬤⬤ (Map LR 53). *Playa La Ropa s/n.* ☎ 554-3752 or ✆ (755) 556-4468. Charming restaurant right next to the estuary.

You can watch the crocodiles while you eat. The food and prices are good and even though they are in a mangrove swamp, I've never experienced a problem with the mosquitoes or "no see-ums."

El Marlin: 🍽🍽 (Map LR 44). *Playa La Ropa.* ☎ 554-3766. The décor has been upgraded, as has the menu. Sushi now being served during season. A nice spot to relax on the beach.

Il Mare: 🍽🍽🍽🍽 (Map LR 46). *Escénico a Playa La Ropa.* Lovely restaurant overlooking the bay serving beautifully prepared Italian dishes. The view is wonderful as is the food. The owner and his wife are a delightful couple and provide super service and perfect pasta dishes. Open lunch and dinner daily.

Jungle Pizza: 🍽🍽 ☎554-7839 or 📱 (755)100-2309. On the *Playa La Ropa* road right where it's divided for 100 feet. Home delivery and I'm told very good pizza.

La Gaviota: 🍽🍽 (Map LR 41). Near end of *Playa La Ropa.* ☎ 554-3816. An institution in *Zihua.* Not much in the way of daytime crowds but popular in the evening.

La Bocana: 🍽🍽 An institution in *Zihua* with a new location on the *Playa La Ropa* road where it divides—just past turn off to *La Perla.*

La Perla: 🍽🍽 (Map LR 43). *Playa La Ropa.* ☎ 554-2700. This restaurant opened as a small palapa hut about 35 years ago. The food is good and the place has expanded over the years to meet increased tourist demand. A favorite spot for locals and tourists. Comfortable lounge chairs and plenty of shade. There is now a charge for using lounge chairs to prevent beach "riff-raff" from using the facilities. Service is the slowest on the beach. Francisco has a walk-in humidor and imports cigars for the discriminating men that want the real deal in *cubanos.* Open for breakfast, lunch, and dinner.

La Escollera: 🍽🍽🍽 (Map LR 54). ☎ 554-2811/2815. A great place to eat and just hang out. Lovely dining area with a piano bar for evening cocktails and dinner, and a pool for afternoon sunning. Open daily. Great view. ✉ **laescollera1@hotmail.com**

Little Suiza: 🍽🍽 *Final de Playa La Ropa:* ☎ 114-1661. Open 6:00-11:00 p.m. except Thursday. They have a rather limited menu but the food is good and their tropical setting is wonderful. During high season, often live music.

Paty's Mar y Mar: 🍽🍽 (Map LR 45). *Playa La Ropa s/n.* ☎ 554-2213 or 📱 (755) 113-366. Another popular beachside restaurant close to the *Sotavento*. Owner Paty goes out of her way to make everyone who enters her place glad they have come. Her prices are very reasonable—very cold beer and good lounge chairs. Open for breakfast, lunch, and dinner. Visit **www.patys-marymar.com** Yoga and spa services offered during high season. Check website for current schedule.

Puerta del Sol: ⦿⦿⦿ (Map LR 42). *Escénico a Playa La Ropa*. ☎ 554-8342. Wonderful bay view. Food is usually very good. Service after 7:00 at night is very slow as they prepare many dishes tableside. Go early to avoid a long wait. Open for dinner.

Rossy's: ⦿⦿ (Map LR 19). Near end of *Playa La Ropa*. ☎ 554-4004. A very favorite watering hole for locals. The food is good, relatively inexpensive, and the beer cold. The best red snapper, *tiritas*, and vegetable soup in town.
✉ **hotelrestaurantrossy@hotmail.com**

ZI: ⦿⦿⦿⦿ (Map LR 35). *Escénico a Playa La Ropa* (Intrawest). ☎ 555-0375. A very special place for a special dinner, the restaurant at Club Intrawest is serving some of the best food in town and the view and decor "to die for!!" Open at 6:00 p.m. daily.

Comidas y Cantinas, Playa Las Gatas

Playa Las Gatas is a must trip for beach lovers. Protected by a man-made reef, this is an ideal spot for snorkeling and perfect for children as there are usually no waves. Usually the water is crystal clear. Be careful of the sharp coral and occasional sea urchin. Access is from the public pier on a small boat. Cost is $40 pesos and the boats leave every fifteen minutes—more or less.

The beach is lined with more than a dozen restaurants and snorkeling gear and floats can be rented for a nominal charge. I didn't map out the restaurants—they are strung out in a row once you leave the dock.

Hidden at the end of this picturesque beach, you will find **Owen's Place**, a group of unique bungalows constructed with raw materials in a setting of tropical beauty. There are five bungalows ranging in capacity and price. Weekly rates are also available. For more information contact **info@lasgatasbeachclub.com**

Amado's: ⦿⦿ Serving good *comida mexicana* and fresh seafood.

Arrecife: ⦿⦿ ☎ 558-0728. With a little notice, they can do a *pescado a la talla.*

Chez Arnoldo's: ¶¶ ☎ 557-8069. Of the 14 or so restaurants on *Playa Las Gatas,* this is my personal favorite. They have been serving wonderful seafood since 1964.

Coco Loco: ¶¶ ☎ 554-5526. Serving fresh fish and seafood daily.

Karitoño: ¶¶ ☎ 558-0307.

La Cabaña: ¶¶ ☎ 558-2242

La Marinera: ¶¶ ☎ 558-0102.

La Mesa Del Pescado: ¶¶ ☎ 556-0891.

Los Mangles: ¶¶ ☎ 556-5767 or 557-3532. House special is a pineapple filled with seafood.

Otilia: ¶¶☎ 554-2119 or 558-0371.

Oliverio's: ¶¶ ☎ 557-4908. Good sushi and sashimi.

Rayito de Sol: ¶¶

Tres Palmas: ¶¶ ☎ 558-1883.

Markets

Our market is somewhat disappointing compared to others in Mexico. It certainly lacks the color of, say, *Cuernavaca's* market with its profusion of flowers or the awesome magnitude of the market in *Oaxaca* with the vibrant hues and colors of its produce and different moles.

Sights in the Market or
Sights not Seen in Safeway

The market contains a potpourri of produce not normally viewed in the Americas. Produce (fresh) usually arrives on Tuesday and Friday. These are the best days to shop as the heat and humidity wreak havoc overnight to the more perishable items. If you're staying for a while and have cooking facilities, do try some of the following:

Aguacates: Originated in the state of Puebla. High in potassium and a rich source of mono unsaturated fats, avocados are one of the healthiest fruits in the world! A diet that includes avocados has been shown by some studies to reduce cholesterol and control high blood pressure.

Camote: Sweet potatoes with orange or purple skin, often the size of footballs. The orange-skinned ones are incredibly sweet, creamy, and delicious. The purple-skinned ones are starchy, stringy, and to be avoided. Sweet potatoes are native to the Americas and are one of the best sources nature provides us for beta-carotene. In Mexico, when sweet potatoes are in season they are lathered with *piloncillo* (unrefined cane sugar) and served as a dessert.

Cecina: In the meat market, many vendors have clotheslines strung in their shops with thin strips of beef hanging out to dry. This is dried, salted beef, very popular with the locals that don't have refrigeration. It can be cooked in a variety of ways, none of which I find palatable.

Chayote: A member of the potato family, *chayote* has pale green striated skin. Sweeter than a potato, these are baked, boiled, sautéed, or used in soups.

Huazontle: Long (two feet or more) green stalks with leafy buds similar to broccoli. These are boiled with the "rocks" that are sold in the market. Served with a zesty tomato sauce. A little stringy, but delicious.

Huitlacoche: Known as corn smut or by the more attractive name

Mexican truffle, it is a type of fungus that grows on corn crops. The Aztecs traditionally encouraged the spread of this fungus among their crops of corn, and throughout Mexico one can order *quesadillas* or other dishes filled with *huitlacoche*. *Huitlacoche* has important amino acids that are surprisingly present in the corn it infects. Apart from its nutritional benefits, *huitlacoche* is becoming prized by chefs around the world for its delicate and appealing flavor. Considered a delicacy by many, the fungus is scraped, cooked and usually served in crepes. The connoisseurs equate it to wild mushrooms (hence, Mexican truffles). Personally, I think it tastes like dirt—many Mexican friends say I've just never experienced it cooked correctly—I'm still waiting.

Jicama: This is a vegetable that looks like an enormous brown turnip. The taste resembles that of an apple. They are delicious in salad and a great substitute for water chestnuts.

Nanches: Tiny yellow berries sold in plastic bags by street vendors. Let your palate be your guide on this one. Much too sour for my taste.

Tomatillos: Member of the nightshade family, related to the cape gooseberry. This is the basis for all green sauces served in restaurants. Different in flavor and usually hotter than the red sauce but equally delicious.

Zapote: A large brown-skinned fruit with a creamy sweet interior. Excellent when mixed with milk and ice in a blender to make *licuados*.

Also seen in the market but not recommended are large glass jars containing *aguas*. This is simply fruit and water blended together to make excellent, refreshing drinks. One cannot be assured the vendor is using purified water and ice. A "must try" at *Michocana*. Often used are the following:

Horchata: Pulverized rice, sugar, and cinnamon mixed with water. Especially good for upset stomachs.

Jamaica: A bright-red drink made from dried blossoms of the hisbiscus flower. The dried flower is boiled in water and then sugar added. The taste is similar to cranberry juice and is considered a great kidney cleanser. The blossoms are sold in the market in small packages and the drink can easily by made at home. Mix one cup of the flowers with one liter of water, boil and add one cup of sugar or honey. Strain.

Tamarindo: A light brown drink made from the pulp of the *tamarindo* bean. It is also sold in packages in the market and is a special favorite of children.

Other mixers include *melón* (cantaloupe), *sandía* (watermelón), *limonada* (lemon), *fresa* (strawberry), *naranja* (orange), *mango, papaya, coco, toronja* (grapefruit) and *piña* (pineapple).

Most of the above-mentioned fruits can be mixed with milk instead of water. This is a called a *licuado*. Let your own personal palate dictate your choice. My personal favorites are *guanábana, papaya,* and *plátano* (banana).

I'm not fond of all the sugar added to the drinks so I carry my own sugar-free packets and they will use these in place of sugar when preparing your drink. Should you have forgotten your Equal, Mexico sells an equivalent called *Canderel*. Most pharmacies and the big grocery stores have this product.

Foods of Mexico

The present-day Mexican cuisine arose from a unique combination of cooking worlds—Aztec, Spanish, and French. To the Spanish conquistadors, the native cuisine of the Aztecs was a delight with many ingredients unknown outside the Americas: chocolate, vanilla, corn, peanuts, tomatoes, avocados, squash, beans, sweet potatoes, pineapple, papaya, and *chiles*. The Spanish added oil and wine, cinnamon and cloves, rice and wheat, and the cattle that provide beef, milk, and butter. Later, during the brief tenure of Maximilian and Carlotta, sophisticated dishes of French, Austrian, and Italian origin were added.

Corn, *chiles*, tomatoes, and beans are the basic ingredients of the indigenous kitchen and are still most important today. The Aztecs and Mayas venerated corn, and no Mexican meal is complete without tortillas. Cooks in Mexico still rely on the ingredients which were popular before the Spanish conquest, corn, beans and squash: The Aztec Trio. Traditional Mexican food is heavy in these three main ingredients. Combined with hunted game meats, such as deer or rabbit, the vegetable and grain trio made for an incredibly healthy diet. Corn, beans, and squash planted together are also a famous example of "companion planting." Known in Mexico as the Aztec Trio and in other countries as The Three Sisters, the plants do marvelously well together. Corn is planted in the middle of a mound of ready dirt. Around the corn, beans are planted to add nitrogen to the soil. The bean vines then climb up the corn stalks as they grow together. On the edges, squash is planted to provide mulch for the other plants. It is no wonder that, before the days of modern industrialized agriculture, native people all over North America used these plants to provide a healthy diet year-round. Centuries old native myths and stories highlight corn, beans, and squash as a magical combination of foods.

The *chiles* are equally important to the Mexican menu. There are an estimated sixty-one classified varieties in Mexico alone, and they come sweet, pungent, and hot. Those used most frequently are in two groups: the red, used dried, and the green, used fresh.

The names of the *chiles* vary from place to place and they can't be trusted. The *chiles* cross-fertilize by themselves so often a mild *chile* (supposedly) will come up hot.

The green *chiles*, usually hotter than the red, are available fresh or pickled in cans. The most common are the *serrano, jalapeño, habanero,* and the *poblano*. To take the heat out of any fresh green *chile*, prepare by removing the seeds, stem and veins, then soak in cold, salted water or water with a little vinegar an hour or more.

Glossary of Food Terms

Bolillos: Crusty rolls with a soft center that can be found at the market (early) or at bakeries.

Buñelos: A large, round, wafer-thin pastry covered with syrup. Traditionally served during the Christmas holidays.

Café de Olla: This deep-brewed coffee, served in small clay mugs, is flavored with brown sugar and dusted with cinnamon.

Cajeta: Thick, sweet sauce made from goat's milk which has been cooked until the sugar caramelizes. Similar to butterscotch, it is delicious served over ice cream or in crepes.

Carne Asada: Thin tenderloin of broiled beef. This typically Mexican dish usually is accompanied by rice, *guacamole,* and refried beans.

Chicharrón: *Moctezuma's* equivalent of crackling, made by rendering the lard from under the skin of the pig and toasting it until golden. Served with lemon and chile sauce or used to dip into guacamole.

Chilaquiles: Also know as the "poor man's dish." This casserole is made from day-old tortillas and shredded chicken. These ingredients, combined with various cheeses, tomatoes, *chiles,* and cream, offer a very delectable and satisfying meal at a very reasonable price.

Chiles Rellenos: Stuffed peppers. This is one of Mexico's best-known dishes. *Chiles poblanos,* similar to bell peppers, are stuffed with either cheese or ground meat, dipped in an egg batter and fried, then topped by a fiery red sauce.

Chiles en Nogado: Created in *Puebla* in 1821 to commemorate the arrival of General Augustín Iturbide to that city after signing the *Treaties of Córdoba*, this seasonal dish was also a salute to Mexico's new green, white, and red flag. Peppers are stuffed with an unusual blend of meat and spices before batter dipping and frying. They are served with a blanched walnut sauce and garnished with red pomegranate seeds and *cilantro* to represent the tricolor flag. No gourmand should miss this delicious dish which is served only in the early fall when the ingredients are in season.

Cilantro: Fresh green coriander. It is a very ancient herb, which was introduced into Europe from Asia by way of Egypt in very remote times. A member of the same natural order as parsley, it looks rather like green Italian parsley, though its flavor is very much more pronounced. It does not dry well and should be used quickly or frozen.

Enchiladas: Tortillas are rolled around cooked meats, usually chicken, then baked with various sauces progressing from moderate to biting—gthen topped with cream and shredded cheese and baked.

Frijoles Refritos: Literally, refried beans. These have been a staple of the Mexican diet for centuries. The most common is the *bayo gordo*, which is similar to the pinto. These are cooked with a bit of smoked meat and onions in a clay pot until tender. They are then transferred to a skillet, mashed and cooked in lard.

Gorditas: "Little fat ones" or round, chunky corn cakes, which are stuffed with various fillings such as sausage, meat, beans, etc. and deep-fried. Garnished with hot sauce and diced onions, they are not for weight watchers.

Guacamole: A salad or sauce made, basically, from avocado, lemon, onions, *chile*, and *cilantro*. Used as a dip for crisp tortilla chips, a filling for tortillas or as a garnish.

Mole: From the *Náhuatl* word *molli*, this was a thick stew in Aztec times. Often made with more than twenty ingredients, including several types of *chile* peppers, crushed sesame seeds or nuts, and pulverized chocolate; this tangy sauce is a sensation to this day. Used with chicken or meat dishes, it is an acquired taste.

Molletes: *Bolillos*, which have been sliced in half diagonally, blanketed with refried beans, topped with cheese and broiled for a few minutes. Delicious as a snack with a spicy salsa splashed on it.

Nopales: The leaves of the prickly-pear cactus are peeled, cooked, and cut into strips or chunks. Mixed with onions, tomatoes, and *cilantro*, they are served in a cold salad that is not unlike a green-bean salad. Combined with eggs, they make a tasty omelet.

Pozole: A stew made with pork and hominy. Now many places are offering chicken *pozole* due to the large number of *gringos*. Served with a side of *chiles, aguacate, cilantro, cebolla,* and *mescal.*

Pulque: Mildly alcoholic brew made from fermentation of the sweet sap (*aqua miel*) of the *maguey* (century) plant. This milky, slightly foamy drink was considered sacred by the pre-hispanic cultures of Mexico.

Queso: Mexico produces a great variety of cheeses that are either fresh, soft, semi-soft, semi firm, or firm. A store, *Genesis* on *Calle Coco,* behind the market, offers most of the following cheeses for sale.

Fresh: *Queso blanco,* which is a creamy, white cheese made from skimmed cow's milk with a fresh distinctive lemon flavor.

Queso fresco is a white cheese made by combining cow's milk and goat's milk.

Queso panela is a soft, white cheese that absorbs other flavors easily, and is often cooked in sauces.

Requesón: a lowfat fresh cheese that is used to finish enchiladas and to make cheese spreads. It is sold most often wrapped in fresh corn husks.

Soft cheese: *Queso añejo* is an aged version of *queso fresco* and can be quite firm and salty as it ages. It is used primarily as a garnish, crumbled or grated over a variety of dishes. Most of the market vendors display large wheels of this type of cheese on the counter. The cheese resembles grated Parmesan. The resemblance stops there. My ex-husband claims it smells like "an old tennis shoe." It is relatively cheap and most often seen sprinkled on *tacos* or *guacamole* at the more inexpensive eateries.

Queso Oaxaca is probably the most popular cheese for *quesadillas.* It is a stretched cheese, kneaded and wound into balls. It is normally pulled apart into thin strings before using to fill tortillas or melted on cooked food.

Queso asadero is used primarily for *queso fundido,* a dish that is usually eaten as a late-night supper.

Queso Chihuahua is a pale yellow and varies in taste from mild to a fairly sharp, it is used in a wide variety of dishes and is especially good breading and frying.

Queso jalapeño is a smooth, soft white cheese with small pieces of *jalapeño chile* in it.

Semi-soft cheeses: *Queso manchego* was introduced to Mexico from Spain and is a buttery yellow color. It is good for melting or for serving with fruit or crackers.

Firm Cheeses: *Queso añejo enchilada* is an aged cheese with a spicy red chile coating.

Queso cotija takes its name from the town of *Cotija* in the state of Michoacán, where it originated. This is basically a sharp, crumbly goat cheese that is primarily served over beans and salads.

Quesadilla: A tortilla, folded into a half-moon pocket, filled with cheese, sausage, meat, or beans and deep-fried or grilled.

Queso Fundido: Individual portions of melted cheese, fondue-style, served with flour tortillas as an appetizer.

Salsa: There is an endless list of these sauces, which are made from a vast assortment of *chiles* ranging from the sweet chile *ancho* to the small, hot chile *piquín*. These are used on anything from soup to nuts and are guaranteed to awaken the most dormant taste buds.

Sangrita: Made from a blend of orange juice, grenadine syrup, cayenne pepper and salt, this tangy brew is used as a chaser for tequila.

Sidral: The brand name of lightly carbonated refreshment made from apples, not too sweet, but very thirst-quenching. *Manzanita* is the brand name of a slightly different mix made along the same lines.

Taco: Corn tortilla wrapped around chicken, meat, or bean filling and deep-fried. Served with shredded lettuce, onion, salsa, and smothered with cream.

Tostada: Same as a taco only served open-faced.

Tamal: One of the most ancient of Mexican dishes. The word *tamal* comes from the *Náhuatl* language. These are made from a finely ground corn dough known as *masa*. This *masa* is then spread on a cornhusk or banana leaf and covered with a meat or sweet filling, rolled, tied, and steamed. Considered a special dish for festive occasions because of the time required to prepare them. Tamales can be scorching hot, or very sweet.

Tehuacán: Centuries before Perrier became fashionable; the Aztecs were sipping water from Mexico's mineral springs. Today, most of the purified water comes from *Tehuacán, Puebla.* If you want bottled water, ask for *agua mineral.* It can be ordered *sin gas* (without carbonation) or *con gas* (bubbly).

Tequila: Renowned Mexican liquor made from the sap of one species of the century plant. This brew is usually clear and colorless and is manufactured in the town of Tequila.

Torta: A sandwich made of a roll (*telera*), usually filled with ham, cheese, avocado, refried beans, and *chile.* There are, of course, many variations.

Tortilla: The staff of Mexican life. They are made from either flour or corn that has been finely ground and formed into dough, which is then flattened and cooked on a griddle. They can be torn into small pieces, or intact, rolled around any kind of food.

Our area now has a local organic growers association representing more than 50 growers in the Zihuatanejo, *Petatlán,* and *Tecpan* areas. They have ten organic ranches that are certified Organic by a private certification association and non-government organization (NGO) that certifies farms so they can sell their products as organic in the United States.

Their main product is the aromatic herb, basil, but they also grow other herbs such as thyme, rosemary, oregano, marjoram, and mint, and they hope to add even more types of produce in the future. They export about 4,000 basil plants at a time, packed in ten pound boxes, a ton a day, and five days a week. They have to be transported in refrigerated trucks and shipped by air to keep them fresh. If you have ever bought organic basil at Trader Joe's in California, you may have eaten Zihuatanejo basil.

The members of these 50 organic farms employ around 200 employees year round. They offer classes once a month teaching small growers the steps necessary to become organic certified and are currently working with fifty additional farms. To avoid the need for chemicals they plant a barrier crop around the perimeter of the cash crop to attract/deflect the bugs. Corn or sunflowers are planted in rows along the outside of the basil rows to stop the bugs before they can reach the basil. They also use natural pesticides and organic fumigation methods that have such benign ingredients such as garlic, onion, cinnamon, vanilla or chrysanthemum.

Life's Little Necessities

The downtown area is full of the "hole-in-the-wall" variety of grocery stores. Most carry staples such as milk, eggs, yogurt, cheese, snacks, and soft drinks. Prices vary greatly. If you're here for a while or shopping for more than a snack, you might want to check out one of the following:

Bodega: Lateral Carr. Acapulco-Zihuatanejo. A full-service grocery store—not really catering to the foreigners but does have better prices on lots of items and generally better produce than *Comercial Mexicana.*

Café Caracol: Two locations: Corner of *Vicente Guerrero y Juan Alvarez* and *Nicolás Bravo*—adjacent to *Paccolos.* Very nice store selling coffee (regular and organic) and nice selection of honey, vanilla, and lots of other items.

Café Zihua: Cuauhtémoc. This place is very proud of its organic coffee. More expensive than the regular coffee.

Comercial Mexicana: *Av. La Boquita s/n.* This full service grocery store opened in July of 2000. As large and clean as any in the States and air conditioned. They carry just about everything but Claussen pickles and Hormel chili. Open daily from 8:00 a.m. until 11:00 p.m. There are also clothing, appliances, furniture, electrical, plumbing, painting supplies, books, and a drugstore. Plastic gladly accepted. More expensive than the market but most people think it's worth it to have air conditioning and one-stop shopping. (Personally, I still go to the market for fruit and vegetables as they are freshly handpicked and delivered almost daily).

From *Topes in Paradise:*

Clotted Sour Cream

After years of being deprived of anything but the basic food necessities or the Mexican breadbasket, I now justify buying anything I want at any price in Comercial Mexicana. I loathe the store but they have so many wonderful, expensive imported items.

However, one of the glaring differences between Mexicans and their North American neighbors is that in Mexico (or at least in Zihua)—the customer is always wrong; whereas in the U.S. the customer is always right! I think Comercial's lack of service and inattentiveness to customer needs is the worst I have experienced anywhere in the world. On a scale of 1-10 with 10 being awful—they are truly a 12-15!

I indulge in real whipping cream for my coffee which they sell at Comercial.

During high season there is a large turnover of expensive items but during low season, it's hard to tell if the product has been on the shelf for ages or not. Also, their refrigeration system is rarely up to standards found in the North so even with an expiration date in the distant future, the item may be spoiled already. Hence, never throw away receipts until you've sampled everything you have bought.

A while back, I had purchased some whipping cream and when I got home and opened it the next morning for coffee—it smelt foul and had great clumps of spoiled cream in the box. I took my receipt, a half a valium, and the cream and returned to the store. (When I know in advance a fight is going to ensue, I try to take drugs to calm me down so my blood pressure doesn't skyrocket and I won't do something that could land me in jail). I took the cream to the desk and politely asked for the manager. He arrived and said, "What can I do for you?"

"I bought this cream yesterday and when I opened it a while ago, I found it was spoiled and I want to exchange it for another cream, please."

"I can't exchange the cream for you—you opened it—we can't take back something that's been opened." He patiently explained.

"I had to open it in order to use it and when I opened it I found it was spoiled. I just want another one." I patiently explained right back at him.

We went back and forth for a good five minutes and finally; I poured the clotted cream on his shoes, and told him to call the police because I was going to get another cream. I left him with his mouth agape, grabbed another cream, and went home to enjoy my coffee. Next time, I'll take a whole valium instead of half.

Merza: Two locations—*Av. Catalina Gonzales* and behind the market on *Los Mangos.* Full service low end grocery store carrying mainly staples **but** they have a huge wine selection with no prices. Very frustrating but there is a little machine to check before you purchase a bottle. All other merchandise is marked.

Adriana y Pancho's: *Esq. Cuauhtémoc y Juan Alvarez.* Centrally located grocery store. Many imported items. Alongside the cash register is a cooler containing imported meats at reasonable prices.

Costa del Sol: *Benito Juárez*—close to market—older men hanging out in front in the mornings drinking coffee. This is the place to buy fresh coffee beans. They will grind to suit your needs. Also vendors of purified water and some staples.

ISSSTE: *Benito Juárez.* This is a government store carrying an eclectic variety of goods. I buy some of my staples here—savings amount to 20% to 40% compared to other stores (with the exception of Waldo's).

Do not shop here at the beginning, the middle, or end of the month. The store is packed around paydays and rarely, if ever, is there more than one checkout counter. A 20-minute wait is not unusual.

Gloria's: *Playa La Ropa* road. Small store with good variety of staples serving the *Playa La Madera* beach area. Gloria carries a wide variety of imported goods—including some wonderful varieties of American cheeses and imported deli meats.

Frutería Hnos. García: *Calle Los Mangos* #14. ☎554-6652. Excellent produce and the biggest variety. The good stuff is in their huge walk-in refrigerator in the back. The problem with this place is they won't let most folks go into the walk-in so you have to know the Spanish names of the produce.

Sam's Club: *Lateral Carr. Acapulco-Zihuatanejo.* Finally it's arrived. Opened August 19th, 2012. Currently stocked with lots of low-end merchandise but they do listen to suggestions and I'm working on it. For example, they had 5 varieties of margarine and no butter–now they are carrying salted *La Gloria*.

Waldos: *Antonio Nava*—close to market. Last but certainly not least— Waldo's purports to be a dollar store. It's not, but is very cheap and carries a potpourri of "stuff" including lots of staples and non-perishable food items. I go in almost daily as you never know what they may have—recently I bought regular size cans of whole tomatoes which no one sells except *Comercial Mexicana* occasionally.

The other kind of junky but wonderful store on *Catalina Gonzales* is called $11.90 *y poco mas.*

Ice Cream and Candy (*Dulces*)

There are numerous stores offering ice cream and Mexican "popsicles." I recommend the following because I know and like them.

Fragolino: (across from basketball court). Gelatos—expensive but very good.

Guadalajara: *Calle Naranjos y Calle Cerezos.* This is a party supply store near the market. They carry bulk candy and other goodies for *piñatas* and party favors. One can always find birthday candles here.

Holanda: *Pedro Ascencio #60.* By the church on *Cinco de Mayo.*

Michoacana: (Located all over town). These stores belong to a major chain and have a variety of wonderful fruit drinks along with yogurt and lots of ice cream. A perfect place to quench your thirst.

Bakeries

Bread, rolls, cookies, and cakes are baked daily. For the best selection, try one of the following. Special orders will be honored, usually with a day's notice.

El Buen Gusto: *Calle Vicente Guerrero* #11. ☎ 100-7685. They have seating inside so you can pick out your favorite sweet and have a cup of coffee or soft drink in the mornings. If you've never tried *pastel tres leches* (cake made with three types of milk), this is the place for your first experience. Fantastic!

La Boquita: *Av. La Boquita* (between town and *Plaza Kyoto*). This bakery specializes in fantasy cakes for all occasions.

Beverages

Purchase soft drinks only in bottles (not in plastic bags from street vendors). These can be bought in any grocery store or supermarket. There are still places that sell glass bottles and you pay a deposit and keep your receipt and get your money back when you leave but these places are becoming extinct as plastic bottles have almost completely replaced glass. On *Nicolás Bravo*, *Atzimba* is still a *depósito* for beers and soft drinks.

Tortillerías

One can't experience Mexico without eating *tortillas*. Flour *tortillas* are not as popular as corn in this part of Mexico. They are sold in most grocery stores in packages of 10. Used for *burritos* (which is not a Mexican dish) and *fajitas* (ditto).

Each neighborhood has its own *tortilla* factory and they do vary in quality. Not being a connoisseur, I can't tell the difference.

Tortillería: *Av. Gonzalez*—across from little market. Little market is named *Mercado Montes de Oca*. I only mention this place because you can get the small tortillas here after 2:00 p.m.

Health, Money, and Legal

Persons arriving in the tropics need to be wary of overdoing it, including drinking and exercising for the heat takes its toll on the body's functions. Fatigue, nausea, and diarrhea will not get you started well! Take precautions with drinking water, things uncooked with water in them, or things washed in water and uncooked. Soak uncooked or unpeeled veggies and fruit for twenty minutes in water to which a couple of drops of *Microdyn* have been added. Be especially careful with strawberries and mushrooms.

New visitors to the area will immediately notice that *Zihua* has lots of pharmacies, dentists, and doctors. Unfortunately, Mexico now ranks as the world's leader in obesity and diabetes. Also most Mexicans have terrible teeth due to the children's huge intake of sugar. A gross tidbit of knowledge—recently the newspaper reported that area hospitals had amputated 800 kilos of limbs due to diabetes—didn't report the time frame but it does give a rather grotesque mental photo of the horrific problem in this country. Certainly not a claim to fame I'd be interested to report to a summit of world leaders. *From Wash Gently:*

Divine Knowledge

Some friends in Guadalajara signed some documents willing their bodies to the medical school there after their deaths. They realized that they had not been given any kind of document or card that would tell others what to do with their bodies in the event of their deaths so they called the school agency and asked about some kind of card to be carried with them or a medical tag or something that would convey their wishes to be sent to the university. They were told that no such cards or certificates were issued and that it was up to the donors to see that their wishes were fulfilled.

"The day before you die you are to call us and we will then come after you the next day," they were told by an official.

They gave up.

Ambulances: *Av. Las Huertas*—close to *Telmex.* ☎ 554-2009. Red Cross (**Cruz Roja**). They are open 24 hours and offer a variety of services. If your injury is not considered life-threatening and you just need a few stitches, they can assist. They also offer dental services on certain days and they are very inexpensive. You can also dial 065 from any phone without a phone card to request emergency service.

Aquario.☎ 554-6231 or 📱 (755)559-7329. Horacio Campusano has oxygen and a heart monitor.

Dr. Moreno Cruz: ☎ 554-2752 or 📱 (755)558-0855. He offers ambulance transportation and can do sutures and injections when applicable.

Air-Evac International: There are several 24-hour medical evacuation units that transport individuals by air-ambulance to appropriate medical facilities in Mexico or elsewhere. Financial arrangements must be made prior to flight. I checked with several of the following—from *Zihua* to Houston cost close to $20,000 U.S. Verify whether your health insurance will reimburse the cost before leaving on vacation.

Aero Medevac-Air Ambulance (Mexico City): ☎ 001(800)832-5087.
Air Ambulance Air Evac: Inside Mexico. ☎ 001(800)321-9522.
Air and Land Ambulance: Zihuatanejo ☎ 554-4825
SkyMed Air Ambulance: Inside Mexico ☎ 001(866)805-9624

Regarding medical care, check with your insurance carrier to see what, if any, medical services will be covered while in a foreign country. Here are some companies who offer health insurance for travelers:

International Association of Medical Assistance to Travelers: ☎ (716)754-4883.
International SOS Assistance: ☎ 1(800)523-8930.
TravMed: ☎ 1(800)732-5309.

Physicians: Doctoring has come a long, long way since I moved to *Zihua*. From *Topes in Paradise:*

Doctor Bravo

Doctor Bravo, a charming married man living in Zihuatanejo, had a fondness for American women. This often led him to practice a brand of medicine sure to get his license revoked if he lived in the states.

My dear friend Diana phoned from Texas and announced she would soon be visiting. Normally, I'm excited about having guests in my home, but I was more or less dreading this particular visit.

Diana, with her platinum blonde hair teased for maximum height, is all of six feet tall. With her high heels on, she could easily strut down the street eye level with John Wayne. Endowed with a body to rival a Vegas showgirl, and always wearing brightly colored hot pants and high heels, she not only turns men's heads, but also I would guess, causes more than a few outright erections. Remarkably, she doesn't seem to realize how hot she really is. Her manner is always shy and helpful, and she never gives eye contact on the street.

I admit I was nervous about how she might handle the overt advances of local males, so until we had a chance to talk about the rioting machismo of Mexican men, I sequestered her in my little house. That first night she suffered an insect bite on the ankle. I knew from the look of the red, swollen, itchy bump that it wasn't a scorpion sting or tarantula bite. Still, Zihuatanejo has lots of spiders that pack a punch. The next morning she insisted we visit a doctor.

Since Doctor Bravo was the only practicing physician in town in those days, I escorted her to his office attached to his home. He wasn't in, but one of his sons went to fetch him.

Doctor Bravo arrived shortly, preceded by an invisible fog of alcohol. The scent of whisky was so strong I envisioned an explosion might ensue if somebody should flick a light switch. Doctor Bravo was tall for a Mexican. His thick black hair was slicked straight back, and he wore dark dress pants with a white shirt open at the collar exposing a crop of unruly chest hair. His bloodshot eyes jumped when he saw Diana. He grinned crookedly, headed right over, and introduced himself, holding her hand much longer than necessary.

I was very reluctant to leave Diana entirely in the doctor's care, but I had already mentioned to her that I had to get to the post office before it closed. I watched the doctor wink at Diana. I think Diana read the frown on my face.

"I'll be fine, honey. Ya'll go on ahead," she said.

"It's only a lil' bite," Doctor Bravo slurred, scanning her luxuriant figure. "But I gonna do a thorough zamination' jus' to be sure."

When I returned, Doctor Bravo was sitting at his desk writing a prescription for what turned out to be a topical ointment. Diana sat along one wall as far from the doctor as possible, looking out the window, her lush lips squeezed tightly together.

"How is she?" I murmured across the desk.

"She gonna be fine, but she a very uncooperative patient," he replied, never raising his head from his writing task.

"Oh." I glanced again at Diana still staring out the window. "I'm terribly sorry," I muttered, "what do we owe you?"

"Oh, nothing," he replied looking up, his bloodshot eyes crinkling at the corners. "The pleasure of you both for lunch at Kau Kan this afer-noon woo' be wonderful."

"Oh, terrific, we'd love to." I said.

As we walked home along the bank of the canal after a wonderful meal of shrimp served in a rich cream sauce, I said, "Diana, what's your problem? You hardly spoke at lunch. The good doctor, although drunk, treated you without charge and tended your bite. He even invited us for lunch. Really, you're a visitor in this country and should show better manners."

She snapped her head around. "Linda, damn it, your good doctor took me down a hall to a little room and told me to take off all my clothes. He said he had to make a thorough examination. I informed him I just had a little ol' bite on my ankle, and have no other symptoms. He said we had to be sure, so to take off my clothes! I turned around to open the door and get out of there and he pinched my butt!"

Diana grabbed my hand and jerked me behind the thick trunk of a tree growing along the canal. She struggled to pull down one side of her hot pants, and sure enough, an angry welt on her behind rivaled the one on her ankle.

Ted Tate's version of Dr. Bravo:

Dr. Bravo

Am extremely attractive lady who was visiting me developed some strange-water-filled blisters on the top of one foot, so we went to consult with Dr. Bravo.

Dr. Bravo looked at the blisters and at the very appealing lines of the lady's figure.

"Please undress and I'll examine you for other blisters or symptoms," he directed.

"There's no more blisters and no other symptoms. I have already been examined very thoroughly," the lady told him.

Dr. Bravo eyed me enviously and suspiciously, then somewhat disappointed turned to the examination of the foot.

After a couple of mumbled "Hummmmms" he gently broke the blisters with a needle, cleaned them, coated the punctures with antiseptic and put a light bandage over the punctures.

"What is it doctor, what's causing those things?" the lady asked.

"I don't know," Dr. Bravo answered seriously, "but you will be OK now."

"How do you know I'll be OK if you don't know what it is?" the somewhat baffled lady asked.

"I know; you just enjoy Mexico, listen to our music, go to the beach, read good books, dance and make love and you will be fine," Dr. Bravo counseled.

The diagnosis, treatment, and counsel were excellent—the lady is now a happy permanent resident of Mexico.

Physicians: There are some very fine physicians in town and every local has his or her favorite.

To the foreigner with limited Spanish, I am only recommending one physician who speaks fluent English. He is conveniently located and **Dr. Rogelio Grayeb** can refer you to a specialist if needed. He makes house calls—even on Sunday! ☎ 554-3334/5041 and 📱 (755)557-8303. He has recently moved to a house on *Calle Zafiro* #12—off *Avenida Palmar.* He shares his practice with Dra. Gudalupe Cendejas—a dental surgeon. ☎ 558-4971. Open 9:00 a.m. until 8:00 p.m. weekdays and 9:00 a.m.-3:00 p.m. on Saturday.

There is also a medical office complex containing over a dozen physicians of all types at the corner of *Nicolás Bravo* and *Vicente Guerrero* inside the courtyard on the second and third floor.

a board certified psychologist with an office in *Zihua* and Chicago. He speaks fluent Spanish and English and can be reached by
✉ drostrov@zihuatanejo.net

Dr. Hugo Alarcón Hernandez. New location by the new Sam's Club. He's above the *FarmaPronto*. ☎ 554-1400. He is a dermatologist and also "rejuvenates skin," has facial fillers, and Botox treatment. He's very professional but I'm not a repeat client.

Dr. M. Becerril: ☎ 554-7366. *Nicolas Bravo.* Another dermatologist located in the big doctor's complex above *Coyuca* pharmacy.

Chiropractors: There are several and three distinctly different chiropractors in the area definitely worth mentioning.

Dr. Fernando Paredes Proa: *Esq. Av. Cosmos y Messier.* (Off the back road to Ixtapa). 📱 (755) 108-8263. Office hours Monday and Tuesday 10:00 a.m-2:00 p.m. and 4:00 p.m.-9:00 p.m. Fernando arrives every week from *Toluca* to give adjustments, acupuncture, or injections if needed. I personally visit him at least every 2 weeks. He's a "little rough" but does the job.

Centro Quirofísico y Massages Profesionales: *Jupiter* #8. (Directly across from side-entrance to *Comercial Mexicana).* ☎ 554-1783/1162. *Isabel Cristina Olivar* uses chiropractic techniques and has helped many of my friends that swear by her. She teaches massage and does a combination massage therapy and spinal adjustments.

Huesero Don Lalo: 📱(755)101-8016. *Don Lalo* has been adjusting backs for as long as I can remember. Many of my friends wouldn't use anyone else and I have had him over for a session or two in times of need. He's very good at what he does but speaks no English.

Dentists: Dental care is cheap. Many foreigners have extensive dental work done here and pay for their vacation in the savings over what they would have spent at home. Ask a local for a recommendation..

Dr. Arturo Perezcano: *H. Colegio Militar* #114. ☏ 554-2344.

Dr. Yolanda Alvarado: *Calle Alejandrina* #4. ☏ 554-2570. Yolanda has been serving the foreign community for over 30 years. She's best used for simple cleanings and quickie fillings.

Smile: *Esq. Calle Amado Nervo y Lateral Carr. Acapulco-Zihuatanejo.* ☏ 554-7236. Dra. Lili and twin Tere are very good dentists and very fun ladies.

Dra. Cecilia Villavicencio: *Antonio Nava.* ☏ 554-3110. Cecilia is a first rate dentist and speaks some English. She's more expensive than other dentists but all her equipment is top of the line (for Mexico) and she does a great job cleaning teeth and filling cavities. Friends having extensive dental work are very pleased with their results.

Dra. Rocía Porcayo: *H. Colegio Militar* #12. ☏ 554-4417 or ☏ (755) 556-0068. A favorite of some of my good friends—I tried her once but with an appointment I was made to wait an unreasonable amount of time. I don't do that.

Optometrists: Eye examinations, glasses, adjustments, or sunglasses are available here. The exam is quite reasonable but the glasses (as they are imports) are very pricey.

Óptica Clínica: *Av. Cuauhtémoc.* ☏ 554-2282. Dr. Dario Cabrera Torres.

Óptica Olmos: *Juan Alvarez*—across from basketball court. ☏ 554-0482.

Clinics and Labs

Clinics are private hospitals and run as such with a doctor always in attendance. Labs perform tests for amoebas, pregnancy, blood sugar, etc.

Hospital de Especialidades: *Av. La Parota.* ☏ 554-7628. Here is a clinic that has been rated highly by the locals. It is close to the *Pemex* station in *El Hujal* and they have access to specialists.

Clinica Maciel: *Las Palmas* #4. ☏ 554-0517. Fax: 554-2380. They have 11 specialists ranging from cardiology to gastroenterology and 24 hour emergency care.

Centro de Salud El Embalse: *Paseo La Boquita* (a couple of blocks past *CM*). Price based on ability to pay. I mention it because if you want to obtain a Mexican driver's license, you must have a blood test and this is where you will be sent. They also will do routine vaccinations cheaply.

Laboratorios Ixta-Zih: Paseo Palmar #8. ☎ 554-2978. This is a modern lab staffed with expert technicians. Next door, is a modern X-ray facility.

Hospitals

Most illnesses can be treated competently at local facilities. Serious conditions are best treated in a major metropolis such as Mexico City or Guadalajara.

Hospital Montejano: Juan Alvarez s/n. ☎ 554-5404. His facility is now mostly specializing in cosmetic procedures.

Hospital General Dr. Bernado Sepulvedo Gutiérrez: Lateral Carr. Acapulco-Zihuatanejo. ☎554-3650. On right hand side of the feeder road leading to Acapulco. This is the general hospital with some excellent physicians in attendance. There is a sliding scale based on ability to pay and the maximum charge for a consultation is $4.00 U.S.

IMSS: Lateral Carr. Acapulco-Zihuatanejo. ☎ 554-2497/2285. Left hand side of the road leading to Acapulco beside *Pemex* station. This is the social security hospital serving the area. All employers must pay social security for their workers and this "tax" entitles individuals to free medical care. This, and all other hospitals, must accept anyone for emergency service, however, unless you are covered by Mexican social security, I strongly recommend you go elsewhere.

MEDICIEL: Avenida Morelos and junction to police station. ☎ 5548617/5824. ✉ **cesar.maciel@terra.com.mx** This very clean modern outpatient hospital has five beds and two emergency beds. It was designed for people needing care after non-life threatening surgery such as hip or knee replacement. Specialist are brought in from Guadalajara to do the surgeries.

Drugstores:

Many Mexicans patronize pharmacies instead of doctors for all their health needs. Good pharmacies have the latest information on drugs. Prescription drugs are sold over the counter at some savings. (The savings over U.S. drugs is no longer what it used to be—but still cheaper than the U.S). There are many drugs that are Class 1 and not available over the counter (Percodan, Valium, etc). For intestinal distress, I recommend either Imodium or Bactrim F. There are now around 50 pharmacies in the area—many of them *Similares* or pharmacies offering generic drugs. Many doctors do not want their patients using these "generics" as they feel they are not quality. A recent newspaper article said that 60% of the drugs sold in Mexico are "pirated" and of lack any quality control. In 2010, Mexico passed a law that you now must have a prescription for antibiotics as they were being over self-prescribed. As a result, many of the pharmacies—generic and regular now have in-house doctors. A visit cost 25 pesos and it's an additional 25 pesos for the prescription.

FarmaPronto: (Numerous locations around town). They offer about a 30% discount over most other pharmacies.

Farmacia Gia-A: *Av. Morelos* by the stoplight and *Coppel.* Upscale with a complete lab that has the ability to do labwork for animals.

ISSTE: *Av. Morelos y Vicente Guerrero.* By far the least expensive.

Koyuca: *Esq. Nicolás Bravo y Vicente Guerrero.*

Similares: These pharmacies are all over—especially around the market area. They advertise savings of up to 80% so are very popular.

Money

Most purchases are made in *pesos*. Most merchants, restaurants and hotels accept credit cards (Visa, MasterCard, and less often, American Express). Personal checks are not accepted unless drawn on a local bank. ★ In Ixtapa, there exists a place to cash foreign-drawn checks *(Intercam)*. First you must register with them and be a resident at least part-time with an established address as well as complying with their other requirements. Once this is done, you can cash checks there and the exchange rate is excellent.

Banks: Banks offer the official money exchange rate that is set by the government and fluctuates hourly. The local banks have specific hours for the changing of traveler's checks and dollars—usually 9:00 a.m. to noon. Remember to bring your passport—many banks insist on this. A small fee is usually charged for each traveler's check cashed regardless of value. In 2010 banks stopped changing pesos to dollars and if you deposit more than $1,500 U.S. or $15,000 pesos to an account, the government charges a 3% "fee." This is to halt drug money deposits and all cash business deposits.

Bank tellers tend to give you only large bills. Try to get "*una cantidad de billetes chicos*" (some smaller bills). Change has always been a major problem here and if you carry small change, it eliminates the situation of waiting "forever" in a restaurant or store while the merchant rushes out to find change for you.

When exchanging a small quantity of money, the *casas de cambio* are much quicker and the service charge is nominal compared to time wasted. With so many ATM's, there are now very few *casas de cambio*. They don't keep banker's hours either.

Now all the banks have automatic machines open 24 hours a day. They often run out of money on the weekends. They accept both debit and credit cards. Remember, your credit card company is charging you a fee to use these foreign machines—usually a minimum of 3%. It's best to have two cards because sometimes the machines are just ornery and won't accept a card. You can no longer go into the banks and get cash withdrawals using your credit card.

I think the following info is informative and interesting regarding Mexican money. Michel Janicot wrote this article for ADIP:

Mexican bills come in six denominations: 20, 50, 100, 200, 500, and 1000 peso notes.

The 20 pesos note shows dapper Benito Juárez. Born in 1806 from a poor, illiterate peasant family. Juárez didn't know how to read or write until he was 12 years old, when he also learned Spanish. He studied Latin, theology, philosophy, arts and sciences then took up law and entered politics. He held several posts in state and national administrations and was twice jailed and once deported for his political beliefs. When the rebellion for Mexican Independence began, he became Minister of Justice and later President of the Republic and was a strong advocate for the poor. He was re-elected president of Mexico in 1867 and died while still in office.

The gentleman with a bandanna covering his head on the 50 pesos bill is José María Morelos y Pavón who was born in September 1765 in Valladolid, renamed Morelia in his honor after his death. His father was a carpenter and mother, a schoolteacher. At age 30, he entered the priesthood, studying under the celebrated Miguel Hidalgo, whose sermons urged independence, freedom and liberty. Morelos offered his services, not asking for weapons or money, and became a victorious rebel leader with many impressive victories. The radical priest/rebel was captured and executed by firing squad on December 22, 1815.

On the 100 pesos bill is Netzahualcóyotl, whose name means "starving coyote." The son of King Chichimeca-Texcocano, the mustached poet king grew up to be a warrior of great courage and valor with a strong interest in science. He assumed the position of governor of Texcoco, capital of the Acolhua and Chichimeca kingdom, in 1431 and held the post for 41 years. He was known as a powerful, civilized man, very intelligent and wise. He built elevated hanging gardens similar to the famed ones in Babylon, as well as palaces, monuments, aqueducts, public baths and a great number of edifices which made the capital a large beautiful city: he studied and cultivated the arts, sciences and literature, passed beneficial laws, wrote poetry and philosophy. He died in 1472.

The 200 pesos note depicts Sor Juana Inés de la Cruz (aka Juana de Asbaje), born in 1651 to a Basque father and a Creole mother. At age 7 or 8 she asked to be sent to a university and at age 8 wrote religious poems. Extremely pious, she entered the convent, San José de las Carmelitas Descalzas in 1667 and was placed in charge of the convent's archives. She acquired some 4,000 books and a considerable knowledge of languages, philosophy, theology, astronomy and art, and became a well-known writer of religious sonnets, musical scores, philosophical theses, biographies, plays and comedies. In the 1690's she sold her library, giving money to the children and the poor. She died in 1695 as various deadly floods and epidemics swept through New Spain. After her death her father confessor nominated her for sainthood.

The 500 pesos note represents Ignacio Zaragoza, known as the "Defender of the Nation." Born in 1829, the son of an Army captain, he became a soldier himself and went on to lead many winning battles in the fight for independence and against foreign invaders. With two other generals, he formed the Liberal Party. With the triumph of the Liberal Party he became Minister of War and fought against the French invasion. Against superior forces, he defeated the French at the decisive battle of Puebla on May 5, 1863. Zaragoza retired soon after and died of typhus in 1862. (Newer bills have Frieda Kallo.)

The 1000 peso note shows the bust of Miguel Hidalgo y Costilla (1753-1831), "Father of the Nation," who initiated and launched the call for Mexican Independence, his now famous "El Grito" on the night of September 15, 1810 from the church of Dolores in the State of Guanajuato. The 57-year-old Catholic priest soon attracted hundreds of disenchanted Mexicans. On December 6, 1810, Hidalgo left Dolores with only 600 insurgents but in a few days that number grew to 100,000. Their first victory was in the taking of the fortified city of Guanajuato. They then marched on to Mexico City and defeated the Spanish at the battle of Monte de las Cruces. However, Hidalgo failed to occupy the town and retreated north. He suffered his first defeat in San Jerónimo Aculco and retired to Guadalajara, gathering more converts. He was finally defeated in Chihuahua where he was captured and executed by firing squad on July 30, 1831. His head was publicly displayed in Guanajuato for 10 years.

If you are using ATM machines, HSBC and Scotia are good because their machines allow you to swipe your card instead of inserting it into the machine. Occasionally, if your card gets eaten, you cannot get it back until the company that issues the card sends a letter to the bank. Not a fax but a letter! If you're a tourist, this could take as long as two weeks so be very careful.

Banamex: (*Esq. Vicente Guerrero y Ejido*). ☏ 554-2181.

Bancomer: *Av. Benito Juárez.* ☏ 554-0670.

Banorte: *Av. Benito Juárez.* ☏ 554-4900.

HSBC: *Av. Colegio Militar.* ☏ 554-5454.

Scotiabank: *Av. Benito Juárez*—closest to canal.

These are all conveniently located in and around *centro*. Most of the banks have an ATM machine at *Comercial Mexicana*. The airport now has an ATM so you can obtain pesos before getting into a taxi if need be.

Money Exchanges or *Casas de Cambio*:

These are generally open from 9:00 a.m. until 10:00 p.m. seven days a week. As stated before, the exchange rate is lower than at the banks but there is no standing in line and no charge for traveler's checks. Some will accept major credit cards. Again, they may ask for identification. There are many in *Centro*, all with large signs. I usually recommend the one at *Pedro Ascencio and Galeana #4*. They can also send a fax for you.

From *Wash Gently, Dry Slowly*:

Chiclets, Dollars and Pesos

Mexico is such a friendly place and its people are so helpful that even an alien gringo who neither speaks nor understands the Spanish language can communicate and survive. It is particularly easy to climb over the speech barrier in a store where you merely point to the articles you want, the clerk writes down the cost, you pay that amount and you are home free. Financial transactions in semi-formal banks are a bit more of a problem.

When I first visited a small Mexican bank to open a very moderate savings account, the president, Mr. Rodriguez, asked that I speak Spanish for it was obvious that I was Mexican and therefore should know the Spanish language. I assured him that I was an Americano of Irish-Indian heritage and that my dark skin and dark hair were generic accidents of the combination. I further assured him that I was sincerely complimented by his mistake and after showing him some identification he reluctantly agreed that perhaps I wasn't Mexican. He approved my check, welcomed me to Mexico and to his bank, and then directed me to the proper window to complete the transaction.

At the window my American dollars check was approved by two more people and converted to pesos. At the next window, a beautiful young lady gave me a slip of paper listing the number of pesos and had me sit at a desk where another young lady skillfully steered me through the proper completion of some routine forms. She gave me a bankbook and directed me toward the "ahorre," or savings window. Several people were ahead of me in the line and a girl about 9 years old was at the head of the line. The savings teller was a stunning, immaculately dressed young lady. She watched the 9-year-old as she chewed vigorously on a wad of gum, leaned over the ledge of the counter to discover a box of Chiclets in the girl's hand, asked for some of them, popped them into her mouth and reverted to a very professional handling of the business at hand.

Suffering from the Gringo, new account, no Spanish trauma as I waited my turn, I needed a gimmick. I left the bank, bought several two-in-a-box Chiclets and got back in line. When I reached the window, I placed my papers on the counter with boxes of Chiclets on top of them. The beautiful young teller blushed, made my day complete with a dazzling smile, processed my papers, thanked me, and bade me "Adios."

The service since that time has always been excellent.

Mr. Rodriguez still thinks I am a Mexican.

Legal

To sell or buy property, make wills, etc., a notary is needed. Notaries handle civil matters (like land transactions) and lawyers deal in criminal matters and other disputes.

Notarios:

#1 Lic. Bolívar Navarrete Herédia: *Alamo #8. (Entre Ahuehuete y Primavera en Col. El Hujal).* ☎ 554-3100, 554-2236, 554-3112.

www.notarialzihuatanejo@prodigy.net.mx

#2 Lic. Carlos Francisco Várgas Nájera: *De Los Deportes s/n.* ☎ 554-5334, 554-2179.

#3 Lic. Saulo Cabrera Barrientos: *H. Colegio Militar #191.* ☎ 554-8260, 554-8261, 554-6160.

#4 Lic. Martín Medina Reyes: Located up the hill at the traffic light across from *Bodega* as you're going to Ixtapa. ☎ 544-7694/6532.

✉ **lmartinm@prodigy.net.mx**

Regular Attorneys: There are at least a dozen attorneys in town but the following I know personally and have done business with them.

Rodrigo Campos: *Mar Negro #8.* ☎ 554-5200.

Agustin Galindo: *Av. Juan Alvarez* #162—across from basketball court. ☎ 554-9915/16. Very popular attorney in town. www.galindoabogados.com

Arquimides Nájera: *Calle Palapas.* ☎ 554-8208.

Peyton & Connell: *Galeana.* ☎ 554-7957 or Fax 554-2035. All employees speak English. ✉ **inquire@mexicolaw.com.mx**

Should you have problems with local authorities and need assistance quickly, the hotline number for the American Embassy in Mexico City is 01(555)080-2000. **Debbie Mioni is our embassy representative with an office located adjacent to the Fontán Ixtapa.** (☎ 553-2100 or 📱 (755)557-1106). Office hours are 12:00 p.m. until 4:00 p.m.

✉ **consularixtapa@prodigy.net.mx** You can also access the consulate through Facebook.

If you should lose one of your credit cards or it is stolen, it should be reported immediately to the credit card company.

★ It is an excellent idea to keep a list of your credit card numbers and copies of your other important papers in a place other than your pocketbook while traveling. Chances are nothing will happen, but if it does, you will be so happy to have that extra list.

This is probably a good place to mention a rather new occurrence in international travel. Many credit card companies become suspicious of charges occurring in locations unusual for you. For this reason, it is a good idea to let your credit card company security team know of your plans to be in a foreign country. Your card could get flagged and you will be denied use of it.

Let's Spend Money!
(Where to Shop)

There are plenty of shops here to please even the most discriminating buyer. Prices are relatively high for handicrafts because the only indigenous craftsmen are the *Náhuatl*-speaking Indians from the village of *Xalitla*. The women and children wear colorful pinafores over their dresses and can be found at the Indian Crafts Market in town (*Cinco de Mayo*) or the Indian Crafts Market on *Playa La Ropa*. Their bargaining skills are legendary and the children, especially, have a fair command of the English language. The crafts market is the one place where bartering is acceptable and necessary. It's a fun place to idle away an afternoon and practice your bargaining skills.

There are shops carrying fine quality goods and then again, there are shops carrying trinkets that they think the tourist will like. From *Topes:*

The Tequila Toad

Dr. Anita Cowan, Professor of Psychology and Doctor of Anthropology, has been in love with Zihua going on five decades. She spent a year in 1980–81 doing research for her doctoral thesis, "Tourism Development in a Mexican Coastal Community", which was published in 1987. I wanted to give her a significant gift to commemorate this happy occasion. Jan Hardy and I were sitting in the street (yes, we were), soaking our feet in a bucket of water preparing for a pedicure and discussing this important matter when our eyes fell on the perfect gift displayed in the beauty shop window. Before our very eyes was a 12-inch high stuffed toad, standing upright, holding an umbrella in one hand and a tequila bottle in the other. This was the perfect gift to commemorate Anita's book on tourism. The toad perfectly exemplified the theme of her book—what tourism has done to a small coastal community. She loved it and it stands in a place of honor on top of her book on her coffee table.

Most stores accept credit cards and very few, if any, of the better shops will barter. Credit card purchases cost the owners 5-7% in fees. If you offer to pay cash, most stores will discount 5-10%. If planning to take more than $400.00 dollars back in purchases, remember the value-added-tax of 16% is included in the purchase price. You do not have to pay duty on tax so get a receipt with the real purchase price listed excluding the tax. Many arts and crafts items are excluded from duty.

It is not a bad idea to have a receipt for all purchases and pack them separately when departing for home. Ninety-nine percent of the time, customs agents won't bother to look at anything but if you fall into that 1% crack, it's best to have everything in order to avoid hassle and delay.

By all means, shop around. Stores off *Cuauhtémoc* are less patronized and they are more apt to bargain.

Most shops are open from 9:00-10:00 a.m. until 8:00-9:00 p.m. Since almost all the *centro* shops are air conditioned, they no longer close between 2:00-4:00 p.m. for siesta. However, I said most—not all.

Art Galleries

Armenta Rodríguez: Local well known artist with shop at *Cuauhtémoc y Pedro Ascencio.*

Galería Casa de Arte: *Av. Cuauhtémoc* #9. Gallery on main street.

Galería Cihuaconatl: *Galeana* #10.

GalArt: Located in the old *Villa del Sol* lobby, this is a first class art gallery and boutique, featuring exquisite jewelry, paintings, folk art, sculptures, and more.

ZIH Galería: *Juan Alvarez* #56—close to pier. Exhibits monthly individual and collective shows throughout the year.

Clothing

All kinds of clothing are available, from native garb to the latest fashions from Mexico City. Prices of clothes here are high. Very few stores ever have anything on sale until low season. Some clothing is of a very high quality. I have some native dresses I've owned over 20 years and still wear. Beware of native cottons. It is best to hand wash whatever you buy here separately the first time. Many of these items are not colorfast and will "run" terribly. In order to fix the colors; soak the cotton goods in cold water to which you have added vinegar. It may be necessary to change the water 4 or 5 times before the dye stops running.

The following are a list of just a few for there are dozens more clothing stores that have quality goods.

Anfibios: *Nicolás Bravo.* Nice selection of sports clothing for surfing, skateboarding, swimming, etc.

Cactus: *Vicente Guerrero*—across from comercial laundry. Carries men and women's fashions from Mexico City. Sometimes some really good bargains.

Coppel: *Av. Morelos*—parking lot by post office is one entrance. Large (for here) department store with a mish mash of furniture, appliances, and clothes.

Eneken: *Juan Alvarez*—across from basketball court. High quality linen goods.

Lupita's: *Esq. Juan Alvarez y Vicente Guerrero.* Lupita, the owner, imports some lovely dresses, vests, shirts, etc. from the *Oaxaca* area and from *Guatemala.*

Mario's: *Vicente Guerrero* #12.—across from Coconuts. Mario has been selling fine leather goods for years.

Tutti Frutti: *Comercial Mexicana.* Of all the "new" Mexican chain stores that are invading our town, this is my favorite. They have women's swimsuits and *pareos*, purses, shoes, scarves, etc. Pricey but really cute stuff.

Crafts and Gifts

Indian Craft Market: *Cinco de Mayo.* The Indians are set up here with over two blocks of craft items from hand-painted plates to hammocks and wind chimes.

Cerámica Tónala: (*Juan Alvarez*—close to basketball court). Blue design plates, vases, etc. from the *Tónala* region of Mexico.

Casa Marina: Adjacent to basketball court. This is a shopping complex owned and operated by the family of the late Helena Krebs. The complex, which is a must to visit, opened in 1965, and contains several shops with unusual items:

Metztli: Wonderful handicraft clothing items.

El Jumil: A large selection of silver from Taxco and indigenous masks from the State of *Guerrero.*

Costa Libre: Lots of crafts and cute clothing.

La Zapoteca: Rugs and hammocks sold here. Often there is a weaving demonstration going on. Without a doubt, the very best quality and selection in town.

Café Marina: Small restaurant specializing in really good pizza and sandwiches at excellent prices. Also has used books for sale at considerable savings. For the last couple of years, Joe has been offering nightly specials, which really appeal to the locals. We can get roast beef and meatloaf and it's terrific!

Mi Cafecita: Coffee, pastries, crepes, and smoothies.

Humane Society: Animals have been cared for here for decades.

Fruity Keiko: Corner Juan Alvarez and Agustin Ramirez. ☎ 112-1011. This store offers a beautiful selection of collectibles for the home with top quality items from the various regions of Mexico. Many items are one-of-a kind pieces from some of Mexico's best artists.

El Arte de Tradicíon: *Cuauhtémoc*—first block from water. Lovely *talavera.*

El Nopal: *Avenida Cinco de Mayo #56.* ☎ and fax 554-7530. Another fantastic gift shop with very unique items. I find a lot of my Christmas presents here. They will also ship DHL for you.

La Catrina: *Av. Cuauhtémoc #16.* This store sells lovely hand crafted items from various parts of Mexico. Specializing in the skeletal dolls of the same name as store.

Lacquer de Olínala: *Cinco de Mayo*—by church. *Olínala* is a very remote small mountain village where they make furniture and decorative items. A solid color paint is applied first and then very gifted artists paint exquisite designs.

Mágicas Manos: *Esq. Cuauhtémoc y Ejido.* Wonderful crafts with lots of ceramics and glass—almost a copy of *Rosimar* further down the street.

Rosimar: *Cuauhtémoc*—way down toward *Morelos.* One of my personal favorites when I want to purchase ceramic gifts.

Jewelry

There are many fine jewelry stores in *Zihua.* Most of them offer high quality silver. The government has ruled that all silver jewelry must be stamped with "sterling" or .925. If you don't see the stamp, go somewhere else to shop. Prices vary but not much. Usually the item is weighed and priced accordingly.

You won't see much gold jewelry except in the very exclusive stores because stores are taxed on a higher tax base if they sell gold. Some of my favorites—all on *Cuauhtémoc* are *Ruby's, Alberto's, Plata de Taxco, Teocali, Escorpíon,* and *Pez y Plata.*

Services A to Z

You might need one of the following services, even if here for only a short time. I've tried to list various selections in each category. I've made comments about various places that I and other locals utilize. Just because there is no comment and only a listing should not be construed as a negative. We all have our favorites and tend to use them often.

A.

Aluminum & glass:
Vidrios y Alumínios Del Puerto: Av. Morelos. ☎ 554-4708.
Vidrios Rodríguez: And. Parque Los Mangos. Frente a Fibazi. ☎ 554-3930.
Vidrios Ramírez: Paseo La Boquita.

Alarm Systems:
Alarm Sales and Service: ☎ (755)100-5858l. By the post office, behind immigration office.

Reparacion y Installacion de Alarmas y Video: *Las Palapas.* ☎ (755)108-7105.

Appliances: There are probably thirty stores selling appliances in town. *ELEKTRA: Esq. Benito Juárez y Av. Morelos* and *Salinas y Rocha:* (on side of market) have good selections, give good service, and do warranty work.

Repair:
Hector Ramírez: Sales, service and installation of major appliances. (Company—Pro-Comfort and Refrigeration ☎ (755)115-0927.

Electrodomésticos Callejas: *Av. Morelos* #37. ☎/fax 112-1419. Small and large appliance repair.

Refriexpress: *Calle Palmar y Esmeralda*—close to Carrier.

Air Conditioning: Carrier—*Calle Palmar.*

Art Supplies: If you're an artist, best to bring your own brushes from home. Local artists tell me you can buy pretty much whatever you need locally.
López Impresores: Benito Juárez. Has a good selection. They also have film development, reproduction equipment, and all occasion gift cards besides general office supplies

Automotive: See Transportation.

B.

Bakeries: See food section.

Banks: Refer to money section.

Barber Shop: *Altamarano y Cuauhtémoc.* Cuts only men's hair—really cheap.

Batteries:

Autopartes del Negro: Lateral Carr. Acapulco-Zihuatanejo (close to hospital).

Ávila: Same as above.

Beer Distributors:

Both carry other brands of beer listed on the big signs outside.

Agencia Corona: Lateral *Carr. Acapulco-Zihuatanejo.*

☎ 554-2910.

Agencia Sol: In same area as above. ☎ 554-2866.

Beauty Shops: There are **dozens** of hair stylists in *Zihua.* Perms, cuts, manicures and pedicures are all inexpensive. I used to recommend you bring your own product but now the beauty supply store is carrying lots of good, imported hair products and *Comercial Mexicana* also has a vast line of beauty supplies and quality products.

Beauty Salón Liliana: *Josefa Ortiz de Dominguez* #5. *Playa La Madera.* Same street as *Margarita's* and *Casa Viejo.* ☎ 544-6344 or 📱 (755)558-0369. Full service salon popular with the locals. She also is a seamstress and makes some cute tropical clothes. English spoken.

Chachis: Nicholas Bravo #13-5. ☎ 554-4836. I "caught" a fungus here six years ago and I still have it. The autoclave (to sterilize tools) is not used. (Thought I should warn people).

Salón de Belleza: Calle Ejido #32. 📱 (755)110-0948.

Estética Unisex: Nicolás Bravo.

Héctor: Calle *Presa de Angostura.* (Next street past intersection of *Benito Juárez y Av. Morelos.*

Zoe Salon: Calle Ejido #32. 📱 (755)1100948.

Beauty Supply:

Comercializadora Tapia: Av. Morelos: ☎ 554-8388.

Probelleza Oline: Nicolás Bravo #15.

Boat Hardware: See hardware

Book Exchange:

Café Marina: Paseo de Pescador.

Flophouse Bar: *Calle Ejido* near Teppan Roll.

C.

Camera Repair: *Tecnicámara: Catalina Gonzales y Cuauhtémoc.*

Canvas and Upholstery:

Decoraciones & Tapicería: Av. Morelos #53. ☎ or ✆ (755)128-7846. They sell some high end fabric and do furniture (fabric) repairs for homes, offices and boats.

La Casa del Tapicería: Av. Morelos. Cushions, fabrics, canvas, zippers and excellent service.

Modatelas: Av. Benito Juárez—block past the market toward *Av. Morelos.*

Paraiso: Av. Benito Juárez across from market.

Tianguis de México: Av. Morelos—just to right of intersection with *Benito Juárez.* I'm always amazed when I come in here. In the back of the store you will find a large variety of fabrics and foam. They will cut to order and/or make your cushions, pillows, whatever.

Carpentry: Take the first left after the fire station as you go toward the beach. Go down to end of block—go left and take first right and then take first left. There is an entire block of carpenters and they can make just about anything you can imagine and cheap!

At the *Playa La Madera* bridge, bamboo furniture is custom made and he does a really good job—he's made several pieces of furniture for me as well as picture frames.

Cell Phones:

You can now buy "throw away" cell phones all over town. They are now requiring photo ID to purchase a phone (they ask foreigners for a passport) and most every store sells time.

TelCel: Vicente Guerrero. ☎ 554-7603. Sales and service for *Zihua* but must go to Ixtapa to reactivate older phone. Many other locations around town but this is the main one.

Chemicals: *Disude: Calle Antonio Nava.* They sell a large assortment of heavy duty cleaning supplies. The only place I've found brass polish and silver cleaner.

Tahuer: Vicente Guerrero #51. Disude copy—do something right and it will be copied here in a heartbeat—hence at least 2-3 Internet places every block and now lots of new coffee shops.

Clock/Watch Repair: See Jewelry and Watch Repair.

Coffee: See Life's Little Necessities.

Computer—Sales, Service and Repair:

Chuatlan Compu-Services: Ejido #32E. ☎ 554-5790. I was told Carlos, Juan Carlos, or Imer were very attentive and good at their job.

Internetplus: Av. Las Huertas esq. Mar Caspio. ☎ 544-8910 or ✆ (755) 104-4096. The largest store in town of its kind selling computers and printers, accessories, etc. Also repair of computers and printers.

Compucity: Av. Morelos y Av. Universidad. ☎ 554-5723. Isidro is the computer fix-it guy of choice among the locals. He makes house or boat calls and is always busy. Visit **www.compucity.com.mx**

Solucion Digital: Cuauhtemoc 44. ☎554-1004: 📱 (755)101-9504.Fabian and his associates really know what they are doing. His techs can fix Apple.

Courier Services:

DHL: Marina Nacional #71. ☎ 554-3747.

Estafeta: Av. Colegio Militar #120. ☎ 554-4888.

RedPak: Av. Colegio Militar #38—across from new OXXO in *Plaza San Rafael.* ☎ 554-9082/3.

D.

Dry Cleaners:

Tintorería America: Catalina Gonzales (close to *Cinco de Mayo*).

Tintorería y Lavandería Express: (same as above).

Tintorería Romero: (same as above).

E.

Electricians:

Florencio Cazaro: 📱 (755)108-1768. Florencio is a charming young go-getter who aims to please and wants to work for the American community. He knows "being on time" is a high priority for those of us that have waited hours and sometimes days for repairmen. He can do just about anything so he really qualifies as an adept handyman and I think he's terrific.

Marcelo Tapia Cortéz: 📱 (755)556-1649.

Electrical Supplies:

Demesa: Av. Morelos. ☎554-3362/7645 Largest and probably best selection of electrical supplies in town.

Electro Iluminación: Vicente Guerrero.

Electro Juárez: Av. Morelos.

Mitron: Vicente Guerrero. Don't really know how to classify this store but they have connectors for computers, cameras, televisions, clock batteries and other "stuff" and they seem to be the only place in town for this stuff that you don't need often but when you do, you do!

F.

Film Development: See Photo Supplies

Flowers:

Florería La Nueva: Vicente Guerrero y Antonio Nava.

Florería Mary: Esq. Cinco de Mayo y Altamirano. ☎ 554-3375/553-0826.
Florería Dany: Antonio Nava esq. Galeana. ☎ 554-2663/8297 or ☎
(755)557-0822. Really nice selection and and can send flowers within
Mexico and worldwide. ☎ **danyfloresmx@yahoo.com.mx**
Foam: See Canvas and Upholstery.
Fumigation:
Clayton: ☎ 554-4535.
Fumigaciones Exter: ☎ 553-0454.
SICOPSA: ☎ 554-8141.
Pasaje Comercial: On the street with all the *Similares* off *Benito Juárez.*
You can buy all kinds of commercial grade insecticides here. Huge
selection.
Funeral Home:
Funerales Carlos. In between light for *Migra* office and light for *Coppel.*
Funerales del Pacífico: Same as above.
Funeraria Miralrio: Catalina Gonzales.
From *Topes in Paradise:*

The Faux Funeral

The steel grey dawn held the promise of another scorcher. By 10:00 a.m. the
hazy skies over Troncones had cleared and a cloudless sky reflecting the sand and
sea where the usually giant breakers were today tamed by a gentle hand and only a
whisper of a breeze, meant the temperatures would soar above 100 degrees. The
twenty-three yellow and white striped beach umbrella tables and scores of plastic
beach chairs advertising Sol beer sat vacant on this Tuesday, save one. Anita,
owner of the Tropic of Cancer restaurant-bar complex had given the staff the week
off for a vacation. I occupied the one chair. I sat silently gazing at the unusually
gentle foaming green surf. From time to time I would reach for a cigarette or take a
swig of lukewarm beer and swipe at the tears making furrows down my cheeks
through the sunscreen. I had come home to mourn. My beloved cocker spaniel
Bambi had died the previous Friday of cancer. I had planned to bring Bambi back
to her birthplace to die on the beach which she had so loved and spent many a happy
day exploring. This was not to be. Bambi simply couldn't hang on to make the
flight the previous Sunday and she went over the rainbow bridge before I could bring
her home.

Hearing the sound of a car pulling into the Tropic I reluctantly got up to
inform the visitor that the establishment was closed for the week. It was a
Zihuatanejo taxi and a man got out of the taxi and reached into the back seat—
removing an enormous bouquet of white roses—a symbol of death in Mexico. "I'm

looking for Linda," he said.
"I'm Linda."
"Well, help me out here—these are for you."
I opened the gate in astonishment as the taxi driver tried to thrust the huge bundle of flowers upon me. "Whoa, wait a minute. You must be mistaken. I didn't order any flowers from Zihuatanejo," I said. The taxi driver staggered to one of the beach tables and plopped down his bundle. "No, you didn't order these flowers. They are a gift from some of your friends in Zihua that heard about the death of your dog." Naturally this started a fresh deluge of tears. The taxi driver threw up his hands and departed. This apparition of roses had attracted the attention of several small children playing just outside the fenced property and three of the bolder ones entered the gate which was now open.
"What are the flowers for?" ask the little ragamuffin with snot clinging to his upper lip and his cheeks grimy with dirt.
"My dog died last week and these are a gift from friends that loved her like I did," I replied.
"Oh, then you are having a funeral?"
"No," I replied. "I don't have her ashes."
"What do you mean—her ashes?" the little urchin asked wide-eyed.
"Well, in the United States, instead of putting the body in the ground, we have it burned and then take the ashes and scatter them in a favorite place. I wanted to bring her ashes here and scatter them on the beach because this was a favorite place but her ashes didn't arrive at my house in time for me to bring them here."
"But you must have a funeral because you have the flowers," interjected one of the other children. One little girl said she would go home and get her stuffed dog and we could have a service on the beach and bury it. I said no—I'd wait until I came back in January and bring the ashes with me then. That was unacceptable to the children. One of the little boys ran over to the big barbecue pit and screamed that there were plenty of ashes in the pit and we could "playlike" they belonged to Bambi. By then I was surrounded by more than a dozen children insisting we have a mock ceremony on the beach. It was finally decided we would have a funeral procession from the Tropic of Cancer to the Burro Borracho some quarter mile down the beach, as Bambi loved the two places equally. We began to dismantle the roses and obtained a bag of ashes. One of the little boys decided we must have a band to accompany us so the kitchen lady was fetched and she provided several of the children with pots and pans and large spoons so we could have a drum brigade. Almost ready, one of the little girls said we couldn't have a funeral procession without covering our heads and I needed a veil. Mind you, I was dressed in a metallic black and blue bikini! Someone went for newspapers and rubber bands which the children

folded over their heads and attached and one little girl went home to get her mother's mantilla for me to wear. By this time, quite a crowd had gathered includeing numerous of my adult friends. We had to open the bodega to get a supply of beer to accompany the cortege and placed beer in buckets with ice along with the two buckets of ashes. This motley crew then made its way down the beach. The boys were banging on their instruments and the little girls were dropping ashes and rose petals only on the beach as Bambi didn't like the water. As we were passing Mallory and Ray's house, a tourist, standing on the outside patio, walked briskly towards our group. He wanted to know what we were doing and I explained about the mock funeral. He was amazed and wanted to know where we were going and what we were going to do. I explained that we would end the ceremony at the Burro and then have a wake at which time I would treat the children to Cokes and the adults to a beer. He then introduced himself and told me that was out of the question. He said he had never encountered anything quite so poignant as our mock funeral and he would like to host the wake and provide food and beverages to one and all. I, of course, said fine and he joined our motley group to walk the rest of the way to the Burro. Marty, the owner, couldn't believe what he was seeing when we entered. This man, Peter Baker, from San Diego, told Marty to run a tab and give anyone and everyone anything on the menu and he would settle up at the end of the day. Peter then ask me to call any other of my friends living on the beach to come on down. By six p.m. the party was in full swing—the children stuffed with Coke, hamburgers, hotdogs, and ice cream, wearily returned to their homes. About 20 of my adult friends stayed and closed the place down (which is nothing new for us). Peter graciously picked up the tab and made me promise to call him before I came back in January. He said he would make every effort to attend the real funeral for Bambi and that he had thoroughly enjoyed the day—no matter how much it had cost him. So a good time was had by all for a momentously sad time of my life and we get to do it all over again in six months when it will be a real deal and many more of my friends will be around to mourn and especially party with me.

Furniture:

Aliza Muebles: Very good quality Mexican furniture on feeder road toward Ixtapa before the gas stations.

Casa de Bambú: Playa La Madera—across from *La Ceiba* condos. They make all kinds of furniture from bamboo and the wife of the owner crafts wonderful lampshades out of coconut husks and old water bottles

Decoré: Blvd. Ixtapa s/n. ☎ 553-3550/3616.   Beautiful but very expensive furniture. Visit **www.decoreixtapa.com**

Muebles Confort: Feeder road toward Ixtapa before gas statio
Segusino Muebles: Nice furniture store on feeder road toward Ixtapa
before *Pemex.*
ZocoZihua: Consignment furniture store next to *Notario #3* on *Colegio Militar.* ✉ zocozihua@hotmail.com

G.

Gas, Vehicle:
PEMEX: Two as you are leaving town toward Acapulco and one
located at the old entrance to the airport. Two on the way to Ixtapa
and one behind Ixtapa on the road to *Lázaro Cárdenas.* One also
located on the road to *Puerto Mio.* All are open 24 hours a day and sell
Magna Sin (unleaded) and *Premium* (unleaded plus) and diesel. Gas is
about the same as the States so expect to pay at least $3.50 U.S. per
gallon. Some stations now accept credit cards.

Gas, Propane:
Every morning, trucks selling propane gas circulate throughout all of
Zihuatanejo. However, if you should need to buy a tank or fitting, you
should go to *Todo Para Gas: Vicente Guerrero*—across from Coconuts.
Fixed tanks can be filled by calling:
Gas de Guerrero: ☎ 554-2080.
Global Gas: ☎ 554-5467/4445

Glass: See **aluminum & glass**

Gyms:
Curves: *Av. Ejido.* ☎ 554-9678. On the second floor of office building
on corner of *Cuauhtémoc and Ejido.* Same as chain started in Canada.
Their hours are a little strange so check first.
Obregón: Calle de Pedregal y Av. Morelos. This is the oldest gym in town
and the equipment is a little shabby but it works! The price is right
also. Cost is $120.00 pesos per month and it is open from 6:00 a.m.
until 10:00 p.m. There are no air conditioners or fans but you expect
to sweat, yes?
Pacific Gold Gym: *Calle Mar Negro #8.* Gym opens daily from 6:00
a.m. until 10:00 p.m and Saturday from 7:00 a.m until 3:00 p.m. They
have an "inscription" of $80 pesos and monthly rate of $225 pesos.
Their music is loud and very disco. I stopped going and a lot of the
Mexicans that do attend wear earplugs.

H.

Hardware: Stores carry the same items as in the States but are not as organized. Try to take in an example of what you need, or drawing paper, as rarely do any of the staff speak English. There are a couple of dozen in town—the following are the ones I have found can almost always come up with what I need and understand my rather crude drawings if I don't know the word for the item.

Tlapalería y Ferretería Del Centro: Calle Cuauhtémoc. One of the best in town. They carry line and stainless nuts, bolts, and screws for boats.

Ferre Mar y Sol: Calle Mediterrano—across from *Telmex.* Very well stocked.

Ferretería Guadalajara: Calle Cerezos. This is a little off the beaten path but it is the most organized hardware store in town in my opinion. Everything is well displayed on walls and behind glass counters. There is a good selection of plumbing and electrical supplies along with a good assortment of tools.

Ferretería Sotelo: Av. Colegio Militar—across from electric company. The largest hardware store in town with home delivery.

Material de Plomería y Eléctrica: Av. Las Huertas. Good selection of plumbing and electrical needs—very helpful owners.

For the sailors, next to the strip club, *Kisses*, to your left on the highway to Ixtapa, is *La Miraflores.* They cater to the fishing fleet and stock stainless hardware, line, Raycor fuel filters, plus a multitude of little items you need to keep your boat running. They are the cheapest in town.

Home Improvement:

Grupo Azteca: Two locations—on *Lateral Carr. Acapulco-Zihuatanejo* on left-hand side after the gas station. Huge sign. Also in town on *Av. Morelos.*

Household Items:

Bazar: Colegio Militar. Carry lots of cheaply made household items you can't live without. Very good selection of plastic pots for plants. They also carry cheap fans and remember you get what you pay for.

I.

Ice: Purified ice can be purchased in bags at most *depósitos.* Almost all of the little *tiendas* in town now carry purified ice. If you need large quantities or blocks of ice, arrangements can be made with *Hielo Ortiz.* ☎ 554-3586. One block off the road to Acapulco, at the last right turn before the entrance to *Agua de Correo.*

J.

Jewelry and Watch Repair:
Calle Presa de Angostura: A couple of doors down from *Hector's Salon.* This man works out of his front yard and is a genius. He's a bit eccentric but I trust him implicitly.
Topacio Azul: Calle Los Mangos. They don't keep banker hours but they do a fine job repairing jewelry and work gold beautifully.

K.

Keys:
Cerrajería Armenta: Av. Vicente Guerrero. Close to *Av. Morelos.* ☎ 554-2633. A fine locksmith and key maker.
Cerrajería Bazar: Jaime Espinoza Esquivel. ☎ 554-8657 or 📱 (755) 100-3595. Comes highly recommended by Lilia (popular beauty salon owner on *Playa La Madera).*
Cerrajería Galeana: Calle Ejido (across from *Los Braseros).*
D' La Cruz: Calle Cuauhtémoc. 📱 (755)557-9700. Very efficient and prompt. Will make 24 hour housecalls.

L.

Language Schools/Spanish Lessons:
Schools seem to come and go.
Diana Fernandez: 📱 (755) 114-5891. Many of the locals take lessons from Diana. I hear she's a very good teacher (and she's a lot of fun).
Juan Luis Navarete: 📱 (755)121-1583. Juan taught high school Spanish to high school teachers in the U.S. His students praise him highly.
Victoria Priani: ☎ 553-3597. She's an excellent teacher and has been in the area over thirty years. Visit **www.vtplanguage.com**
Laundry: Laundry service here is fairly inexpensive. Ironing is available for an additional charge. Generally open from 8:00 a.m. until 8:00 p.m. If you take items in early, same day service is available.
Lavandería y Tintoría Express: Catalina Gonzales #35. ☎ 554-4393. Dry-cleaning available.
Lavandería Kyoto: Located at canal bridge at edge of *Playa La Madera.*
Lavandería Centro: Vicente Guerrero—next to *Mi Chayita.* I mention this one as it is self-service and full service and they have oversized machines for rugs and bedspreads.
Lavanderia Turbo: Av. La Boquita. ☎ 554-7171/4888. Home pick-up and delivery.
Tintorería Romero: Catalina Gonzales #44. Dry-cleaning only.
Turbo Laundry: Av. Palmar—next to Lab and X-Ray facility. They have a couple of large commercial machines.

Liquor Stores:
There are lots of stores selling liquor but the following have the best selection/prices.
Bodega: Lateral Carr. Acapulco-Zihuatanejo.
Comercial Mexicana: La Boquita s/n.
ISSTE: Benito Juárez s/n.
Sam's Club: *Lateral Carr. Acapulco-Zihuatanejo.*
Vinoteca: Corner of *Ejido y Cuauhtémoc.* ☎ or fax: 112-1392. Wonderful selection of domestic and imported wines and with a smaller selection of imported alcohol.
Visit **www.vinoteca.com** or ✉ **vinoixtapa@vinoteca.com**
Wine & Spirits: Two large liquor stores on *Nicolás Bravo*—both owned by Andy who was on the other side of the street in a very small store.

M.

Massage: *Playa La Ropa* has several massage stations all along the beach. The prices are generally in the $200-$300 pesos range—negotiable during low season.
Centro Quirofísico Isabella: ☎ 554-1783/1162. Isabella has an office across from *Comercial Mexicana* on *Av. Jupiter.* Appointment necessary.
Masaje Holístico: Calle Alejandrina. ☎ 554-5904 or 📱 (755)108-2729. Guadalupe Salas is a lovely lady that does very fine massages out of her home. She has strong hands so can give a really good deep massage.
Ana Scales gives wonderful massages in her home at the end of *Playa La Ropa.* 📱 (755) 111-0857.
Medical Supply Sales: *Av. Morelos.* Sale of crutches, wheelchairs, hospital beds, etc.
Medical Equiptment Sales: *Mar Negro* #60. ☎ 554-8320 or ✉ **ortozagro@hotmail.com**
Mechanics: Ask a local for a reference but if you're in a bind, the following three come highly recommended.
Mario: 📱 (755)558-4013. He works out of a yard across the street from the loading dock of *Comericial Mexicana.* He's been my mechanic since 1982.
Christian Moreno: ☎ 554-7633. *La Boquita* #513. *Col. Industrial.*
Beto: 📱 (755)559-0027. Has yard on feeder road toward airport right before last *Pemex* station on the right.
Moving Service: Trucks are parked alongside *Comercial Mexicana* and can be rented by the hour or negotiate for a "house" moving price.
Musicians: ☎ or fax 554-3256. This is the number for the musicians'

syndicate or union. They don't have demo tapes for you to listen to but they can give you a list of bands, duos, trios, marimbas, pianist, etc. and tell you where they are currently playing and arrange for you to go listen to them.

N.

Nurseries: On the way to the airport there is a very large nursery on the right hand side of the road. They have a huge selection of plants and pots. Also on Highway 200, going toward *Playa Troncones*, there are several nurseries. At the end of *Playa La Ropa*, right past *Gaviota*, a large property on the left advertising *regaderas* or showers has a vast selection of indigenous plants at ridiculously low prices. My favorite in-town nursery on *Av. Palmar* is *Viva Vida Vivero*. Lovely family and nice selection of indigenous plants at fair prices.

O.

Office Supplies and Equipment: See Printing and Copying.

Oil, Lubricant: *Lateral Carr.Acapulco-Zihuatanejo.* On both sides of the highway toward Acapulco, there are dozens of small shops with the Quaker State sign out front. You can buy oil at any of these.

Outboard Repair:
Yamaha: Cinco de Mayo before *Altamirano.*

P.

Paint Stores:
Acuario: Esq. Av. Morelos y Cinco de Mayo. (Across street from *Comex*).
Comex: Esq. Av. Morelos y Cinco de Mayo.
Sherwin Williams: Av. Morelos. Same side of street as *Comex.*

Plexiglass:
Vidrios Rodriguez: And. Parque Los Mangos. Frente a FIBAZI. ☎ 554-3930.
There is also a man named *Baltazar* who lives in *La Noria*. The fishermen told me to ask for him at the little *tienda* directly across from the Port Captain's office.

Party Supplies:
Dulcería El Caramado: Calle Naranjos. Across the street from back of market. They carry bulk candy and goodies for piñatas as well as plastic goods and party favors.
Guadalajara: Calle Cerezos #5. Same as above but they have a different selection.

Pet Supplies:
Farm. Veterinario Zihuatanejo: Calle Los Mangos. This place and the following sell medications, various dog foods and heartworm and flea and tick control pills.
*Nutrizoo: Calle Los Mangos-*fish side of market.
Veterinario Campos: Calle Ejido.
Comercial Mexicana: Av. La Boquita s/n.
Bodega: Lateral Carr. Acapulco-Zihuatanejo.
Photo Supplies: Film is expensive here. It is wise to pack plenty of rolls before leaving home. Processing is also high and, if you possibly can, wait until you return home for developing. Most places advertise 24-hour service.
*López Impresores: Benito Juárez—*canal end.
*Foto 30 de Uruapan: Nicolás Bravo—*by Dr. Campos' (vet) office.
Kodak Dígital: Across the street from *Mi Chayito.*
Photography: *Foto Durán: Vicente Guerrero.* Professional photos and **the guy** for passport and FM2/3 photos.
Arte Visual: Directly across the street from the *bomberos* (fire station). Edson Hernandez Quiroz is a terrific photographer and makes great videos. He is quite in demand for special occasion parties. ☎ 554-7856 or ✆ (755)108-5198.
Visit **www.eartevisual.com**
Elizabeth Brady Photography: ✆ (755)120-3633. Elizabeth enjoys photographing weddings or doing portraits of your family. Visit ebradyphotography.com or ✉ **elizabeth@ebradyphotography.com**
Picture Framing:
Rodríguez: And. Parque Los Mangos. Fuente a FIBAZIi. ☎554-3930/4335.
Plumbers:
Seth: ☎ 554-7164 or ✆ (755)558-6157.
Florencio Cazaro: ✆ (755)556-3290.
Printing and Copying:
López Impresores: Benito Juárez.
Tetes: Calle Palapas. (My favorite and very reasonable).
Imprenta Roque: Vicente Guerrero #228ª. ☎ 554-7141
Public Restrooms: Next to basketball court and in parking lot of pier. Also the market has restrooms. $3.00 to $5.00 pesos.
Pumps Repair:
Electro Bombeos: ✆ (755)121-1456. Visit **www.bombasgucasa.net** or ✉ **bombasgucasa@hotmail.com** They sell and repair pumps of all

types. I bought a tiny pump from them for my fountain and getting them to come to the house was a major project and then they installed the fountain incorrectly even when I told them it was wrong. But they seem to be the only game in town to my knowledge, so it's important that they be listed.

Purified Water: Purified water is sold in a five gallon *garrafón*. The price is approximately $1.00 to $2.00 U.S. Purified water is also sold in small bottles in almost all the stores, but you'll pay almost the same for one liter as you do for five. If you're here for a while, buy a large *garrafón* off one of the circulating men/boys on bicycles that travel the streets daily or from the *Agua Santorini* truck. You'll pay a deposit but it should be returned when you leave.

R.

Rental Equipment: *Equirentazihua. Avenida Universidad s/n* (on the corner of *Av. Morelos* where you turn to go to police station). Finally, a place to rent heavy duty equipment such as drills, power washers, chain saws, etc. ☎/Fax 554-7933 and 📱 (755) 225-1092.

Restaurant equipment and supplies: *Proesa. Av. Marina Nacional* #71. (Adjacent to DHL off *Av. Morelos*). ☎ 544-6302/4816. Huge array of professional stoves, refrigerators, sinks, and professional pots and pans.

S.

Satellite and Cable TV:
Megacable: ☎ 554-3356. *Kyoto Circle.* This is cable TV and Internet connection combo for about one-third the cost of SKY.
Sky TV: ☎ 01(800)475-9759. Local office now at *Esq. Calle de Pedregal y Av. Morelos.*

Seamstress/Tailor:
Librería y Artículos Religiosos: 📱 (755)113-7561. The owner Delia has been making and repairing my clothes for the last 10-12 years. She's very reasonable and perfect for simple items such as hemming a dress or sewing a tablecloth. She's been ill so perhaps is no longer sewing. *Sastreria Ortiz: Calle Las Palapas.*

Shoe Shine: At the intersection of *Benito Juárez* and *Avenida Morelos* is a park. All around the park are shoeshine stands.

Shoe Repair: There are several in town but I use *El Rápido* on *Catalina Gonzales* because they do a really good job and fast.

Spas:

Casa que Canta: ☏ 555-7030 ext. 207. A variety of 8 different kinds of massages, facials, body wraps, etc.

The Tides: ☏ 555-5500.

Renaissance Day Spa at *Hotel Barceló*: ☏ 553-0369/0562. In addition to regular spa services (manis, pedis, massage, etc) they have a variety of machines that do wonderful things to your body. Often specials so ask. If the owner is there you can communicate in English.

Hotel Melía Azul: ☏ 555-0000 ext 8161. No real spa but they do have a room set aside with two ENERVITA machines—physical therapy system that is based on the Chinese techniques that applies heat to acupressure points along the spine.

Intrawest: ☏ 555-0350. They do massages, manicures, pedicures, and facials at this time.

Sporting Goods:
Deportes Nauticos: Esqu. Galeana y Bravo.
Nauticos: Nicolás Bravo—next to above. (Mostly clothes but some equiptment).
Sport Aquique: And. Parque Los Mangos. Frente a Fibazi.
Stainless Hardware: See Hardware Stores.

T.

Telephone and Fax: There are numerous long distance places in *Zihua* where one can make a call. Most are open from 9:00 a.m. until 9:00 p.m. These calls can be very expensive. The cheapest way to call is directly from one of the many pay phones around town using a calling card that can be purchased at most of the drugstores in town. The phones say *"LADATEL."* They come in all denominations. You insert the card and punch in the number you want. They also work for local calls.

For national long distance direct in Mexico, dial 01+ area code + number.

To dial directory assistance for anywhere in Mexico, dial 040.

To make an operator assisted call to anywhere in Mexico dial 020.

To speak to an international operator in Mexico dial 090.

To call a cellular telephone from a landline dial 044 + area code + number. To call a cellular telephone outside your area code, you must now dial 045 + area code + number.

To call direct to the U.S. or Canada, dial 001 +area code + number.

To call an 800 or 888 number in the U.S. and Canada **usually** the company you are calling has not paid for Mexico to be included in his toll free service so you must pay *Telmex* a connection fee and the way to do that is to dial 001 (880 instead of 800 and 881 instead of 888) plus the number.

Telmex: *Esq. Las Huertas y Calle Medeterreano.* Billing information 01(800)980-0700 and (555)212-1010.

Television Repair:
Audio Vision: Calle Cuauhtémoc #68. ☎ 554-2218 or 556-8523 or ☎ (755)558-0678. Very good service here with Angel Torres. He charges a small fee to look at your TV and applies it to price if you have it repaired here.

Tires:
Euzkadi Radial: Lateral Carr. Acapulco-Zihuatanejo—right past *CM.*
Goodyear : Lateral Carr. Acapulco-Zihuatanejo after *Euzkadi*).

Towing Service: *Apzide.* ☎ 554-3411. You'll see signs around town indicating towing enforced if you park in a prohibited area. Towing is almost never enforced unless they are clearing the streets for a parade. They will take your plates instead.

Translators:
Veronica Gonzales, is a lovely Mexican local who is a court certified translator—especially important for legal documents. ☎544-7687. She speaks perfect English.
Victoria Priani is also a skilled translator. Her attention to detail is quite amazing and is very important for translating documents from one langage to another. ☎ 553-3597. Visit **www.vtplanguage.com**

V.

Video Rental: You will find a pretty good selection of DVD's— almost all of which are in English.
Comercial Mexicana: Av. La Boquita s/n.
Pirated DVD's are sold all over town for the price of 3 for $50.00 pesos. The quality varies greatly but you can't beat the price and if you get a bad copy, they will exchange the film. They have driven out the video rental stores except for above.

W.

Watering Holes: The most popular drinking spots in town for locals and visitors alike would be The Fishing Hole, *La Playa*, The Flophouse, *Paccolos, Zorro's, Barracuda,* and *Casa Arcadia.* These are the popular ones in town. **Zorro's** opens real early as does **Casa Arcadia**. Opening at noon is **The Fishing Hole** and at 2:00 p.m. **The Flophouse** followed by *Barracruda, Paccolos* and *La Playa*. ***Bandido's*** is also popular among tourists—mainly men waiting for wives or girlfriends to shop at the Indian market. Go into any of the above and you're sure to encounter locals who can entertain you or answer your questions about the area. All have about the same pricing for beer, soft drinks, and alcohol with the exception of *Bandido's*. He's significantly higher on drinks so you won't encounter many locals there unless it's the weekend or Monday night football. *Bandido's* is the only place in town offering dish network with consistency. In 2009, I bought friend Graham and myself piggy banks so we could save money for a year in order to go to *Bandido's* and catch UT football on Saturday. We never got out of there for less than $500 pesos so the piggy banks worked for us.

Weddings:

Wedding Planner: ☎ 554-2700/554-5092. Francisco Ibarra of *La Perla* on *Playa La Ropa* will handle all aspects of your wedding needs if you book the restaurant. ✉ **weddings@zihua.net**

Isabel País has been planning weddings in the area for a number of years. She can assist you in finding the perfect locale and take care of all the details. ☎ 554-7905 or Fax 554-3517 or 📱 (755)559-4452. ✉ **weddings1@prodigy.net.mx**

Ixtapa Bridal: ☎ or Fax 553-1690. ✉ **bridal@yahoo.com**

If you opt to have your wedding in a private home or "party room" instead of a restaurant, *Villa Chefs* will be happy to consult with you regarding catering needs. ☎ 554-1194. ✉ **lrfox2@yahoo.com**

Welding:

Refrigeración Zihua: Cinco de Mayo. They are the only welders of stainless steel.

Wood:

Madera de la Costa Grande: Lateral Carr. Acapulco-Zihuatanejo before last *Pemex* on right.

El Colonial: Av. Morelos. Close to *Cinco de Mayo*.

Y.

Yacht Services:

Artículos de Pesca—La Bahía: Juan Alvarez #58. Carries same items as the following.

Casa Lobata Piñeda: Juan Alvarez—upstairs across from basketball court. This store carries a wide assortment of fishing tackle, boating gear, and supplies.

Servicios Técnicos: Marina Ixtapa. ☎ 553-0080/2099.

Yoga: There are generally 4 yoga locations in the area—high and low season.

Paty's Mar y Mar. ☎ 554-2213. Classes held at least twice daily during high season and sometimes during rainy season. Call for class schedule as her website doesn't specify when there are no classes. Beautiful setting facing the ocean. $10.00 U.S. for visitors.

Hotel Irma: Playa La Madera. Currently classes at 7:30-8:30 a.m. Monday, Wednesday and Friday. ☎ 103-8582. Classes are held on the lower level patio and the ocean view and breeze are wonderful. Cost is $50.00 pesos. If raining, classes held across the street from hotel entrance.

Yoga with Victoria: ☎ 116-7314 After missing a year Victoria has decided to return for the 2013 high season. As of this printing, no location has been determined.

Nat Sam Yoga: *Calle Ejido* above *Banamex.* ☎ (755)114-0862.

Z.

and zat about covers it!

Churches, Plazas, Public Buildings and Important Offices

Churches: Zihuatanejo did not have a Catholic church until 1954. A wealthy businessman from the U.S donated $2,000 dollars to the town council and the church; *La Virgin Señora de Guadalupe* was built. Perhaps only half of the *Zihua* population is Catholic. A second larger Catholic church was finished in 1997 at *Plaza Kyoto*.

There are many Jehovah's Witnesses, Mormons, Spiritualists, and Baptists living here. *La Iglesia de Jesucristo de los Santos de los Últimos Días* is on the road to Acapulco on the right hand side before the Circle of the Sun.

Also we have the Zihuatanejo and Ixtapa Christian Fellowship open to all religious faiths and services are conducted in English. Please see clubs and organizations for more information.

Plazas: There are numerous small plazas scattered throughout town, the most important being the municipal plaza or *zócalo*. It is located right in *centro* and used for government speeches, celebrations, and dances.

Public Buildings:

Centro Social: Av. Morelos. This building can be rented to hold special events such as wedding receptions, parties, etc.

Biblioteca (library): *Cuauhtémoc.* Some books in English.

Important Locations:

The following is a list of offices you may need to use, or want to visit, whether you are a visitor or resident.

Archeological Museum: South end of *Paseo del Pescador.* Construction of the museum was begun in 1948 and completed in 1951. The structure was home to the post and telegraph offices, customs, treasury, immigration, harbor master, and registry of fishing boats.

When finished, then President Alemán flew in an amphibious seaplane with his current mistress, famed film star María Felix, for the inauguration of the new Federal Building (*El Palacio*) as it was called back then.

Measuring 22 by 38 meters, the structure also features two rectangular stones embedded on the exterior wall of Room 4, which indicate the geographic coordinates of the city, Latitude North 17-38-14 and Longitude West 101-33-48.

El Palacio was closed from 1988 to 1992 for remodeling and re-opened on May 22, 1992.

To this day, City Hall is the trustee of the institution with the goal "to conserve and display the historical artifacts, adding to the historical value of the city." The large collection of local artifacts—donated for the most part by Anita Hahner—is thus preserved, exhibited, and provides a permanent safekeeping to the local history. *From Wash Gently:*

'Tis Not The Gift But 'Tis The Giver

A group of us displaced Americans who were residents of the coastal area of Mexico were privileged to learn of an unexplored pyramid that was only a few kilometers from our town. The pyramid was more of a hill with an entrance that was very low and narrow and covered with heavy undergrowth. The permanent inhabitants of the pyramid were scorpions, snakes, spiders and bats, so it was only those of great curiosity, courage, or general stupidity who ventured inside. I made one trip inside but after being greeted by a bunch of waltzing spiders, a snake of unknown breed and an entire air force of bats I retreated and elected to never again enter that place.

By searching around the exterior of the pyramid one could find bits and pieces of sculptured figurines, clay pots and ceremonial decorations. This method of digging out our own pieces of pre-Columbian art had its drawbacks as the ground was iron-tough, the scorpions and snakes resented the intrusions and we were getting too old to climb the surrounding cliff-like hillsides so we found an easier way to accumulate the desired treasures, we bought them from the children of a nearby village. These children knew how the rains flowed and that with the little streams that came from the pyramid there would be lots of the broken little critters that we sought. Whenever we would come into the village the children would run to greet us, each one screaming for attention to her or his little bag of clay figures. We would sort through them and buy those that pleased us and always gave the children more for them than they asked. Each of us soon had a marvelous collection of pre-Columbian art, little clay animals, dolls, whistles and pots.

During one of these trips I noticed a little girl among the group that was selling their treasures who seemed shy and was not aggressive as the others. She was a small girl of seven years with eyes that were like polished obsidian and the prettiest smile that I had ever seen. Her dress was stained and badly worn but she didn't need the trappings of dress to be beautiful. All that she had to sell was a clay monkey's head with one of the ears broken but I bought it and thanked her profusely. After we left the village I could not get the picture of that beautiful child from the mirror of my mind so I went back to visit her.

I found her house, a small but meticulously clean adobe with the decorations of a devout Catholic family. I asked the little girl's mother if it would be OK for me to buy her some presents for Christmas and she then told me what the little girl,

162

Veronica by name, needed the most. I went to a nearby "traveling" market and bought underclothes, dresses, shoes, hair ribbons, candy, picture books and combs.

When I presented Veronica with these gifts she would not believe that they were for her and she seemed somewhat stunned. She didn't thank me but just stared at me with those big dark and misty eyes. I left and wandered down the hill, feeling somewhat smug for having assuaged my own feelings and having given her some needed things.

A moment later Veronica came flying down the hill and tugged at my shirt tail, and yelling for me to stop. I stopped and she shyly handed me something and then turned to run back up the hill to avoid the embarrassment of my thank you. I looked at the gift, a small black engraved bead that had come from the pyramid. It was the size of a small marble with a face engraved upon it and several bands of lines about its edges with a hole drilled through it. It obviously had been a decorative bead of some special person from long ago.

Veronica stood at the top of the hill watching while I inspected the bead and when I blew her a kiss she ran into the house. She thought that she had only given me a muddy old bead that she had found but to me it was The Star of Mexico.

Airport: The airport is located on the *Lateral Carr. Acapulco-Zihuatanejo* about fifteen minutes south of *El Centro.* ☎ 554-2070. From *Topes:*

A Comfort for the Bum

While true, soldiers did arrive in 1932 and built an airstrip—it was soon neglected by the authorities just like many of the later public works projects completed and abandoned in town.

The air service was a twin Otter seating sixteen passengers who arrived on a twice-weekly schedule out of Mexico City. The Zafari hotel on the outskirts of town (current site of Colegio Bertha Van Glummer) had been established in the early 1950's as a hotel for big game hunters. Cougars, jaguars, and other esoteric wildlife roamed the mountains and were plentiful. There was a large grassy area behind the main hotel grounds where pigs, cows, and horses grazed. When the pilot of the Otter was approaching, he would sweep the field once with the plane sending a message to the proprietor, and one of the staff would run out onto the field with a broom and shoo the livestock away long enough for the plane to make a safe landing.

I had been living in Zihuatanejo about four months when I finally received a letter saying two of my best friends in the whole world would be arriving on the Otter mid-September. The letter had of course been sent "por avion" but delivered by burro—arriving two months after the postmark. Naturally Diane had offered to bring any creature comforts I needed from the states so I rushed to the Telmex office *on Cinco de Mayo to wait seven hours for a phone call to be completed. It wasn't a total hardship because I could wait at the corner watering hole, Tortugas, and by the time my call went through I was totally snockered. I ran up a $200 pesos phone tab (which was really expensive in those days) but didn't really remember much of the conversation. Fortunately I had the letter with the date of Diane and husband Mike's arrival.*

Knowing that Diane would arrive with a ton of suitcases I maneuvered my car out of my front yard on Playa La Madera to make the treacherous trip to the Zafari. The "road" was filled with potholes the size and depth of infinity pools and strewn with boulders the size of pregnant sows. There was a reason there were only four cars in town, one of which was mine.

I reached the airport as the plane was circling the field and waited patiently for the arrival of my friends. When the plane taxied onto the field and the door opened I heard a terrible commotion from inside the plane. First to descend was Diane with her behemoth bouffant hair and shame written all over her face. Next off the plane was the pilot escorting my drunken friend Mike down the stairs. Around Mike's neck was a toilet seat and in Diane's six suitcases were enough rolls of toilet paper to last even someone with serious Montezuma's revenge six months!

Apparently in my lengthy and rambling phone conversation, I had groused about the fact that not a single toilet in all of town had a seat—including my apartment, all four restaurants, and the five hotels. They didn't stock toilet paper in the grocery stores with any regularity and usually there was a nail in the restroom with old pages of a comic book to be used in place of toilet paper.

Mike was very drunk and the pilot was not a happy camper so I discreetly slipped him a $100 pesos note (about $12.00 U.S. dollars) which produced a dazzling smile and a helpful hand getting the luggage and Mike into the car.

News travels fast in small, sleepy fishing villages, and I had a procession of neighbors and friends wanting to come by and see me and avail themselves of my facilities—so many in fact, we ran out of water in the tinaco and had to wait two days for it to refill. (No pipa trucks in those days). Fortunately I had rented the adjoining bungalow for Mike and Diane and we rationed out the water judiouosly. I hoarded the toilet paper and made it last a very long time and the seat traveled with me to my various residences until 1979, when I left Zihuatanejo to move temporarily to Florida. I figured I wouldn't need it and friend Ted Tate with his super skinny ass could enjoy the seat for many years to come.

Car Registration: *Calle Universidad*—police station. If you buy a car from a dealer in Mexico, he should do all the paperwork for you. If buying from an individual, you will need to do the following to get plates and papers. You must have 1) original car purchase papers-*factura*, 2) the old registration (*Registro Federal de Vehiculos*), 3) the document describing the vehicle (*tarjetón*) and 4) the receipt for all previous years' license plates (*tenencia*). Mexican vehicles require renewal stickers by March 31st. All is done at the *Finanzas* office.

City Hall: Around the corner from *Bodega*. ☏ 554-2082. The Mayor's office is located in City Hall, *ayuntamiento*. Local government is headed by a *Presidente Municipal*, *regidores* (town council), and a set of *vocales*, representatives from the *colonias* or various neighborhoods. They serve a three-year term.

Customs: ☏ 554-3262. Customs (*aduana*) are located at the airport. Should you need to leave the country for an emergency and entered with a car or a tourist permit, you must obtain special permission from this office. Usually your car can be left with a friend, or Customs may insist you leave it at their offices. They will attach a note to your Tourist Card indicating you have permission to leave the country without your vehicle. This rule only applies to a tourist card—has nothing to do with FM2/3.

Electric Company: *Av. Colegio Militar*. You may pay your bills in person here. Check bills very carefully, as the company has a great propensity for overcharging.

FIBAZI: (*Fideicomisión de la Bahía de Zihuatanejo*). *Av. Universidad y Lateral Carr. Acapulco-Zihuatanejo*. ☏ 554-2472. Trust established to finance infrastructure and regularize land in *Zihua*. This very large complex has maps of the area with a list of the property owners' names and addresses. This is a good place to find out what property is available in the area but it is best if you know someone at *FIBAZI* before making this type of inquiry.

Fire Station: *Paseo a Playa La Ropa* past the canal. ☏ 554-2075. The Rotary Club was instrumental in getting this fire station built and equipped with a real fire truck.

Immigration: *Colegio Militar*. ☏ 554-2795. As a tourist, you can legally stay in Mexico up to six months. If arriving by plane, Immigration officials may only stamp your Tourist Card for thirty days. You can, however, request that it be stamped for up to 180 days. Should you want to stay longer than the period provided on your tourist card, pay a visit to this office. There is never a problem in obtaining an extension up to a maximum of 180 days.

Mexican Police Corps: ☏ 554-2040. To summon the police, call this number.

In Mexico, there are several police departments with distinct areas of responsibility. The following is a summary of the specific duties of some of the police departments you may need to deal with.

Judicial Police: The Judicial Police are under federal jurisdiction. You will need this reference only should the unthinkable happen and you or one of your friends be detained by the Judicial Police. You do not want to get involved with the Hoodies (pronounced Who-dees), in any way, shape, form, or fashion. The word "Hoodies" come from the pronunciation of the Spanish *Judicial*. They wear plain clothes and drive black Suburbans with tinted windows and carry big guns. They tend to circulate in groups of four to six. The Judicial Police handle all drug-related matters.

From *Wash Gently, Dry Slowly:*

The Pot and the Air Conditioner

In all walks of life we all try to improve our status and standard of living by using whatever talents or means that are available. Often those means are used for simple survival while in other cases they flirt with million dollar situations. As in most things, the larceny and chicanery which we all practice, differs only by degree. In a small tourist-oriented coastal town I saw a beautiful display of the flexibility of this talent, of human vulnerability to moral criticism and a logical conclusion to a business deal. This happened in Mexico, but it could just as easily been in Boston, St. Louis, or Shreveport.

Francisco, the young owner of the nice hotel, answered a knock at his door to find a very serious policeman waiting there.

"Francisco, you have marijuana in your house and I must arrest you," the policeman announced.

"You are mistaken," Francisco pleaded. "I don't use it and I don't have any of it."

After asking for and getting permission to enter the hotel apartment, the policeman went directly to Francisco's secret place and drew out a box filled with the weed.

Francisco protested that he was the victim of a "plant," both figurative and literal.

"You must come with me to jail, for I now have the evidencia," the proud policeman insisted.

Francisco, solidly maintaining his innocence, poured generous drinks for him and the policeman and they entered into a gentlemanly discussion of the situation. The policeman refused an offer of money but after several drinks, he made Francisco an offer.

"I will not arrest you if you will give me your air conditioner for my house," he stated.

"But you live in a bamboo house with no electricity and my air conditioner is mounted into the concrete of the wall," Francisco argued.

"No matter, you will run a wire from your hotel to my house and we will put the machine on a table you will provide," the policeman instructed.

After several more drinks the policeman's position hadn't changed, so he and Francisco removed the air conditioning unit and loaded it into a wheelbarrow to truck it to the policeman's lean-to.

As they trundled down a steep, cobblestone paved street, Francisco lashed out verbally at the policeman. Francisco and the policeman were very drunk and very emotional.

"You are no longer my friend, you are not a good policeman, you are not a good person and you certainly are not a good Mexican. We know each other for years and now you take my air conditioner. Things between us will not be the same and you will not be welcome in my house," Francisco fumed.

"You are right, Francisco. To take your air conditioner would be wrong and I am not a good person. Let's return it to your house," the conscience-stricken policeman agreed.

They trudged back up the hill, wrestled the now mangled air conditioner back into place in the wall and relaxed with a few more sips of the nectar of the cactus.

Francisco beamed. He was victorious. He had shown the policeman the error of his ways, saved his air conditioner and avoided a trip to jail.

"Francisco, you are a good man. I am glad I didn't take your air conditioner. That would have been wrong. We are friends for a long time and I should not thought of such a thing. A simple 5,000 pesos is better for both of us," the policeman said.

Francisco counted out the money.

"Now you're being reasonable and honest."

Tránsito: *Av. Universidad.* ☎ 554-5265. The *Tránsito* police survey vehicular traffic in cities and towns. They wear uniforms. This is where the jail is and where they hold your license plates if you park in a prohibited area. When you park illegally, policemen remove a plate. Should this happen, you must go to the *Tránsito* office and pay a fine to get your plate back. The rectangular signs with a slash through the large capital "E" mean "no parking." Even if you see lots of cars parked illegally, don't make the mistake of thinking its fine to park along with the other cars. Foreign plates are like a magnet and draw Mexican police to them. The fine for illegal parking is about $200 pesos.

Traffic Accidents: In the event of a traffic accident, ask to see the other driver's license if, by some miracle, he has stopped. Jot down his license number, address, etc. No license, automatic responsibility for any accident! Notify your insurance company of the particulars and whose fault it was. Your insurance company will likely pay. Report the accident to the *Policia Tránsito* if the accident is the other driver's fault or if your car is totaled and you can't drive it away. If in doubt about calling the police, contact your insurance company and they will advise you. If the accident occurs on the highway, report the accident to the highway patrol following the above guidelines.

Jail: If you find yourself in jail, ask to call your lawyer or a friend who can call one for you. Remember, the Mexican judicial system is based on Roman law and on the Napoleonic code. A person being judged for an offense is presumed guilty until proven innocent. If you become a victim of any incident during your stay in Mexico and require assistance, you can communicate with the Tourism Secretariat offices or call the Hot Line Emergency Telephone at the appropriate Embassy, or if a U.S. citizen, contact Debbie Mioni, our Embassy representative, at 553-2100.

I might mention under the jail heading, that the possession or trafficking of narcotics is considered a federal offense in Mexico. Only the possession of medicinal drugs prescribed by a physician is legal. Mexican law is extremely severe in narcotics trafficking cases. Possession and trafficking of any drug could result in a prison sentence of at least seven years. You might be offered drugs on the streets by someone and the situation might be very tempting—who hasn't heard of Acapulco Gold—but many of these individuals are undercover agents or police informers. It's not worth the risk.

People often ask me about drugs in "the old days" and since the statute of limitations has long since expired on some of my past antics I've decided to share with my readers one of my favorite adventures. From *Topes in Paradise:*

Curtsy to the Queen

I was delivering a boat to Puerto Vallarta from Acapulco in the fall of 1974 when I met a wonderful couple heading south on their beautiful wooden sailboat.

When T.J. and Karen found out I lived in Zihua and had spent time in Oaxaca, they became my new bestest friends. Their "goal" was to score about 200 kilos of marijuana from the Oaxaca region and sail it back to the States. They enlisted my help in this endeavor and it was agreed that T.J. and I would fly to Oaxaca and try and set something up.

T.J. was a gorgeous 6'3" hunk of humanity with dazzling blue eyes and sun-bleached blonde hair. His presence with me in Oaxaca made us stand out like sore thumbs. I couldn't rustle up any of my contacts in or out of town so it was agreed that T.J. would go back to his boat in Puerto Vallarta and they would sail to Zihua and meet me there and I would stick around Oaxaca for another week and try to obtain some "product samples" for T.J. to enjoy before I returned to Zihua.

As soon as he left, my hiding friends descended on me in the zócalo and in the blink of an eye, I had 4 different types of samples for T.J. to peruse within hours of his departure. I immediately booked a flight back to Zihua via Acapulco and sequestered the samples in my bra. I was sitting at the airport waiting for my flight when several trucks loaded with soldiers screamed to a halt outside the terminal. They rushed into the terminal with guns at the ready and screamed for everyone to stand up and put their hands in the air. I had not the foggiest idea of what was going on but it wasn't looking good for the little fox.

The commandante announced that everyone would be searched thoroughly and two soldiers held guns on individuals while another soldier patted each person down. There were only three women in the lounge and we were separated from the men being searched. The commandante had a conference with several soldiers and one of them boldly approached one of the Mexican women and started to pat her down. She screamed at him and kicked him in his cojones and that was the end of the female pat down. After the men's examination it was explained that the Queen of England was arriving for a state visit in Oaxaca and they had to make sure there were no armed individuals in the airport.

The Queen's plane landed and our plane to Acapulco was called to board. As I walked to my plane, I passed the Queen as she was entering the airport. I did a quick little curtsey and a small prayer of thankfulness that the Mexican Army did not allow females in the Army or I would have been patted down and not writing this story today.

When I returned to Zihuatanejo, T.J. and Karen's sailboat was gently rocking in the bay and they certainly enjoyed my samples. However, in my absence, they had made the acquaintance of some locals and decided to purchase "local product."

Highway Patrol: ☏ 554-3122. The *Policía Federal de Caminos* is in charge of enforcing the rules and regulations on the national highways.

Ministerio Público: *Calle Presa de Angostura.* ☏ 554-2900. When you are the victim of a crime, the appropriate authority to which this should be denounced is the *Agente del Ministerio Público* (Public Prosecutor). If you are robbed or mugged, go immediately to the *Ministerio Público* to report the crime. At this office you will be provided with appropriate certifications and will be instructed on the procedures that need to be followed for the investigation and determination of offenders' responsibilities. You may need an interpreter. I recommend taking a good book, as they are slow.

Most people here will tell you it is a waste of time to report a crime, since the police don't really pursue the matter. Yes and no. If you have homeowner's insurance, the loss can be reported when you return home and usually you are covered. You must have a police report detailing the items stolen and the circumstances. A word of advice: most hotels offer safety deposit boxes. Use them. Don't take lots of money or valuables to the beach and leave them unattended. Find a restaurant you like to patronize at the beach and ask the owner to watch your valuables. Watch out for the children vendors—we have some really clever thieves. If staying somewhere with balconies, don't leave anything hanging outside overnight (even on the second or third floor). Don't take a walk during daylight hours and leave your room door open. If you observe these precautions, you shouldn't have a problem.

Post Office: *Av. Telegrafías.* Between the light at *Migra* and the light at *Coppel.* The post office is open Monday thru Saturday. Behind the counter is a schedule of postal rates. If you need a post office box, you must get on a list. Renewals are due in January and this is the best time to apply for a box. Many people receive mail through General Delivery (*lista de correos*). A list is posted on the wall. If you don't pick up General Delivery mail within ten days, it is returned to sender.

Mail service to and from foreign countries is slow, varying usually from one to two weeks. Don't ask friends and relatives to send you items to Mexico through the mail. Postal thievery is a big problem.

One time my mom sent my three spring-form pans when I had my cheesecake business. They arrived fine and in the bottom I found two Hershey's candy kisses. Next time I talked to mom, I asked why she sent only two kisses. She said she had sent two packages!! The thieves were kind enough to leave me a couple.

Port Captain: Pier. ☏ 554-2195. This office is located near the pier and the Port Captain is in charge of regulating boat traffic in the bay.

Public Works: ☎ 554-3964. This office issues building permits and accepts complaints about roads and roadwork, etc.

PROFECO: Calle Presa de Angostura. Federal Consumer Protection Agency. ☎ 554-5236. Tourist *PROFECO* ☎ 554-2007. *Av. Morelos.*

Registro Civil: Ayutamiento or city hall. This office is where one goes to register births or deaths or obtain a marriage license.

It is quite easy for a foreigner to marry another foreigner in Mexico. All that is needed are 3 copies of your passports, 3 copies of your Mexican tourist cards, a list of 4 *testigos* (witnesses) and copies of their passports or other photo ID, and maybe a blood test at the nearest *Centro de Salud.* You fill out a form, tell the judge where the ceremony will be held and he/she will arrive and officiate in a simple civil ceremony. Charges vary.

Social Security: *Lateral Carr. Zihuatanejo-Morelia* (left hand side before the road to Ixtapa divides). ☎ 554-2088. This office takes care of collecting benefit payments for workers and provides said benefits.

Tax Office: Intersection of *Colegio Militar y Av. Morelos.* ☎ 554-3644. Anything relating to city taxes should be addressed to *FINANZAS.*

Telephone Office: *Calle Mediterraneo.* To arrange telephone service, pay overdue bills, etc. you must go to this office. Repairs can be requested by dialing 050 and bills not overdue can be paid at *Comercial Mexicana* or via Internet direct from your Mexican bank account.

Telegraph Office: Next door to Post Office. ☎ 554-2163. Many people have successfully had money wired to them in *Zihua.* I personally prefer bank-to-bank transfers.

Tourist Service: *(PROFECO). Av. Morelos*—close to *centro social.* ☎ 554-2575. Since tourism is so vital to Mexico, the country has set up tourism offices all over the country to assist in handling complaints of all types. Complaints are noted and appropriate action taken. The only problem is that most people staffing these offices do not speak English, so try to find a friendly foreigner to assist you. The most common complaints involve taxi fares and harassment by time-share people.

Water Department: *Esq. Las Huertas y Colegio Militar.* To pay water bills, arrange for service, or make complaints, appear at this office. Must pay bills here—can't pay online or at the grocery store. ☎ 554-2358. This phone number is the emergency number to report a broken pipe flooding the streets or a dangerous manhole cover missing.

.Sports, Entertainment, Clubs, and Pets

The title is self-explanatory, and facilities and organizations come and go, as do their personnel, meeting times, and places. Check with a local for specific information.

Adventours: This company offers biking, kayaking, snorkeling, and bird watching. Tel. 553-3584 or 📱 101-8556. or ✉️ **pablomendezabal@gmail.com**

Adventure Divers: *Calle Adelita.* ☎ 554-9191 or 📱 (755)557-9787. They offer certified dive courses and various snorkeling tours including one to the "King of Kings"—the "blessed" 15 foot bronze statue that sits on a pedestal sunk into the bay close to *Playa Las Gatas.* Visit **www.adventuredivers.com.mx** or ✉️ **adventurediversmx@gmail.com**.

Bike Rental: *Bizihuanas* is a bike shop on *Cuauhtémoc* #39. ☎ 544-6495 or 📱 102-3558. ✉️ **alejandro@bi-zihuanas.com** Also location in Ixtapa at *Plaza Hacienda* #6. ☎ 553-0312. Daily and hourly rental of bicycles. In Ixtapa, there is the very fine bike path that goes all the way to *Playa Linda* and is now patrolled by the police after a serious mugging and shooting incident in 2010.

Cultural Sundays: Every Sunday evening sometime between 6:00 p.m. and 8:00 p.m. It's hard to be more specific since we are discussing Mexico. Almost every Sunday, there is some type of cultural event, sponsored by the city, at the basketball court. You never know what you are going to see—a skateboard competition, children dancing, famous singers from Mexico City or perhaps a world famous orchestra!

Casa de Cultura: Esq. *Ejido y Cinco de Mayo.* New home for the arts. Classes in dance, guitar, painting, ceremics, etc. All age groups.

El Refugio de Potosí: ☎ (775) 100-0743. Open Sunday, Monday, and Thursday from 10:00 a.m to 5:00 p.m. Here is a wonderful nature preserve with tropical trees, flowers, plants, birds, insects, animals, etc. It is a non-profit started by Laurel Patrick and it just keeps getting better and better. Visit **www.elrefugiodepotosi.org** or ✉️ **laurel@elrefugiodepotosi.org**.

Golf: Two beautiful golf courses, one a Robert Trent Jones, are located in Ixtapa. They do not take reserved tee-times and it is no problem to play anytime except during the very busy Christmas and Easter weeks. Very expensive.

Palma Real : ☎553-1163 or ✉ <u>palmarealixtapa@hotmail.com</u>
Here you will find four tennis courts and two paddle courts.

Club de Golf Marina: ☎553-1410

Horseback Riding: Arrangements for horseback riding can be made by going out to *Playa Linda*, the beach across from *Isla Ixtapa*. There are several *palapa* restaurants and anyone can direct you to the man renting horses. Hotels can also make arrangements for you (more costly of course). The going rate is about $30.00 U.S. for a two-hour ride. **Ignacio Mendiola** 📞 (755)559-8884 offers beach and country tours by horseback and he speaks a little English. *Playa Blanca* location. *Mexico Horizons:* ☎ 554-7970 or 📞 (755)557-0800. Horse rental at *Playa Linda* and *Linda Vista*. ✉ <u>mexicanhorizons@yahoo.com</u>

Hunting: There is a wide range of game to hunt in the surrounding areas but a permit must be obtained beforehand from the Ministry for Urban Development and Ecology. (I honestly can't find their office). They provide a free hunting calendar with full information on species of animal and respective open seasons. Hunting arrangements should be made before your trip through the Mexican Consulate, since, if you want to hunt, you must have a weapon and you can't get a license for a weapon without a hunting permit.

Kayaking: ☎ 553-0496. Zoe Kayak Tours will take you on a wonderful adventure into the lagoon at *Barra de Potosí*. Bryan, your knowledgeable host, will point out the wildlife and fauna of the area. ✉ <u>zoe5@aol.com</u> or broadband ☎ 1(518)213-4122.
Kayaks can also be rented on *Playa La Ropa*.

Motor Bike Rental: *Calle H. Galeana.* (Close to *Zorro's*). Also several places to rent these in Ixtapa. I think it's crazy to rent a bike, as Mexicans are not known for their defensive driving skills.

Para Sailing: There are several of these operations on *Playa La Ropa*. If they are not very busy, the price of $20.00 U.S. is negotiable. An occasional accident has occurred but these guys have a lot of experience and the equipment and boats are first rate.

Parque Aventura: 📞 (755)115-1733/4. A "theme park" located on the far side of the mountain separating *Zihua* from Ixtapa. They have all sorts of exercise driven activities including a zip line, rope climbing, etc. They claim to have 22 different activities. Visit <u>www.parrque-aventura.com</u> or ✉ <u>parque-aventura@hotmail.com</u> Open daily between 8:30 a.m and 6:30 p.m.

Sailing: ☎ 554-2694/8270. If you can afford it a must do on your vacation is a cruise on the *Picante,* a beautiful catamaran that can hold upwards of 100 people, operating out of *Puerto Mío*. They excel in making sure everyone has a wonderful time and the public has given them rave reviews. A day trip is from 10:00 a.m. until 2:30 p.m. and the sunset cruise from 6:00 p.m. until 8:30 p.m. It's a spectacular vision to sail toward the sunset and watch the moonrise over the jagged mountain peaks surrounding the area. A "Pacific Discovery Cruise" is offered during high season leaving at 9:00 a.m. and returning at 12:30 p.m. The price includes full open bar and light hors d'oeuvres or coffee and pan dulces for the Discovery Cruise. Occasionally, live entertainment is offered. Reservations necessary.

✉ **ydelsol@prodigy.net.mx** or visit **www.picantecruises.com**

SportFishing: (Pier). ☎ 554-2056. The pier is the place to go to sign up for a fishing boat. The waters around the area are rich in sea life and it would be unusual to go out fishing and return empty-handed. Most boats leave the pier around 7:00 a.m. and trips are of seven hours duration. Usually, after catching your fish, the boat captain takes you to Ixtapa Island where your fresh catch is cooked up by a local restaurant, or should you wish to save your fish, most restaurants in town will be most happy to cook your fish for a small service charge. It is not mandatory to give the boat captain your catch despite anything he may tell you. Make arrangements for a boat 24 hours in advance. Prices are fixed by the co-op and start at approximately $150.00 U.S. for 4 people. Boat sizes range from 25 to 36 feet. Luxurious sport fishing boats can be rented at the marina in Ixtapa.

Numerous captains now offer catch and release fishing trips. The fishermen at the pier can guide you to one of them or you can contact one of the following if you don't want to be bothered by dealing directly with the fishermen.

Capítán Moses: ☎ (755)100-4007. Moses has been around forever and knows all the captains. He tends to walk *Playa La Ropa* in the mornings and afternoons arranging fishing trips for tourists. He currently is booking on the vessel *Goyita*. He speaks excellent English and I think very highly of him.

Zihuatanejo Sportfishing Charters: ☎ 559-7208.

✉ **sportfishingcharters@hotmail.com**

Swimming: *Av. Universidad* (on the grounds of *FIBAZI*). Here is an Olympic pool open to the public for a nominal charge. Behind the pool area are several soccer fields where locals can practice and in the evening have competitive games, which are also open to the public.

Scuba Diving: The *Ixtapa-Zihua* seabed is home to a wide variety of marine life. There are more than 30 different dive sites.

Carlo Scuba and Sports: *Playa Las Gatas* beach location. ☎ 554-6003 or ✉ **carloscuba@yahoo.com**   This dive center has been in operation on *Playa Las Gatas* beach for as long as I can remember. Satisfied customers come back yearly for a dive experience and take home fond memories.

Ixtapa *Aqua* Paradise: Three locations to serve you. The *Los Patios* shopping center in Ixtapa. ☎ 553-1510 or Fax 553-1547. *Hotel Barceló*. ☎ 555-2078. *Puerto Mío* in Zihuatanejo. ☎ 554-0460.

Ixtapa Divers: *(Plaza Ambiente*—Ixtapa). ☎ 553-0118/2104.

Dive Zihuat: *Juan Alvarez*—across from basketball court. They have lots of experience in the area and can offer complete diving courses or refresher course—whatever your needs may be. (New ownership–Carlos left because his family was threatened.) ✆ 755-102-3738. www.divezihuatanejo.com

Snorkeling: Snorkeling equipment can be rented at several places on *Playa Las Gatas*. The boat shuttle to *Playa Las Gatas* leaves the pier every fifteen minutes from 8:00 a.m. until 5:00 p.m. Cost is about $4.00. U.S. Also rental at *Playa La Ropa* in front of the *Hotel Sotavento* and at the end of the beach by *La Gaviota*.

Tennis: In Zihuatanejo, only *The Tides* has two courts—primarily for the use of guests. If it's low season, they will rent to outsiders. The *Club de Golf* in Ixtapa has courts open to the public for a nominal charge. ☎ 553-1062/1163. Almost all the hotels in Ixtapa have courts for rent. Naturally, preference is given to their own guests.

Water Skiing: Arrangements for this sport can be made at the pier. Also in front of *The Tides*, there is a water-ski concession. There are also jet skis available for rent on *Playa La Ropa*. Prices vary and may be open to negotiation depending on time of year.

Windsurfing and small Sailboats: There are several wind-surfers and catamarans available on *Playa La Ropa*.

Yoga: See A to Z guide for list of yoga places and times.

Entertainment

Zihua is not the entertainment capital of the world but there are a variety of activities from time to time. During high season, there is usually live music at *Paccolos*, and *David's* on the *Paseo del Pescador*. *Mariachi* groups like to stroll the boardwalk nightly and will play at your restaurant table. Sunday evenings, there are entertainment groups at the basketball court.

Circus: The circus comes to town often during high season and the small town Mexican circus is great fun and definitely worth a trip

As in most things, some of the performers are masters while others need to polish their act a bit. From *Wash Gently, Dry Slowly*:

The Circus

The small town Mexican circus is a most informal affair where performer and spectator are on an eye-to-eye relationship. Most of the performers work at many tasks and in the lot outside of the Big Top it is not unusual to see talented trapeze artist carrying water to the elephants. Here too, the spectator can walk freely among the tethered elephants, camels, bears, and other animals. Only the lions and tigers are caged.

These circuses are delightful and seem to be the reality of what circuses are all about. As in most things, some of the performers are masters while others are need to polish their act a bit. Whatever the act or however talented the performer, Mexican rural circuses are a helluva lot of fun.

Whenever the circus comes to our town, as a cover for my wanting to go, I round up some neighbor kids and we make a big production of going. Sometimes we can get the bus and other times we hitch rides on the back of trucks. The free rides on the trucks give us more money to spend on circus goodies.

During one of our afternoons of planning for a circus visit, a very attractive American lady visitor decided to go with us. She added a real touch of class to our shabby group and we were delighted to have her.

We bought the usual inexpensive seats and as soon as we were seated, a Mexican strongman with the most incredible muscles I've ever seen stopped in front of us. His head was shaved, his face akin to that of Anthony Quinn, he was dressed in black and silver, a tight-fitting vest with silver conchas, black tights, and silver bracelets around both of his enormous wrists.

He stared intently at the lady with us, extended his ham of a hand and introduced himself as the lion tamer, the elephant trainer, the man who gets shot out of the cannon, and the trick motorcycle rider. We all shook hands with him; the kids were most impressed, the lady was flattered and I was grateful to get my hand back in one piece. He kept his attention riveted on the lady.

The lion tamer's command of English was as limited as ours was of Spanish and I'm sure there was a severe loss in translations. He asked, we thought, if we

would like to see his trained lion. Thinking that he was talking about his circus act, we all agreed that we were looking forward to seeing his act.

"And you, Señorita?" he asked our lady guest.

"Oh yes, I particularly enjoy animal acts," she answered and treated him to a dazzling smile.

He smiled, seemingly well pleased, gave a formal bow and left. We were all glad that he had chosen us to talk with because it makes you feel a bit special if you have some personal touch with the star of the show.

A few moments later our newfound friend returned, leading a gigantic male African lion. The leash on the lion looked inadequate, the lion snarled unhappily, and we were a deep shade of uncomfortable. They stayed with us for the opening acts of the circus and left only when their act was on.

We all enjoyed the circus tremendously, especially with our two extra guests.

The lion wasn't too impressed; he went to sleep during the grand entry march.

Dancing and Disco: *Black Bull,* corner of *Vicente Guerrero y Nicolás Bravo, Rumba Caliente,* corner of *Ejido y Vicente Guerrero,* and *Tequila Town,* first block of *Cuauhtémoc,* are the local disco hangouts for the young set.

Disco Gato Pardo: *Esq. Colegio Militar y Palmar.* Usually, ladies in some form of undress perform "shows" during the evening. *From Wash Gently, Dry Slowly:*

The Misunderstanding

Once each year a group of Alaskan pipeline workers chartered an airplane for a flight to Zihuatanejo. Once there, they proceeded to raise all manner of hell. Whenever they couldn't get connecting rooms they bought a chainsaw and sawed doorways between the rooms they were assigned They rented entire restaurants and kept the waiters there for days and nights with a loud party blasting that could be heard for miles. Some of these guys brought their own female playmates, some had local girl friends, some picked up a few strays, and some turned to the professional ladies for their bedroom fun.

One of these giants selected an unusually pretty girl from the assortment at El Coyote, the local bordello and offered her more money than the girl had ever received before. When they got to her room the girl took a silver crucifix from a drawer and hung it on the wall. Then she took a religious picture from the same drawer and placed it in view on the dresser. She followed this by lighting two candles and placing them beside the bed with a short prayer. The "Customer" was so touched by this display of concern for what the girl was doing that he didn't have the heart to be a part of her transgression so he just paid her the promised fee and left. Back at the bar where his friends were partying he related the story of the strange and religious girl. One of the local patrons, hearing the story, leaned over the guy's shoulder and told him that he had totally misunderstood the girl's actions.

"Man, she wasn't offering a prayer for forgivness, she was just giving thanks for having such a high paying customer."

El Canto de las Sirenas: Across the street from the big bus station. ☎ 554-6709. Our own "king of strings," José Luis Cobo, has his own bar with a late night venue. Opens at 9:00 p.m. but doesn't get going until at least midnight. Worth a visit but if you can't make it, you can listen to him at *El Pueblito* on Thursdays between 3:00 p.m. and 5:00 p.m.

Movies: Zihuatanejo has one non air conditioned movie house.

Cine Paráiso: *Cuauhtémoc.* Has three screens with weekly features— usually American films. This theater usually starts at 4:30 p.m. Movies change once a week and a billboard out front posts feature presentations and time. The price has escalated greatly and very few folks attend anymore as you can buy pirated DVD's for less than $1.50 U.S. Since the movies (at the theaters) are sub-titled in Spanish, the crowd feels free to talk the entire presentation and this is most annoying. Brand new to Mexico is NETFLIX which arrived mid-September 2011 at a cost of $99 pesos per month.

Cinema Flamingo: Located behind the main shopping plaza in Ixtapa, this theater is air conditioned and exactly like theaters in the United States. Movies here generally start at 5:00 p.m. and the cost is $60.00. From *Wash Gently, Dry Slowly:*

Friday Night at the Movies

A special double-feature at the movies, Leadbelly and Slapshot. Because it was the special feature night, the cost of admission was raised to ten pesos.

The movie house in Zihuatanejo is a real outdoor theatre. A vacant lot between two buildings was closed in at each end, a door was added, a ticket window-chipped out of the bricks, the far wall painted white, and there was the movie. A platform was raised, a tiny cubicle erected and a projection booth was added.

Long, wooden benches are provided for seats but somewhere during the construction of the benches, little attention was devoted to balance. Should the majority of the occupants of a bench lean forward or backward at the same time, the bench yields to gravity and tumbles.

Regardless of the bench peril of the movie, a bunch of us from the poverty end of La Ropa Beach loaded on the bus and headed for town and the movie.

About halfway to town, a man stepped from one of the houses beside the road and hailed the bus. The driver stopped and opened the door.

"Fiesta, quince años, a party, 15 years," the man beside the road shouted.

The fifteenth birthday of a girl in Mexico is a very big event in her life. It is the day when she is no longer regarded as a girl, but as a señorita. So it was this type of fiesta, or party, to which the bus driver was invited.

The driver parked the bus and joined the party. The host invited all of us aboard the bus to join the celebration, but we declined and walked the rest of the way into town.

We were late and missed Leadbelly and saw only Slapshot.

We should have gone to the party.

Star Gazing: I suppose another form of entertainment would be looking for "celebrities." A couple of our more famous celebrities arrived even before the airport was constructed in 1932. That would be Ernest Hemingway and Zane Grey. They were both avid sport fisherman and Grey wrote, "Zihuatanejo has more authetic South Sea atmosphere that the South Sea islands themselves."

More recently, we have had our fair share of "stars" who have vacationed here for long periods of time over many years including John Wayne, Marty Feldman, Lauren Hutton, Xaviera Hollander, Bianca Jagger, and the Rolling Stones. Nowadays celebrities generally stay at *La Casa Que Canta* or rent a private home and you rarely see them but back in the olden days, there was lots of local interaction. From *Wash Gently*:

Fleeting Fame

Fame is a most elusive commodity and when the famous one gets out of the environment where his fame is recognized he is often treated as harshly as the next guy and it happened often in Zihuatanejo.

Larry Rivers, the famous New York artist, usually had a group of friends and admirers around him when he was at the beach. He was very demanding and his entourage seemed to bend to his every whim as did the restaurant waiters and cooks. His manner was strictly gruff New York and he got away with it most of the time, until...

Mr. Rivers had brought a beach chair to the beach, had drink in hand and entourage around him when a young couple took up a position near him on the beach. The young man turned on a cassette tape with the volume that created the term "ghetto buster" and Mister Rivers became annoyed immediately.

Mr. Rivers approached the young man and told him, "Turn that damned thing down or move somewhere else!"

The young man, with a voice that sounded as if he had just gargled with beach sand and ground glass, looked up and asked, "Who the hell are you?"

"Larry Rivers, the artist," the famous one replied.

The young man got up, poked a finger in Mr. Rivers' ribs and with his face thrust in his growled, "Well, I don't tell you how to paint your damned pictures, so you don't tell me how to play my radio. Understand?"

Mr. Rivers gathered up belongings and guests and left the beach for the day.

Like Mr. Rivers' friend Andy Warhol said, "Everyone is famous for at least fifteen minutes once in their lifetime."

Clubs & Organizations

There are numerous clubs and organizations in the area. Tourists are welcome to attend any of the meetings without prior notification. If someone who lives here complains about boredom, I just throw a copy of ADIP at them with the "get involved" page earmarked.

Alcoholics Anonymous: Recovery 12 Step house. English speaking recovery groups. Directly across from the *bibiloteca* (library) on *Cuauhtémoc*, AA—Monday, Wednesday and Friday at 6:00 p.m. NA—Thursday at 6:00 p.m. Additional meetings November through April. For more information call Bob P. at ☏ 554-2034 ✉ **Qigongporvida@yahoo.com**, or Nick ☏ (755)112-2124.

Baby Bundle Project: This group of American and Canadian women create bundles of baby products required by new mothers. The group meets at a private home in Ixtapa every 2-3 months year round for snacks around the pool and social time all the while creating bundles to help economically challenged, unwed teenage mothers living in the Ixtapa-Zihuatanejo community. The group donates around 300 bundles per year. Social workers from the local hospitals assist in pinpointing those children who are having children in need. For more information or to get involved contact Joan at ☏553-1618 or ✉ **playaobispo@yahoo.com**, or Elizabeth at ✉**bnfotografia@hotmail.com**

***Fundacion* Rene Ferguson A.C:** This Foundation was set up in memory of Rene Ferguson and its objective is to support able young women who need financial help to complete college. For more information contact Erica Islas at *La Quinta Troppo* or at ✉ **mexdrop@prodigy.net.mx**

Ixtapa Christian Fellowship: Non-denominational Elglish language service every Sunday at 10am at *Villas Pariso* in Ixtapa. Contact Ron at ☎ 554-5919 or Joan and John at ☎ 553-1618.

Niños Adelante: Until 1974, only six years of schooling was offered in *Zihua*. Education becomes expensive for children going on to high school. For this reason, a group of Americans formed the *Niños Adelante* program to offer *becas* (scholarships) to those promising children here in *Zihua*, who, for economic reasons, could not continue their studies. Individuals "adopt" a child, and help pay tuition throughout his/her school years. Since the program was implemented, hundreds of children have been able to obtain a high-school diploma. Many of these have gone on to college with help from their sponsors and are now productive members of the community. Local contact is José Bustos at ☎ 553-8712.

Por los niños de Zihuatanejo A.C.: Non-profit organization consisting of a board of 4 bi-lingual Mexicans and 5 year-round foreign residents. The monies collected at Sailfest go to this organization and they are responsible for distribution to schools in need. *Por los Niños* supports learning and school repair projects at more than 12 under-funded primary schools and kindergartens. Contact: Lorenzo Marbut at ☎554-2115 or 📱 (755) 102-4463. ✉ **Lorenzo@porlosninos.info**

Rotary Clubs: There are two Rotary Clubs operating in the area. They operate like any chapter in the States and welcome Rotarians from elsewhere to participate in their weekly gatherings. *Club Rotario* Ixtapa—*Nuevas Generaciones:* ☎ 553-0018. They meet Thursday evenings 8:30 p.m. at *Dal Toscano Ristorante*.

Club Rotario Zihuatanejo: ☎ 554-9321. They meet at the *Hotel Catalina* on *Playa La Ropa*.

SOS Bahía, A.C: Non-profit organization dedicated to the rescue and long-term preservation of the ecological integrity of the Bay of Zihuatanejo. Promotes environmental awareness, advocates the sustainable development of the bay's surroundings, and works to stop water pollution and the destruction of wildlife habitat in and around the bay. They have fund-raisers and days when beach garbage in and out of the water is picked up. Visit www.sosbahia.org or ✉info@sosbahia.org

SPAZ: *Paseo del Pescador.* ☎ 554-2373. Basically the equivalent of the SPCA, located at the *Casa Marina* complex and founded by Helena Krebs. They care for and give refuge to all kinds of animals. They also provide sterilization clinics, free adoptions, educational outreach programs, treatment and rehabilitation for wounded, homeless, or abandoned animals. Sells t-shirts and memberships to raise funds and gladly accepts donations. Family members are on the board but anyone wishing to help can attend one of the meetings the first Saturday of each month at 8:00 p.m. Open 7 days a week from 10:00 a.m. until 9:00 p.m. Contact www.zihuatanejo.net/spaz/ or ✉ animals.zihua@hotmail.com

The Angel Tree Program: This is a worldwide organization and a branch was started in Zihuatanejo in 1993. They organize gifts for the children of people incarcerated in the local jail. Gifts are delivered on January 6th of each year (King's Day). The inmates also create high quality hammocks which are sold through local churches including Ziuatanejo Christian Fellowship and at Ixtapa Christian Fellowship. The revenues of the hammocks go to offset their expenses while incarcerated and to support their families. If interested in helping contact Patti at ✉ ixtapapatti@hotmail.com

The NETZA Project: The Netza Project is a U.S. and Mexico registered non-profit organization that works to advance literacy, education and economic opportunity for all, in particular supporting the vision and expansion of The *Netzahualcoyotl* School and Kindergarten for Indigenous Children in Zihuatanejo, which today educates over 400 migrant, native, and street children—many of whom speak *Náhuatl, Mixteco, Amusgo,* and *Tlapaneco,* and who otherwise might not be in school. The *Netza* Project also advocates equality and social justice through dormitory shelter, health, programs, women's micro-finance, adult literacy, scholarships, and international volunteerism by fostering respect for diversity and celebrating native culture. See www.netzaproject.org or contact Lisa Martin at ✉ info@netzaproject.org or U.S. ☎ 1(508)284-0078, or Mexico ☎ (755)100-1173.

Zihuatanejo Christian Fellowship: Non-denominational English language service every Sunday morning at *Nardo's* restaurant on *Playa*

La Madera. Contact John and Betty at ☎ 554-7178.

ZI-Guitar-FEST A.C: The Zihuatanejo International Guitar festival brings musicians to *Zihua* from all corners of the world. A percentage of festival proceeds go toward supporting music, art, and cultural education in the community. Sponsors, donors, and volunteers always needed. **www.zihuafest.info** or ✉ **info@zihuafest.info**

Pets

Pets can be brought into Mexico with very little hassle. Birds are a different story altogether and extensive research is needed before attempting to bring any type of bird into Mexico. Some hotels, in *Zihua*, have no objection to your bringing an animal onto their premises. It is, of course, advisable to check with the management first. All one needs is a health certificate issued by a vet proving that the animal has been vaccinated against rabies, hepatitis, pip, and leptospirosis. This certificate must be dated within 10 days of your arrival in Mexico. In researching material for this edition I ran across a great website that answers all your questions about pet travel in Mexico and has a list of hotels in various cities that accept animals! **www.gringodog.com**

Effective June 2012, none of the airlines flying into our area will accept pets in cabin unless they are service animals. Absolutely no exceptions. Check above website for more information.

A major concern of tourists is whether their pet can get good health care here should the animal become sick. *Zihua* has some very fine vets. One precaution I do recommend is, just as you sould not drink tap water, neither should your animals. Give them purified water.

My friend Joan and I were laughing about our dogs—not only do they refuse to drink tap water—they insist on cold water from the *garrafón*.

There are a couple of places in town to buy pet food, and now you can obtain your loved ones favorite. For years there was no variety. *Veterinario Campos: Calle Ejido.* ☎ 554-2042.
Veterinaria del Centro: *Vicente Guerrero*. Rafael Castro. ☎ 554-2628.
Dr. Jorge Islas: *Pelícanos, Ixtapa.* ☎ 553-1324 or ☎ (755)551-8705 or Emergency ☎ 553-2222. He is a fantastic vet who speaks pretty good English, with lots of love and compassion for all animals. He makes house calls and will get up in the middle of the night for an emergency.

Pet foods and supplies can be purchased at Dr. Campos or over by the market on *Calle Los Mangos.* Also good variety at *Comercial Mexicana* and *Bodega.*

Many tourists that visit often ask about our street dogs. A favorite dog story is from Ted Tate's *Wash Gently, Dry Slowly.*

SECO

Seco is the Spanish name of the Mexican dog that lived for years at La Perla Restaurant. Since Seco loosely means, "dried up" in English, it is clear that some thought went into naming Seco.

Dried up he was. Also banged up, beaten up, and broken down. Seco's face was grizzled gray with time and pockmarked with miscellaneous scars showing the ravages of disease and the marks of battles. His undersized body was bony and the agony of bones that had never known a protective layer of flesh. Each and every bone seemed to have developed on its own—improperly.

To see Seco run was to see nothing coming together with everything trying. All parts seemed to fly in all directions and forward progress appeared to be achieved only accidentally.

A part of Seco's running problem was due to a crooked right hind leg— not crooked once but several times. The leg, broken in the long forgotten past, was never set. It mended casually, still useable but never again coordinating with the rest of his body. The legs independent actions showed when Seco scratched fleas on his right side. In a standing position his right hind leg rotated like an eccentric wheel, creating jerky, wobbly motions in the air near his body but with no body contact at all. When Seco scratched with that leg, lots of air got scratched but no skin and no fleas. If there was a psychic benefit from scratching air around fleas, Seco achieved it. Apparently the psychic benefit was there, for several times a day Seco would stop what he was doing and, standing patiently, would jab the air violently with his hind leg, searching in vain for the fleas that should be occupying the space he was scratching. Each time, judging from Seco's expressions, something good had happened when he scratched. Perhaps, with his strong imagination, a hundred fleas would have tumbled off onto the ground, leaving him a few flealess moments once again.

Although Seco could qualify as the most battered and broken down dog in all Zihuatanejo dog history, broken in spirit he was not. Seco was—in Seco's mind—a dog descended from the dogs of conquistadors and Aztec warriors. Seco was—in Seco's mind—a young, powerful, well-coordinated, attractive, male canine specimen, ready and willing to take on all dog comers and capable of challenging and vanquishing any of them.

And challenge he did—every male dog that wandered down the beach and into Seco's territory. He would jerk from his resting position at La Perla and with legs and parts flying in all directions make his wild run on the terrified intruder, baying deeply, though somewhat cracked.

Almost always the intruder would flee, more in fear of the unknown than of the oncoming Seco. It is a dog's instinctive lot to fear the inexplicable. Even the strongest minded dogs bay helplessly in fear of the full moon when inexplicable feelings well deep down inside. And to see Seco descending from all directions simultaneously was more than the average dog could take. He had met the inexplicable.

However, there was an occasional dog challenger—likely born under the no nonsense sign of Virgo—who stood his ground, questioning that the apparition he saw was supernatural and correctly deducing that the mass of flying bones hurtling at him was nothing more than an old decrepit, disjointed dog, possibly, like Custer, making his last stand.

That clear-sighted Virgo challenger would stand his ground. Seco, when confronted with an upstart would come to a quick stop, right hind leg folding as he skidded, while the other three legs shook and bent. Never did he back off. This Mexican standoff could go on for as long as five minutes. Eventually Seco would approach the challenger cautiously. The hairs on both dogs' backs would rise and both dogs would sniff each other. While the challenger slowly circled Seco, Seco would stand firm—as firm as he could on his twisted legs and crooked back, supported more by heart than body. It was a noble stand. He made it clear he would give no ground. When the challenger's inspection circle was completed, he would stand back and relax, convinced now in his Virgo mind that no real threat ever existed and that it would be socially undignified to spend more time jousting with this old dog. He would then depart. Seco would watch the departing intruder for a few seconds, then offer up two sharp staccato barks to seal the victory. He could then safely return to his resting-place, satisfied with his victory.

While Seco was never very socially acceptable to most dogs, to humans he was even less so. More often than not, when Seco rested beneath one of the La Perla tables, that table would remain empty.

Seco remained eternally grateful to the rare human who dared to touch the mangy-looking hide and pass on a few loving words with some understanding scratches. It was his deepest and most tender need. From his resting-place at La Perla, Seco was ever vigilant for that rare human who might speak kindly to him and scratch the patch that his pitiful broken leg would never reach.

To see Seco recognize such a friend was to see a new Seco in action.

His deep, challenging, cracked bay became an eager and emotional whine, more like a human high in ecstasy, or deep in trouble, than a dog. With pure adoration shining from his eyes, Seco's voice would quiver; ranging up and down with the same emotion a human would use to vocally greet his loving family after years of separation.

In Seco's world where humans mostly stopped to stare in disbelief, shudder and move away, Seco was deeply appreciative of the rare compassionate one who had the vision to see that beautiful Seco shining deep inside. For the enlightened human, Seco became again—in Seco's mind—a charming puppy, asking after his master's health and dogging his master's steps wherever he went. When master stopped, Seco stopped. When master sat and rested, Seco would lie down and rest, laying his scarred head heavy on his master's foot, content now to drowse, knowing master could not get away because he has his foot so well nailed down. Under that warm reassuring blanket of love, Seco could sleep.

To sleep—perchance to dream—to dream that, had life turned a few less corners, this temporary master might have been the one—the one true master love that had remained forever out of reach—the one true master who could recognize the gallant heart, the loyal spirit and, above all, the beauty of this deserving puppy, now turned dog.

It has been many years now since Seco went over the Rainbow Bridge to dog heaven. I visualized that on his judgment day his presence was announced.

And here comes Seco...a Mexican dog from Zihuatanejo..."

And at that moment, the beaded one, robe flowing, would stand, turn his soulful eyes to our long-suffering friend and say, "Seco? Not Seco. Welcome home friend. Welcome home...Don Quixote."

Transportation

Entering Mexico: You can only enter Mexico with a valid passport. For the motor vehicle, the original title must be presented. Notarized affidavits of ownership may or may not be accepted.

Airplane

The preferred method of travel to and from *Zihua* is by air. The international airport opened in 1975 and since then *Zihua* has become readily accessible to the world. Following are the major airlines.

Aeroméxico: Corner of *Juan Alvarez* and *Cinco de Mayo*. ☎ 554-2018.

Alaska Airline: ☎ 554-8457. No local office—airport location only.

America West Airline: ☎ 554-8634. No local office—airport location only.

Continental Airline: ☎ 554-4219. No local office—airport location only.

Interjet: ☎112-1928 (inside *Comerical Mexicana)* or airport 553-7002. Mainly service to Mexico City or *Toluca*.

Car

Arriving by private car now costs as much as air travel and with all the problems with violence in the country, it's probably not a good idea to drive unless of course you're me and don't mind the "Highway of Death." Most major roads are good but jammed with *doble remolques*. High gas prices have caused most companies to "double up" their transports so now you don't have to pass one truck—you pass a truck and a half. Most major highways are now three lanes and passing is easy. Furthermore the high price of gas has made highway driving prohibitive for most people so there's very little traffic on any of the roads outside major cities. The new toll roads are in good condition, mostly, with two or more lanes each way and dividers down the center; however, they are very expensive. From Laredo to Acapulco, plan to spend at least $150.00 U.S. one-way. Try to avoid Mexico City at all cost—it's dangerous.

A new law passed in June of 2011 requires a bond of $200-$400 U.S. to cross into Mexico if you have a car registered in a country other than Mexico. The price relates to car year model. The monies are returned to you if you leave the country in a timely fashion or you take your car papers and FM3 to the nearest regional customs headquarters (*Lazaro Cardenas*) and have them issue an extension. If you fail to get the extension, then the monies are forfeited.

Careful preparation is most important before an auto trip into Mexico. Find out, if possible, whether your make and model of vehicle is sold in Mexico. This will give you an idea of what spare parts to take. Mexican car mechanics are marvels at improvisation but many are not familiar with newer computer systems. A spare fan belt is a must and make sure your tires are in good shape.

Be careful how you pack the car. You will be stopped lots of time for inspection and easy access for the police saves a lot of time. Don't leave valuables in plain sight—an invitation to steal.

If you're coming into the country as a tourist, insurance should be purchased prior to entering Mexico. It is expensive but necessary. Remember, the Mexican judicial system is based on the old Roman law and on the Napoleonic code. You are presumed guilty until proven innocent. Some people buy insurance only for highway travel days. If you don't plan to use your vehicle once you reach your destination, this is an ideal way to save money.

A list of articles allowed into Mexico without paying duty is obtainable from the Internet, consular office, or at customs. If bringing in new items have your receipts handy and be prepared to pay duty.

If you have car trouble, the equivalent of "911" in Mexico is "060." You may also call the Ministry of Tourism's hotline at (01) 555-250-0027/0123/0292/0493 or toll free at (01) 800-903-9200. The Ministry can dispatch the "Green Angels," a motorist assistance service. They have a fleet of trucks with bilingual crews and operate daily on all the major roads. The Green Angels may be reached directly at (01) 555-250-8221/4737/4644. If you are unable to call them, pull off the road and lift the hood of your car; chances are they will eventually find you.

The only gas stations in Mexico are government-owned *PEMEX* stations. When filling the tank, remain to watch that the attendant doesn't cheat. Make sure the meter is turned back to zero at the start. There are restrooms at all *Pemex* stations but it is a good idea to carry along toilet paper. There are five *PEMEX* stations in Zihuatanejo. Two located on the road toward Ixtapa and two on the road toward Acapulco. The latest addition is located on the road to *Puerto Mío*.

It is customary to tip gas station attendants at least a few pesos when you fill up. Gas is comparable to stateside prices—close to $3.50 U.S. for unleaded.

When driving in Mexico, drive defensively and avoid driving at night since animals and people walk on the roads.

Car Rental

One can rent a car in *Zihua*. You need only a valid driver's license and a credit card. Be prepared to pay through the nose. A jeep can fetch up to $75.00 U.S. A weekly rental of a sub-compact can be as much as $400.00. It's best to make your reservations from home. Rates are about half of what you pay here and are honored. Remember the quoted rate outside Mexico does not include the *IVA* tax. From *Topes:*

Car Troubles

I favor AVIS when renting cars, but they have pulled out of this area. One year I reserved a sub-compact from AVIS and was quoted a price of $300.00 for a month. When I arrived, with my reservation number in hand, no sub-compacts were available and I was "upgraded" to an antique piece of garbage Dodge Dart. It got me where I wanted to go so I didn't complain. However, the day of my departure, the AVIS manager presented me with a bill in excess of $1,500.00 dollars. I was charged a daily Mexican rate for the car since I hadn't specifically reserved a bigger model. Outraged, I argued with him to no avail and swore vengeance.

Returning to the States, I dashed off numerous nasty letters to AVIS. Several weeks went by but finally I received a credit on my VISA for the total amount charged and a letter of apology. I had, in my correspondence, denounced the AVIS manager in no uncertain terms and praised the secretary who seemed to do all the work and was most pleasant. Returning the following year with another AVIS reservation I was greeted by the new manager—the secretary from the previous year. She gave me a very fine, brand-new car and told me that my letter was responsible for her new position and the old manager's firing. Ah, sweet vengeance!

Alamo: (Airport). ☎ 554-8429. (*La Puerta—Ixtapa*) ☎ 553-0206. A newer location at south entrance to Ixtapa by *Banamex*.
Budget: (Airport). ☎ 554-4837 and ☎ 553-0397 (*Plaza Ambiente—* Ixtapa*)
Dollar: (Airport). ☎ 554-5366.
Europcar: (Airport and Ixtapa). ☎ 553-7158.
Green Motion: ☎ 553-0397. *Plaza Ambiente—Blvd. Ixtapa.*

Hertz: (Airport). ☎ (755)109-0022/23. Ixtapa—*Emporio.*
Thrifty: (Airport). ☎ 553-7020. *Barceló*—Ixtapa. ☎ 553-2019
    ★Important tip: If you are already here and decide you can't live without a rental car, call from *Zihua* to the States to make your reservation or do this by Internet—it will save you money.

Car Sales
    Foreigners who live in Mexico often buy a used or new car and must have a Mexican driver's license to operate it. Cars are very expensive in Mexico.
    The new car showrooms are located alongside one another on the *Lateral Carr. Acapulco-Zihuatanejo.*
Dodge dealership: *Lateral Carr. Acapulco-Zihuatanejo.* Adjacent to General Hospital.
Ford dealership: (same as above).
Honda dealership: *Ave. La Boquita s/n.* Located in *Comercial Mexicana* complex.
Nissan dealership: (Same as Dodge and Ford).

Car Parking: Parking downtown is a hassle. If you walk around in *centro*, town is full of cars but all the shops are empty. That is becaue nowadays everyone has a car—long-term financing is encouraged. If you walk in town before 9:00 a.m. town is empty of cars but after 9:00 a.m. is full. The shopkeepers take up all the spaces so very few people go to town except to visit the banks. The city provides some parking areas free of charge all along most of *Cinco de Mayo.* There are several lots available in town for about $10 pesos/hour. Beware of the sign with a slash through a big E. This means no parking and your plates may be removed.
Car Parts: The road to Acapulco is lined with *Refaccionarías* (Auto Parts stores). Now have an **Auto Zone** that's stocked with parts.
Car Mechanics and Service: The availability of expert and inexpensive repairs makes owning a car pleasurable (if parts can be found). Most mechanics are specialists. My car goes to one mechanic for brakes, another for electrical work, etc. Mexican mechanics are master wizards—given enough tin foil, rubber bands, and duct tape, they can keep a car running forever. Ask a local for references. All the locals have their personal favorites and are happy to share that information.

Boats

Many individuals trailer their boats down from Canada or the States. There are several places to have boat repairs or boat engine repairs made. See Services A-Z.

Bus

Bus is by far the cheapest way to travel in Mexico. The big bus station, housing most bus lines is located on *Lateral Carr. Acapulco-Zihuatanejo,* across from the gas station. ***Estrella Blanca:*** *Lateral Carr. Acapulco-Zihuatanejo.* ☎ 554-3476. The new buses are clean, comfortable, and most offer air conditioning. Service is almost continuous, with a stand-down time only in the wee hours of the morning. Many offer service *sin escala* (non-stop) but the lines change their schedules often. ***Ejecutivo*** and ***Futura*** services are offered on many routes—featuring movies, soft drinks, air conditioning and comfortable lounge chairs. They are much more expensive than ordinary buses but worth every penny. Best to go a day in advance to purchase your ticket and choose the class and seat you want. It can take as little as three hours or as much as six hours to reach Acapulco. ***Estrella de Oro:*** *Lateral Carr. Acapulco-Zihuatanejo y Jupiter.* ☎ 554-2175. They offer the same above services with their first class called *Diamante.*

Beware: Although many types of bus service purport to offer toilets on board, be prepared for them not working or at the very least being absolutely filthy and without paper. Only on the top-notch buses can one be sure of finding adequate facilities. Even the *directos* make stops to give clients an opportunity to buy snacks and use the facilities.

Small buses operate between *Zihua-Ixtapa* and outlying towns on a regular basis from 6:00 a.m. until 11:00 p.m. *Esq. Av. Morelos y Benito Juárez.* Buses leave for Ixtapa and other close destinations when they are full, about every ten minutes. Priced at eight pesos.

Combis or *micros* (small vans) run continuously between *Zihua* and Ixtapa and throughout town. The *combi* and bus stops are recognizable because of their bright blue awnings. These little *micros* will have the destination plainly visible in their window. Slightly more expensive than local buses, they get you to your destination a little faster. From *Topes:*

THE ROAD TRIP TO HELL

Dawn arrived sluggishly this late August morning in Zihuatanejo. The serrated edges of the majestic palm fronds were motionless against a molten grey sky. It felt as if a wet serape had been draped over this small fishing village and everyone appeared to be moving in slow motion.

A hurricane had recently yo-yoed up the coast from Hualtulco to Baja, narrowly missing the major port cities, but dumping two feet of rain along the entire coast over a two-week period. Jan Hardy arrived on my doorstep drenched in sweat and went into an instant tirade against the stifling heat and humidity. She'd been grousing about the weather for weeks. We'd been talking about a road trip to Guatemala all summer and in an epiphany I was to dearly regret later, "I said, "Let's get out of her tonight. We'll take the bus to Puerto Escondido and on down the coast to Tapachula and come back via San Cristóbal. It should be cool in the highlands. If we don't get out of here soon, we'll have mildew growing on our feet just like it's invaded our shoes and clothes." This made Jan immensely happy and we agreed to meet at the bus station at about 8:30 for the night bus to Acapulco. Jan suggested she take traveler's checks and pay for everything and we would split the cost. I readily agreed but decided to take along a few pesos just for my own sense of well being. I packed two small canvas bags, one with summer clothing and one with heavier jeans and sweaters for the chill mountain air. It was more luggage than I really needed for a bus trip but I figured I could carry both a few blocks without having a heart attack so what the hell.

Jan and I met as planned at the bus station and bought our tickets to Acapulco. We figured total it was about a nine hour trip to Puerto Escondido with a change of buses in Acapulco and we would arrive at a decent morning hour and have a day or two on the beach in a town we didn't know well. Also, we were paying for one of the newer first-class buses and we thought we'd get a good night's sleep on the bus.

The sky had been grumbling all evening and just as we boarded the bus, it started to rain. Although a weekday evening, the bus was almost full and we were forced to find window seats in the very rear over a wheel well. Not my favorite seat but it beats standing up. Before taking off, I reached out to open my window which was cracked about four inches because the bus driver had not yet turned on the air conditioning and it was stifling inside with humidity and ripe bodies. The window wouldn't open or close but I decided this was tolerable since we were leaving imminently. Since Jan and I both wanted window seats, the aisle seats were vacant for a few minutes but mine was quickly grabbed by a rather tubby little man that had yet to learn the secrets of deodorant. As friend Anita Cowan would say, "He smelled like a ripe old goat" and his pores were oozing the Presidente brandy he had consumed prior to boarding the bus. At least he wasn't trying to hide his body odor with noxious smelling cologne as so many Mexican men did at that time.

The rain was falling in sheets and the bus driver was doing about eighty miles an hour which meant that the four inch crack in my window was an entry point for the pounding cold rain. Within minutes I was cold, wet, and miserable as opposed to dry, damp, and sticky. I stepped over my companion to reach one of my bags in the overhead and inadvertently fell in his lap. I apologized profusely but he immediately took this as a sexual come-on because he instantly got a hard-on and I knew this was not going to be a good beginning to a two-week trip. I managed to retrieve the bag and pulled out a towel to stuff in the window and my trusty foul weather jacket to drape over my now shivering body. This stopped the major flow of water but didn't begin to solve the problem of my bus companion or the trickle of cold rainwater dripping from the overhead onto me. I curled in the seat as best I could and tried to ignore my companions chatter and the Chinese water torture being performed on my forehead. The lights in the bus had been extinguished and with the pelting rain outside, the interior was as dark as a broom closet. I pride myself on being able to sleep almost anywhere and even with this adversity I managed to doze off lightly for a while. Glancing over at Jan, she was oblivious to my plight as her window was not leaking and she had both seats to herself.

I was awakened suddenly by a feeling all was not right. Bus companion had one of his hands on my privates and one hand on himself. He was copping a feel and jerking off. I swore abruptly, jumped up, stomped on his feet and woke up Jan. I made her make room for me and pulled my foul weather gear over me and was just getting comfortable as we pulled into Acapulco and had to change buses.

I grabbed my now sopping towel out of the window and my luggage and we trudged into the terminal at midnight to buy our tickets to Escondido. We fared much better on this particular bus as it was less crowded and we both slept until it pulled into the deserted bus station at Escondido before dawn.

Puerto Escondido is a beautiful little town lying approximately two hundred miles south of Acapulco. Town itself sits on top of a towering cliffside that abruptly ends on a wide sand beach facing the open ocean. The waves are tremendous and it has always been known as a spot for old hippies and Europeans. It is much more laid back than most parts of Mexico, Zihuatanejo included.

However, it was hard to think about the beauty of this small hamlet when it was pitch black outside and hours before sunrise. From a previous jaunt to Escondido, I remembered a small, inexpensive hotel was to our right about midway down the steep hillside. Since we were tired and grumpy and our choice was to wait or walk, we picked up our luggage and literally stumbled down the hill toward where

I thought the hotel was located. My memory served me righteously and we found the San Felipe Hotel. After banging on the door for what seemed to be an eternity, the night watchman was roused from a drunken stupor and we got a room. We fell into an exhausted sleep and finally roused ourselves about noon to go exploring. There's not a lot to Escondido and we ended up at a beachside bistro by mid-afternoon. It was frequented by many of the locals and we had the good fortune to strike up a conversation with Mimmie Dalberg, an expatriate from Germany who had built a charming little hotel right above the beach. She invited us to stay at her hotel and join the locals for a fiesta that evening at a local night spot.

Jan and I decided this would be fun but we should make it an early evening in order to catch the bus to Salina Cruz early the next morning as we were anxious to get into a temperate altitude and have a chance to wear our winter garb. We spent a most enjoyable evening with the locals and departed about eight the next morning, in a taxi this time, to the bus station where we bought tickets to Salina Cruz. That was the end of the line for this particular bus route and we were told we would have to change bus stations in Salina Cruz to get to Tapachula. This was an ordinary bus and the driver made numerous stops to pick up those folks waiting by the side of the road. As usual, Jan and I both wanted window seats and for most of the ride the aisle seats remained unoccupied. However, the closer to Salina Cruz we drew, the more crowded the bus became. Only the seat next to me was vacant when the bus driver pulled off the road once again to take on a passenger. This particular passenger was a middle-aged women carrying a baby in one arm and two live chickens in the other. Naturally she approached the only seat available which was next to me and ask me very politely would I prefer to hold the baby or the chickens! As I could tell from the smell, the baby's diaper needed changing and I opted for the chickens. Although the bus was full, the driver continued to pull over and more and more passengers boarded. Several were laughing and pointing at the little gringa holding gingerly to two live chickens. I took this in stride as just another adventure in Mexico and laughed with them. When we finally reached Salina Cruz around noon, my seat companion graciously thanked me and left with baby and chickens in tow.

Jan and I grabbed our luggage and seeing no taxis around trudged up several blocks to the other bus station. There we were informed there were no first-class buses leaving for what could be several days. Rio Tehuantepec's bridge on the only road to Tapachula had washed out and was impassable. Those trying to pass were being ferried one car, bus, or truck at a time thru the raging torrent of water so first-class buses were cancelled. We ask if there was any option and the ticket lady said we could take third-class buses up to the river, wade across and catch a first-class bus on the other side. Jan and I looked at the dismal town with no redeeming features and decided to literally forge onward. Jan said, "I can swim—how about you?" Another three blocks walk brought us to the third-class bus station and we boarded an ancient gas-choking monstrosity to travel another thirty miles toward our destination. We disembarked once again in Tehuantepec and changed one antique for another. The bus driver informed everyone that he would take us as close to the river as he could and then we were on our own. After a short ride the bus abruptly halted behind a line of similar vehicles. The bus driver informed us that was the end of the trip and he was turning around and going back. Stupidly I said, "How far to the river?" He replied, "At the front of this line of cars and busses."

It was now mid-afternoon and blazing hot. At least it wasn't raining. Again we hoisted our bags and took off walking toward the river with a group of other stragglers wanting to get across. None of the cars or trucks we walked past had their engines on and most folks were just wandering about drinking beer and eating fruit. Jan asked one man how long he had been waiting to cross the bridge and he said three days! But not to worry—there were plenty of trucks with perishable goods on them and several beer trucks in the line and we would have plenty to eat and drink during our perhaps prolonged stay on the highway. Naturally that was comforting. Sure enough, a few hundred yards further we passed a beer truck and we were handed two lukewarm coronas which went down our parched throats just fine. As we were greedily drinking another man walked up and gave us mangos and apples to eat. When we offered to pay, he declined saying all his food would rot in the heat anyway. When we asked how much further to the river, he replied, "Probably only four or five more kilometers. A couple of hours on foot if you keep up a good pace."

Jan groaned and I sighed. Our feet were already hurting and our luggage, which was weighty to begin with was feeling like it was packed with barbells instead of bathing suits. Jan was looking around frantically for some type of vehicle to convey us to the river when she spied a young man with a bicycle. She immediately approached him and yelled in Spanish, "How much to rent your bicycle to transport my luggage to the river?" He looked at her in wonder and said," you honestly want to rent my bike to carry your maleta?" "Yes, how much?" she cried desperately. "Fifty pesos," he tentatively replied. "Bueno, it's a deal," said Jan.

Jan swung her two bags on the handlebars of the bike and off we went. It was dusk by the time we reached the river and fortunately there were several more beer trucks dispensing free suds so we weren't dehydrated—just sunburned and a little lightheaded from the tortuous walk and warm beer.

As we had been told, one vehicle at a time was being roped across the raging torrents of water. At the head of the line was a truck with only the driver inside. I asked if he would give us a ride to the other side and he said sure—hop in. With our bags and Jan and I in the front seat it was a very tight fit but we managed to squeeze in and just as night settled we were finally across the river.

There were, of course, no buses on the other side to take us to the next town so the truck driver graciously gave us a ride to some god awful little place where he was going to spend the night. We offered to buy him dinner which he accepted and then we took a taxi to the bus station. By now it was midnight and we were exhausted. At the deserted bus station, we were told there wouldn't be a bus until seven in the morning and no, there were no hotels in town so we camped out at the bus station until daylight where another third-class bus took us to a bigger town so that we could catch another bus to Tapachula.

We finally arrived in Tapachula about dark and found a modest hotel in town where we instantly fell into an exhausted sleep. We were in good spirits as we were close to our goal of Guatemala.

The following morning we arrived at the consulate, and with only a short wait, obtained our visas to Guatemala. We then took a third class bus (all that was available) to the frontera or border. We were told by the bus driver we would have to cross into Guatemala by foot and catch a Guatemalan bus for the rest of our trip. We disembarked and walked a short way to the border crossing where there were dozens of folks milling about. We managed to push and shove our way up to the booth where immigration stamps your visa and it was closed. Finally spying a man in an official looking outfit, I ask what was going on. He replied, "Oh, the immigration man hasn't shown up yet. He called in sick and they are trying to find a replacement."

Finally, after about an hour wait, someone showed up and opened the window to start stamping passports and visas. Jan and I got in line and after only about ten minutes, the window closed again.

"Now what?" I said to the man in line behind me.

"Oh, it's eleven and time for their break."

"But he just opened!"

"No importa, a break is más importante."

After another wait of half an hour, the window reopened and the line slowly moved forward. Jan and I finally had our visas but were running way behind our sel- imposed schedule. We had planned to be in Panajachel by dark and this was becoming a remote possibility.

As soon as we crossed into Guatemala we were besieged by money exchange folks offering to give us quetzals for pesos or dollars. Jan didn't want to exchange one of her hundred dollars traveler's checks as she was certain the bank rate would be more favorable. I agreed and we both changed twenty dollars in pesos for *quetzals figuring forty dollars would easily get us to Panajachel and we could go to the bank the next day.*

We found the bus station without any difficulty and boarded a bus that, with numerous stops, would take us to Quezaltenango which is a major city in Guatemala and from there catch a bus to Panajachel.

The bus was packed and Jan and I had to stand for the next couple of hours. We finally pulled into a San Marcos and Jan noticed it was market day. When we disembarked, the next bus was getting ready to pull out from town but it to was filled to overflowing. Jan pleaded to wait for the next bus and let us tour the market.

Why not? We weren't on any real schedule and after asking around were told the next bus would depart at three in the afternoon. According to our watches it was about one thirty so we asked if the bus driver would guard our luggage so we could go to the market. He agreed readily and we entered the bus and put our two suitcases with only clothes on the back luggage rack. Keeping one duffel each we took a walk to the market and stood in awe at the vast array of colorful clothing and vibrant flowers.

Each town in Guatemala has their own signature huipils—the hand-embroidered blouses worn by the natives. The huipils here were all done in rainbow hues with flowers embroidered on the front. I'm a collector of these fabulous woven pieces and had never seen this particular design. We negotiated for two of these exquisite huipils and bought them for the princely sum of fifteen dollars each. We now had ten dollars in quetzals to get us to our destination but weren't worried as ten dollars in Guatemala goes a long way or normally it does. We stopped for a bit to eat and leisurely made our way back to the bus station arriving at two forty five—plenty of time to board the bus and obtain a seat.

We arrived back at the bus station which was bustling with activity but saw no sign of our bus. We checked our watches again and perplexed asked at the ticket window what had happened to our bus. The man informed us it had left on time at three in the afternoon.

"No, no," we shouted. "It's not three yet."

Patiently, he explained, "senoritas, it is now almost four in the afternoon—you missed your bus by almost one hour."

With a feeling of horror, I realized that Mexico was on daylight-savings time and Guatemala was not—a small fact that Jan and I had overlooked in planning our trip. All I could envision in this moment was freezing in the mountains without any warm clothing. Jan was fit to be tied and screamed, "we've got to find a taxi and catch up with the bus." We frantically started running up and down the streets screaming for a taxi. We found a taxi with no driver parked outside a small cantina. We barged in screaming, "Where's the taxi driver of the taxi parked outside." The cantina was obviously for men only and the few patrons looked at us like we had just been released from a mental hospital.

Finally, one man stumbled to his feet and admitted he was the taxi driver. We rapidly explained our problem and he reluctantly agreed to chase down the bus for us. First we had to buy gas for the taxi which took almost all our remaining quetzals and then we were off—speeding up a torturous road into the mountains. As we swayed around corners, Jan whispered, "Linda, we're in serious trouble. I only have a fifty dollar bill and the rest are one hundred dollar traveler's checks. What are we going to do?"

In our haste to catch the bus, we hadn't even begun to negotiate a price with the taxi driver.

"I don't think we have a choice in the matter Jan. Obviously we can't ask him for change for a fifty so we'll just have to give him that." Jan was horrified at the thought but the reality of the situation was now beyond our control.

We passed numerous buses but not the one with our luggage. It's of course hard to tell them apart but we had placed our luggage in the very back top rack of the bus. Unless someone had already stolen our bags, they were readily recognizable by the distinct yellow and red canvas.

We rounded an especially sharp curve and were fast approaching a bus when I spied our luggage still in the back rack.

"That's it!" I screamed at the taxi driver. We could see the bus was chock-full of people and our taxi driver started honking his horn and waving for the bus driver to pull over. We could see in the side-view mirror the bus driver shrug his shoulders and continue on.

"We'll have to pass them and block the road." I said.

The taxi driver ever vigilant to the fact he had two gringas as passengers said, "Oh, that's very dangerous and will cost you extra."

"Not a problem" we said.

The taxi driver rounded a sharp curve and sped ahead of the bus. About fifty feet further he put his taxi in the path of the bus and slammed on his brakes.

Jan and I jumped out and started waving our arms frantically for the bus driver to pull over. With great reluctance he did. The bus door opened and we were told there was no room on the bus by the driver's assistant. It was readily obvious there was no room on the bus but we insisted. Finally the bus driver turned off the bus and climbed out. He recognized us as the gringas that had left our luggage in his care and after a shouting match about bus capacity with his assistant, agreed we could board.

Jan reluctantly handed over her fifty-dollar bill to the taxi driver and he left happy as a pig in shit. We then crammed our bodies onto the bus and the driver took off. Jan was shoved against the driver so tightly her rather large breasts covered each of his ears. I, on the other had, was shoved flat against the accordion door. As we slowly made our way up the treacherous mountain road, the driver would occasionally pull to the side to let off a passenger after a scream of "Parada," or stop. The door would swing open and I would immediately go flying out like the wind up Jack-in-the-Box of childhood memories. At one point, the bus driver's assistant asked us for our tickets and when I replied we didn't have them he said to pay him or get kicked off the bus. My arms were pinned against my sides and my head was smashed into the door. I lost it and yelled like a banshee that we would pay when we reached Quetzaltenango and not a second before.

Finally, at four-thirty Guatemala time we pulled into a shabby bus station on the outskirts of a large town and were able to disembark and stretch our very exhausted bodies. We paid our bus fare and were left with one dollar and ten cents in quetzals and five hundred dollars in traveler's checks. We ask when the next bus to Panajachel was and were told no buses traveled after five and we couldn't catch a bus until the next morning.

We found a taxi and ask how much to go to the center of town and a nice hotel.

"Three quetzals," He replied.

We explained about our riches-to-rags situation and he was unsympathetic. Another taxi driver told us there was a nice hotel a few blocks away and he would take us for our last dollar. Without much choice in the matter, we reluctantly entered the taxi and were driven to a fine accommodation that had a sign announcing they took plastic, so we paid off the taxi driver and entered.

We tried to explain our situation to the owner and ask if we could pay double for the room on plastic and have him give us the extra in quetzals.

Not to our surprise, he refused.

Here we were on the outskirts of a bustling city with ten centavos to our name. We asked if there was a bus to town and how much it would be and he said "five centavos" pointing to a bus stop at the end of the street.

We settled in our very fine room and decided to spend our last monies and see what we could do downtown.

We caught a bus to the center of town and were immediately ecstatic as several banks were still open. However, when we went in to exchange one of the traveler's checks, we were told they only did money exchange from nine until noon with no exceptions. I asked if we could draw some money on our plastic and that could only be done between nine and five daily, again no exceptions.

199

Frustrated beyond belief, I asked one of the clerks where the best hotel in town was and she directed us across the plaza.

As we crossed the plaza, I sought out a taxi driver and asked how much to take us back to our hotel tonight and then pick us up in the morning. He said "six quetzals"

All we really needed was dinner plus six quetzals to get us through this nightmare so we entered the hotel and ask for the manager.

The clerk wanted to know if there was a problem and we said no—just get the manager.

We were shortly greeted by a gracious middle-aged man that listened to our problem and finally gave us the sympathy we were craving. Since we weren't staying at the hotel, he couldn't cash a traveler's check but would be willing to let us eat dinner, pay with plastic and overcharge us the six quetzals to catch a taxi round trip so we could return to the bank the next morning.

With a huge sigh of relief, we were escorted into the dining room by this charming man and he explained to our waitress what was to transpire.

We ordered a huge expensive dinner and for the first time since our breakfast which seemed years ago, we were able to relax.

Tired but sated we finally pushed away from the table and asked for the check. The waitress brought it and Jan signed. He returned with our six quetzals "extra" and Jan in dismay said, "Oh my god. I forgot to include a tip. Now we can't afford one!"

When the waitress returned to our table, Jan profusely apologized and pulled out of her purse a traveling make-up kit which she offered to the young girl in lieu of a tip.

The young girl obviously wore no make-up but graciously accepted this "gift."

The next morning, things seemed much brighter especially after exchanging a hundred dollars at one of the banks. Again we returned to the bus station for the "last leg" of the trip to Panajachel.

Again, we boarded a bus designed for eighty people but filled with at least one hundred and fifty. All buses in Guatemala are former United States school buses from the forties and fifties. They have wooden bench seats designed for two children yet usually there is a minimum of three or four adults seated on each one. The buses are always a cornucopia of colors and designs limited in scope only to the imagination of the artist.

As we slowly made our way down the road, the bus driver suddenly yelled something unintelligible in Spanish and everyone standing in the aisle and seated would duck down to the floor of the bus. It happened very suddenly and Jan and I were the only ones not to respond. People around us were frantically yanking on our shirttails from the floor so we squatted also.

"What's going on?"

A little old lady of about ninety with a seamed face and few teeth explained to me as if I were a stupid child that there were laws in Guatemala that buses could only carry a certain number of passengers. If they exceeded the limit, which they all did, then the bus driver would be fined and the people on the bus were expected to pay the fine for him. So, when the bus driver saw an Army vehicle he would yell and everyone would duck down and the Army patrol would assume he was not exceeding the limit.

This scenario was played out several times on our way to Panajachel and I found it amusing to say the least.

We finally reached our destination and checked into a lovely, cheap hotel near the center of "town."

Actually Panajachel is more a village than a town but with a cosmopolitan air to it. There are many Americans living here and this is reflected in the quality of the fine restaurants, bars, and shops in town. It is situated on a lake containing seven inactive volcanos and is as charming as can be. The mountain air is cool and clean, tinged with the scent of eucalyptus and rich soil. We were in the highlands of Guatemala where the coffee beans are grown. The soil is rich and fertile and while men toil in the coffee plantations, the women weave their magical huipils to be sold at the major market of Chichicastenango.

Jan and I spent a wonderful week there—taking photos and purchasing huipils. After a week of exploration, Jan and I decided to move on to San Cristóbal. Not nearly as eventful as the trip to Guatemala but still nine bus rides later we arrived in this jewel of town set high in the mountains of Southern Mexico in the state of Chiapas.

We finally returned to Zihuatanejo after a two week jaunt and 57 bus rides! A record by any standards.

Taxi: Rates are set by the taxi-cooperative but not always honored. Make sure to reach an agreement on the price before embarking. A trip to the airport will cost about $10.00 U.S. (per cab not per person). Fares are set from the airport and are much higher. Fares increase 40% after midnight. From the airport to *Zihua* the price is $25 to $40 U.S. If you don't want to pay this amount and aren't burdened with lots of luggage, walk off the airport grounds and go over to one of the little restaurants about 100 yards from the airport door. There are local taxis there and the charge will be much lower.

In *Zihua*, expect to spend from 20 to 40 pesos between destinations. In Ixtapa, expect to spend double that amount. Between *Zihua* and Ixtapa, you'll pay about 55 to 120 pesos. Add 5 pesos to the price if you call for a cab and if you ask the driver to use the AC, there will be additional charges—so find out first.

Try to write down or remember the cab number before entering the taxi in case you accidentally leave valuables inside. This a a very common occurrence.

A taxi co-op operates from the market area to Ixtapa all day. Easiest is to hail them on the street or call from your hotel. There are three companies working out of *Zihua:*

Apaaz: ☎ 554-3680 & 554-8809 and ☎ 554-8772

Utaaz: ☎ 554-3311/4583.

UTZI: ☎ 554-4763

If a problem arises regarding price or service, get the number (circled in blue) on the exterior of the taxi and report the offense to *PROFECO*. They will try to rectify the problem.

Sightseeing and Travel
Beaches South

The names of the beaches south of town can get confusing. From *Playa Las Gatas* to the airport is 13 miles. This whole beach area is collectively called *Playa Blanca* officially, but locals designate certain "beach" areas by different names.

I've only listed a very few of the hotels, B &B's, inns, guest cottages, etc. For both areas, north and south, people came—they saw—they loved the area—and they built a "hotel." There are literally dozens and dozens and dozen of accommadations from **Barra de Potosí to Saladitas.** My guidebook is not an ad for these places but information about the area. The whole area is beautiful and secluded. Wonderful and charming to visit but I wouldn't want to live there.

Playa Manzanillo: This secluded beach is accessible from *Playa Las Gatas*. There is a footpath behind the restaurants. Ask any local for directions once you get to *Playa Las Gatas*. This path will also direct you to the lighthouse with its breathtaking views. Definitely worth the walk—early or late in the day.

Playa Larga: About 5 kilometers out of town on the Acapulco highway, this jewel of a beach has nicely paved road, and numerous restaurants. My personal favorite is *Popeye's*. Their *camaronillas* (shrimp and cheese stuffed *empanadas*) are fabulous. A couple of the restaurants have built "swimming pools" for the kids as the waves are very high and the undertow wicked.

Las Posas: Another favorite beach of mine. It is located adjacent to the airport. As you approach the airport, right before the speed bump there is a dirt road to the right along a chain link fence. Drive slowly about 3 km. and you come to a fine little beach with *palapa* restaurants. It's next to the lagoon so take some mosquito repellent.

Barra de Potosí: This is a tiny fishing village very popular with tourists and visiting Mexicans. Some lovely homes have been built here. To get there, take the *Carr. Acapulco-Zihuatanejo*. Just past the *Puente Achotes* is a sign on the right indicating *Laguna de Potosí*. The road is paved after you get through town. Also you can reach here by taking the road that goes around the airport and passing *Las Posas*.

In *Barra de Potosí*, there are numerous palm-thatched restaurants or *enramadas*—everyone has his/her favorite. The prices are reasonable and the food good, also the only place you can be assured you will get abalone.

Rumor has it that there is a pirate cache buried on the backside of the mountain and an archaeological site was discovered in the 80's (2 pyramids).

For bird watchers or nature lovers, a boat tour of *Laguna Potosí* is a must. Ask any of the restaurant owners to point out one of the boat guides. For about $100 pesos you will see flocks of rare roseate spoonbills, blue herons, ibis, egret, cranes, pelicans, sea gulls, and frigate birds. Also for rent at a couple of the restaurants closest to the lagoon are kayaks. For a guided tour, contact Zoe Kayak Tours at ☎ 553-0496 or ✉ **zoe5@aol.com**. Bring binoculars if you plan to do this trip.

Our House B&B: ★ ★ ★ 📱 Karen(755)113-6114 or 📱 Cecil(755)114-0069 . The house has three rooms and a studio for rent. Breakfast included and lunch and dinner upon request. They also have facilities for people with special needs. Furthermore, there is hook-up for 3 RV's on site. They have a tour bus with a wheelchair lift. Wheelchairs available if necessary. Visit **www.ourhouse-zihua.com** or ✉ourhousezihua@yahoo.com

Casa Frida: ★ ★ ☎ 557-0049. Another fantastic 3 room B&B located on the beach at *Barra*. Service and hospitality are top of the line. The entire house can be rented. Visit **www.casafrida.net** or ✉ **request@casafrida.net**

Hotel Las Palmas: ★ ★ ★ ★ 📱 (755)557-0634. This is truly an incredible B&B located on a very secluded strip of beach on *Playa Blanca*. There are ten very different guest suites with only the best amenities. Visit **www.hotellaspalmas.net** ✉ **reservations@hotellaspalmas.net**

Tree Tops Bungalows: ★ ★ 📱 (755)115-5671/4521. Located at the north end of *Playa Blanca* (on the oceanside of airport). There are 4 really cute bungalows built on stilts located here on a section of very secluded beach. There is a restaurant—bar on site and the beer ice cold.

Visit **www.zihuatanejo.net/bungalowstreetops/bungalows** or ✉ bungalowstreetop@hotmail.com

Beaches North

Playa Mahagua: This small beach is located between *Zihua* and Ixtapa on the back road to Ixtapa. Unfortunately, developers came in the mid 90's and started a huge project and now it is part of *Monte Cristo.*

Playa Hermosa: This is the beach for the *Las Brisas* Hotel in Ixtapa. It's a small crescent-shaped cove bordered by dramatic black rocks. Non-guests of *Las Brisas* sometimes frequent this beach as it is not as rough as *Palmar*—being protected by the rocks. Perch under one of the many comfortable *palapas* and get a waiter's attention by running a little red flag up a pole. Good snorkeling around the rocks.

Playa Palmar: The main Ixtapa beach containing all the major hotels with the exception of *Las Brisas*. This beach is on open-ocean so the waves are often large and undertows tricky. The red danger flag is up almost all the time.

Playa Quieta: This beach is home to the Club Med and *Melia Azul*. It is also the jumping off point for the short boat-ride to *Isla* Ixtapa located at the north end of the beach. There are now several restaurants to choose from. The parking lot is filled with vendors hawking their wares.

Ixtapa Island: A short boat-ride from *Playa Linda*. The island is a wildlife sanctuary but chances of seeing the iguanas or raccoons are slim. There are four beaches on the island with their own distinctive characteristics. Each has numerous restaurants and snorkeling and scuba gear can be rented on the island.

Snorkeling is popular at the island as the water is normally very clear and there are abundant fish. There are several seafood restaurants with the *Marlin* being the most popular. Take your trip during the week as the island becomes very crowded on weekends.

Playa Troncones: This beautiful beach has exploded with growth since the early 90's, largely due to Dewey McMillan and Anita Lapointe. It's a half-hour drive north of *Zihua* with the turn-off sign clearly marked. The paved road is a joy to ride on as the old one had potholes the size of small cars and it was rough traveling. Since the *ejido* land was opened in the mid 90's, real estate prices have soared. As in Zihuatanejo, there were about sixty families who owned all the land and farmed jointly. Since the mid-90's, the members of the *ejido* have titled the land and have been able to sell lots since late 1995. Land prices have gone from about $3,500 U.S. to $300,000 U.S. per lot.

Tour guides used to use *Troncones* as their "typical Mexican village" but not anymore. One of my sources claims it is just too difficult to explain how *Troncones* got from then to now! In the not too distant past, the village consisted of a few palm-thatched huts on the ocean side of the street (and I use the term loosely) selling lukewarm beer and mediocre food. The other side of the street had small dirt-floored wooden shacks. Traversing them, then as now, down the dirt street, are pigs, donkeys, cows, horses, and flea bitten dogs.

Now along four miles of the ocean side of the road are multi-million dollar homes, gorgeous B&B's, and hotels. I defy anyone to find a more glaring difference between the "have's" and the "have-not's" in such as short distance!

Troncones is truly a lovely spot and repeat visitors abound. However, it is not for everyone. It is the perfect vacation getaway for those truly wanting "to get away from it all." It's also a very popular surf spot. If you enjoy the nightlife and a variety of menus, again *Zihua*/Ixtapa are the better choices.

I recommend folks break up their vacation and spend a few days at *Troncones*. It is truly relaxing and soothing to the soul and it's hard to find a more spectacular sunset. If you're lucky, you'll spot dolphins frolicking in the waves and whales cruising the coast. At certain times of the year, the sea turtles struggle up the beach to lay their eggs. The locals protect the endangered turtle eggs and many places have ponds to place the newly hatched turtles in so they might have a better chance at survival. A "sea turtle release party" is quite the event.

Troncones B&B's

Since the vast majority of folks use the Internet, I am not going into lengthy descriptions of all the amenities of each of the following. As they say, a picture is worth a thousand words and all can be viewed in living color at **www.troncones.com.mx**.

All the accommodations are located on the beach so a map is really not necessary. Prices are listed for high season, which is December through April with Christmas and Easter priced somewhat higher. Low season rentals are about 30% less and you can really bargain in September and October. July and August are when the Mexicans take their vacations and they have discovered *Troncones,* so don't expect discounts then. All accommodations have hot water and ceiling fans at the very least. Most now have air conditioned rooms and I'll try to make note when applicable. There are several taxi stands in *Troncones*, most around the T-intersection of the beach road with the road leading to the main highway.

Vacation Rentals and Bungalows

Alegría: ★ ★ ★ ☏ 553-2815.   This is a really cute house steps away from the *Tropic of Cancer* restaurant complex.   There are two very large bedrooms each with a king size bed and a single and an en-suite bath, full kitchen, large living area with sofa bed and private porch and gardens overlooking the ocean. Visit **www.tronconestropic.com**. ✉ **casacanela@yahoo.com**

Casa Canela: ★ ★ ★ Contact information same as above. A private 2-bedroom house located across from the old *El Burro Borracho* with a large, fully-equipped kitchen, living room and covered porch.   The house sleeps six. Visit : **www.tronconestropic.com**. ✉ casacanela@yahoo.com

Behind the house are two bungalows called *Canelita* ★ ★ each providing very adequate accommodations for two.   They share a kitchen. Perfect for the budget minded.

Santa Benita: ★ ★ ★ Contact information same as above. Two charming, air conditioned rooms for rent at the Tropic of Cancer complex. These rooms share a very large open-air palapa style living area and kitchen located above the rooms. The building is steps from the pool, bar, and ocean—my personal favorite.
Visit **www.tronconestropic.com**. ✉ **casacanela@yahoo.com**.

Casa de Eva : ★ ★ On same property as *Alegría and Santa Benita* but a little more economical. All three can be rented as one complex.

Casablanca: ★ ★ ★   One of the oldest homes in *Troncones*. Completely renovated, now offering a two-bedroom first floor apartment for rent with owners living on the second floor. Visit **www.casablanca-troncones.net** ✉ **casablanca@troncones.net**

Casa Colorida/Casa Palapa: ★ ★ ★ ★ ☏ 553-2820. These are two lovely homes on three landscaped acres. *Casa Colorida* is 3000 square feet of living space. *Casa Palapa* is 2000 square feet.

Casa de la Sirena: ★ ★ ★ ★ Here there are private villas, bungalows and mini-villas with total accommodations for 2-20 people. Owners Mike and Debbie go that "extra mile" to make your stay the best vacation of your life. Visit **www.casadelasirena.net** or ✉

casasirena@gmail.com

Casa Las Piedras: ★★★★☎ 1(650)559-0687 or local ☎ 553-2876. Luxury B&B located in Troncones with four beautiful suites. Price includes breakfast.

Casa Delfín Sonriente: ★★★ ☎ Stateside call 1(831)688-6578. This charming house can be rented in its entirety or private rooms and bungalows are available. Visit **www.casadelfinsonriente.com** or ✉ **enovey@casadelfin@cruzio.com**

Casa Escondida: ★★★ 🕿 (755)558-3672. This is a private villa with two guest cottages and two apartments on the beach with pool. Visit **www.tronconesbeach.com** or✉ **tileman66@hotmail.com**

Casa Ki: ★★★ ☎ 553-2815. This is one of my favorites. There are five very private bungalows sitting in a tropical garden. Breakfast included during high season. Ed, Ellen, and Tina work very hard to make their guests feel welcome. Great library and game selection. Visit **www.casaki.com** ✉ **casaki@yahoo.com**

Casa Viva: ★★★ ☎ 553-2913.(Not for reservations). Reservation number 1(650)585-6770. The house has an eco-friendly design with solar energy and recycling systems for water. The entire house can be rented or individual bungalows. Visit **www.casavivatroncones.com** ✉ **guzykan@hotmail.com**

La Morada: ★★★ ☎ 553-2804 or 1(512)263-2548 in U.S. Four luxury suites with air conditioning and pool. ✉ **TheLaMorada@aol.com**

La Puesta del Sol: ★★★ ☎ 557-0503 or in U.S. 1(818) 553-3311 or Fax (323) 913-1246. Right on the beach, this lovely home has several housing options for all budgets. There's a very nice penthouse with great ocean views, 2 mini-suites and even a surfer room. Visit **www.thepuestadelsol.com** or ✉ **troncones@yahoo.com**

Quinta d'Liz: ★ ☎ 553-2914. Luis, the charming and affable Mexican host, is filling a gap in *Troncones* by offering 4 small, clean rooms, very inexpensive with fans.

Tres Mujeres Paradise: ★★★ Located right on the beach with six beautifully appointed rooms, this is a new addition to the area and a delightful one. Visit **www.tresmujerestroncones.com** or ✉ tresmujeresparadise@gmail.com

Playa Manzanillo

This beach is adjacent to *Troncones* and is considered an excellent surfing spot. Very popular all year round. There are several accommodations here to suit various budgets.

Casa de Helen: ★★★★ ☏ 553-2800 in Troncones or (541)908-8999. This is a luxurious three-bedroom house with a pool right on the beach. A/C in the bedrooms, satellite TV, and fully staffed. There is a three-night minimum. ✉ **troncoseshelen@yahoo.com**, Visit **www.troncones.helen.com**

Casa de los Sueños Tropicales: ★★ A vacation home on the point of *Playa Manzanillo* with two bedrooms. ✉ **edgorrie@telus.net**

Eden Hacienda & Restaurant: ★★★ ☏ 553-2802. There are six rooms in the main hotel and four beach bungalows and four suites. Breakfast included. Visit **www.edenmexico.com** ✉ **evaandjim@aol.com**

La Posada de los Raqueros: ★★★ There are (2) two-story *casitas* and two bedrooms in the main house. *Casita del Pelícano*, *Casita del Mariposa*, *Cuarto Caballo* and *Cuarto del Viejo del Mar*. ✉ **raqueros@raqueros.com**

Las Tejas: ★★★★ For true luxury, this four-bedroom vacation home on the beach is ideal for a large group. Open-air living and dining rooms. Bedrooms all open onto a terrace facing the ocean. A large *palapa* relaxation area fronts the beachfront pool. Two rooms have king-sized beds and A/C. The other two rooms have twin beds and fans. Visit **www.casalastejas.com** ✉ **lastejas@zihuatanejo.net**

The Inn at Manzanillo Bay: ★★★ ☏ 553-2884 or Fax 553-2883. An eco-lodging located on the beach with 8 individual bungalows around a pool and restaurant. ✉ **manzanillobay@aol.com**

Troncones Point Surf Club: ☏ 553-2886. Eco-complex. Hard to price as they have full bungalow rental, room rentals, and dorm-like bunk-beds setting with board rentals and repairs. Meals served family - style. Really cute place and well maintained. ✉**hostel@tronconesPoint.com** or visit **www.tronconespoint.com**

La Majahua
When you run out of road going north from the village of *Troncones,* you reach *Playa La Majahua.* This is primarily a fishing village with several small eateries serving good seafood at excellent prices. This is the place to swim if you doubt your abilities at toughing the surf in *Troncones.* The little bay is protected and there is no undertow to speak of. Perfectly safe.

Abadia B&B: ★★★☎ 1(541)389-8142 or 📱 1(541)390-4355. There are five good-sized rooms with refrigerators, terraces and pool. Visit **www.abadiamexico.com** or ✉ **info@abadiamexico.com**

Saladitas
Saladitas, for a very long time was pristine and quaint. Now, it also is home to million dollar homes. The road leading to it is a left at a town called *Los Llanos* (plains) and there is a huge tire at the top of a hill.

House of Waves: ★★ ☎ 554-4532. Two story home with three rooms and separate bungalow for rent. Visit **www.houseofwaves.net**
✉ Elsa: **elsavale29@hotmail.com**

La Chuparosa de Saladita: ★★★ There are two complete villas and two *casitas* for rent at this luxurious home. Naturally, all amenities. Visit **www.lachuparosadesaladita.com** or
✉ **chuparosasaladita@gmail.com**

Saladitas **Surf Camp**: ★★ These are rustic beach bungalows on stilts and the old time surfers wish they had been able to keep this spot a secret. Visit **www.salidatas.com** or ✉ **surfcampmx@aol.com**

Wining & Dining in *Troncones* Area
Jardín del Eden: 🍽🍽🍽 ☎ 553-2899. Located at *Hacienda Eden* on *Playa Manzanillo.* A varied menu and the staff will make you feel at home. Dinner reservations required.

La Costa Brava: 🍽🍽 ☎ 553-2808. This is a great little restaurant specializing in seafood. It is on the beach by the bridge and *laguna.*. For a super treat, get a group together and have the owner do a *pescado a la talla* (whole fish, stuffed and grilled over an open fire). Fantastic! Closed Saturday.

The Inn at Manzanillo Bay: 🍽🍽🍽 ☎ 553-2884. The chef/owner is a graduate of the California Culinary Academy and his menu is eclectic and versatile.

Troncones Activities

Present Moment Retreat: ☎ U.S. 1(916)580-3418 or local ☎103-0011.   Ten bungalows. Rates for one week are $1,795.00 U.S. per person and include a variety of activities.

Visit **www.**presentmomentretreat**.com** or

✉**reserve@presentmomentretreat.com**

Ixtapa—History

Tourism development, as a source of income for Mexico, began on a national level after the Mexican Revolution. With the country stabilized, thousands of tourists came to Mexico seeking adventure and travel.

Mexico City hosted a convention in 1935, for 8,000 Rotarians with a speech delivered at the *"Bellas Artes"* by then President Lázaro Cárdenas.

Mexico then hosted the Second International Pan-American Congress of Tourism in 1941 and the need for tourism development on a national level became firmly entrenched with the Mexican government as an economic theme.

Along these lines, Mexico introduced legislation to promote and facilitate foreign investment in the nation's tourism industry. The World Bank and other lending institutions made loans to Mexico for tourism facilities.

The father of Acapulco's tourist boom, President *Alemán Valdés* (1946-1952), ideas led to a blueprint for tourism used for later development.

FOGATUR was created in the 1950's as a development bank fund for the provision of credits, loan guarantees, and infrastructure investment. By the end of the 1960's the government had created *INFRATUR* to channel money into tourist development areas, both old and new.

In 1965, the Mexican government decided to conduct surveys to pinpoint desirable tourist zones; taking into accounts not only beautiful tourist spots but also the economic needs of various areas.

An incredible amount of data was gathered and areas selected included Cabo San Lucas, Bay of Banderas, Puerto Escondido, Cancún, and Zihuatanejo-Ixtapa.

A master plan for development was completed in 1968 and officials in Zihuatanejo were aware of the changes a mega-resort would bring to the area. *Zihua* was earmarked as a service city with a tourism component, while Ixtapa was to be built into a fully equipped resort community. Bob Schulman, a freelance writer who specializes in Mexico has a different take of how Ixtapa was "born."

Ixtapa—*A Computer Found It*

In 1969 the Mexican government decided to go all out to boost tourism. It started by creating a high-level agency tasked to build super resorts—from scratch—named the Fondo Nacional de Fomento al Turismo (the National Fund to Promote Tourism), or FONATUR for short.

Experts in fields ranging from marketing to land management, backed up by economists, archaeologists, sociologists, entomologists, and a few programmers for those then newfangled computers, staffed the agency.

As things turned out, Fonatur's computer whizzes came up with some of the tourism world's best investments. After sizing up possible resort locations all over Mexico from data collected during an earlier two-year study, the computer cranked out its first two selections: Ixtapa, and an uninhabited, 14 mile-long island running along the Caribbean shoreline on the tip of the Yucatán Peninsula. First up for development in 1972 was the computer's find on the Yucatán. It was called Cancún. Ixtapa ran a close second on the development time-line, having been designed and built about a half-year behind Cancún. Cancún opened for business in late 1974. Ixtapa's first hotel, the Aristos, opened in 1975.

Negotiations to acquire land were begun—not without problems. The beachfront was subdivided into lots for sale to hotels, a golf course plotted, and residential areas around the golf course containing 500 lots were planned. Also laid out were plans for a commercial center with space for 76 shops, a housing area for workers, health clinic, security office, fire station, laundry, and nursery.

Excitement over the project ran high in Zihuatanejo. Ixtapa was looked upon as a project producing thousands of jobs for locals. Thousands of laborers flocked to the area in search of work—taxing public services and housing beyond capacity.

Efforts were made by government and local officials to avoid the creation of another Acapulco at all costs.

FONATUR was created to channel money into development of Ixtapa, combining the previous two organizations of FOGATUR & INFRATUR.

Goals laid down by previous administrations were realized when, by 1979, tourism was generating more revenue than oil.

Unfortunately for Mexico, tourism began a decline from the high reported in 1979. Inflation was a major factor. A vacation in the U.S. was 10-20% less expensive than a vacation in Mexico. A major devaluation in February 1982 reversed this trend to some extent. This created economic hardship for the local population, especially for the owners of craft stores and restaurants.

The tourism market fluctuated dramatically in the 80's and 90's.

Concern for tourist safety, the earthquake of 1985, and the hurricane of 1988, curtailed the flow of tourists "south of the border." By 1990, the number of tourists "south of the border" begin to increase dramatically. The Internet created free publicity for this area and despite the "narco-wars" going on all over the country, tourists continue to flock to Ixtapa. (I am referring to national —not international tourists).

Since the first hotel in Ixtapa opened in 1975, it has grown according to plan and continues to be a model resort.

Orientation

Ixtapa is located approximately seven kilometers north of Zihuatanejo and is a 25-minute ride from the airport. The resort covers an area of four square miles.

The *Bahía del Palmar* is the principal beach and the largest of the hotels are grouped in this area. Complementing the hotel zone is the Robert Trent Jones Golf Course, shopping center, and a number of smaller villas and condominiums.

The beach is 2 kilometers long, ending at the breakwater for the marina on the northern boundary. *Palmar* was designated a "clean beach" by the government in 2010. The city fathers were desperate for this designation and achieved this accolade with much hard work and lots of fanfare. The water itself is dangerous for swimming most of the time, having large waves and always with an undertow.

Please remember, Ixtapa is a resort created for tourists. The infrastructure necessary to a functional town is found in Zihuatanejo. Public offices, stores, pharmacies, food markets, etc. are abundant in *Zihua*. Ixtapa stores, pharmacies, etc. are geared to provide minimal necessities for a "short term" tourist visit. Please refer to appropriate sections in the Zihuatanejo part of this book for more comprehensive information.

Accommodations
Hotels

Ixtapa is filled with luxury hotels staffed with English speaking personnel. The differences between *Zihua* and Ixtapa are most evident when one enters the lobby of one of these elegant hotels. You could swear you were in a clone in Hawaii or perhaps Miami Beach, an impression one is not likely to get in *Zihua*.

Barceló: ★★★★ (Map I2), ☎ 552-0000. This very nice all-inclusive hotel contains 333 rooms and 12 suites—all with AC, radio, cable TV, mini-bar and private terraces. The rooms surround a giant atrium, which gives the lobby and adjoining restaurants an open, airy feeling. A high degree of personal attention and the friendliness of the staff are features which serve to distinguish this delightful, comfortable hotel. Amenities include a large swimming pool, 3 tennis courts, and game room with movies, children's playground, pharmacy, tobacconist's, travel agency, and in-house physician. For conferences, there are four suites, each with a capacity for 200 individuals. The lobby bar features a fine guitarist-vocalist and the Sanka Bar is a popular spot for late evening usually featuring live entertainment. It's very much a family-oriented hotel with maximum capacity all year round by Mexican nationals. Book online at wwwbarcelo.com/barcelohotels

CLUB MED: ★★★★ (*Playa Quieta*). ☎ 552-0044 or Fax 553-0344. Club Med opened in 1981 on 21 acres of land. The complex contains 298 rooms and 15 suites with all amenities. Currently geared toward family vacations with mini-club activities for children 4 months to 12 years of age. Prices are all inclusive. Book online at **www.clubmed.com**

DIF: ★★ (Map I12). This facility is not available to foreigners but for your information, the initials stand for the National Program for Family Welfare. It contains dormitories for guests, with a sports court and swimming pool. It was the idea of the Mexican government to provide some very low-cost accommodations so the Ixtapa resort complex would be within the budget reach of all Mexicans.

Emporio Ixtapa: ★★★★ (Map I6). ☎ 01(866)280-6073. This hotel opened in 1979 and contains 173 rooms and 8 suites with AC, mini-bar, music, and cable television. Facilities include 2 pools, 2 tennis courts, 2 restaurants, and a coffee shop. The grounds are lovely and the lobby centers around an indoor garden.

Visit www.emporiohotels.com

Holiday Inn Ixtapa: ★★★ Esq. *Paseo de las Palmas y Agua de Correa.* ☏ or fax 01(800)560-0500. Visit www.holidayinn.com (Couldn't locate e-mail address). This hotel is not on the beach—about a 15 minute comfortable, level walk.

Hotel Dorado Pacífico: ★★★★(Map I7), ☏ 553-2025 or Fax 553-0126. The hotel opened in 1982 and contains 285 rooms and numerous suites each with its own terrace with sea view. All rooms have AC, satellite television, a mini-bar and music. The hotel boasts two hard tennis courts, an Olympic-sized pool, and organized social activities. There are four restaurants and convention facilities to accommodate 1500 people.

✉ reser@doradopacifico.com

Hotel Fontán: ★★★★ (Map I3), ☏ 553-1666. This hotel opened for business in 1980 and features 462 rooms, and 18 suites all with AC., cable television, and radio. The hotel has three pools, a game room, and convention suites, which can handle up to 1200 people.

★The American Consulate is located on the hotel grounds.

Hotel Presidente Inter-Continental: ★★★★ (Map I4), Tel. 553-0018 or Fax 553-2312. This hotel opened in 1977. Its eleven stories contain 408 rooms and 11 junior suites. The rooms have AC, music, and cable television. There are four restaurants and numerous bars. Facilities further include three swimming pools, two hard tennis courts, and three convention suites. *Fiesta Mexicana* show once a week and numerous guided activities.

Krystal: ★★★★ (Map I8). ☏ 553-0333 or 01(800)087-4887. Opened in 1980 containing 255 rooms and 19 suites equipped with satellite television, AC, mini-bar, music, and nice terraces with sea views. The hotel has 2 pools, 2 clay tennis courts, a basketball court, and a games room. On the premises is the fabulous restaurant Bogart's as well as two other fine restaurants. There is a lobby bar with live music and the famous disco Christine, which is open to the wee hours of the morning. The hotel has one of the largest convention centers in Ixtapa with a capacity for 1400 people. Visit www.krystal-hotels.com

Las Brisas: ★★★★ (Map I1). ☏ 553-2121. This hotel was opened in 1982 and contains 428 rooms, 13 junior suites, and 6 master suites with private pools on the top floor. All rooms have AC, color television and large balconies with hammocks. There are 5 good restaurants, four swimming pools, and four lighted tennis courts. The hotel furthermore contains seven convention suites, which may accommodate from 40 to 650. The lobby bar offers a happy hour and serves giant margaritas the sunset view is one of the finest in the area. The *Vista Hermosa* is the hotel's private beach with transportation provided during the day. The hotel is an architectural marvel and most people either love it or loathe it. It sits on a steep hill and is isolated from the rest of the hotel zone and shopping centers. This is not a major problem as taxis are plentiful but it is the major complaint I hear from tourists staying here. Visit wwwbrisashotels.online.com. Their website wouldn't let me pull up Ixtapa or maybe it's because I'm computer ignorant.

Posada Real Ixtapa: ★ ★ ★ (Map I10). ☎ 553-1925.

Melía Azul Ixtapa: ★ ★ ★ ★ *(Playa Quieta)* ☎ 555-0000. This all inclusive facility has 400 rooms, 5 restaurants, 3 pools, gym and 2 tennis courts. Also convention center for up to 2400 people.

Qualton Club Ixtapa: ★ ★ ★ ★ *(Playa Linda)* ☎ 552-0083 or 01(800)90-MELIA. This hotel contains 150 all-inclusive rooms. Visit **www.qualton.com** or ✉reserva@qualton.com

Park Royal Hotel: ★ ★ ★ ★ (Map I9). ☎ 555-0550. This hotel opened in August 1989. The hotel has over 275 rooms. Rooms are lavishly decorated and equipped with AC, safety deposit boxes, mini-bar, music, satellite television, and each has a balcony with bay view. There are two restaurants, a cafeteria, pool, and 5 convention suites with facilities for 400. ✉reservations@parkroyalhotels.com.mx

Tesoro Ixtapa: ★ ★ ★ ★ (Map I11). ☎ 753-1175 or 555-0600. This hotel is now a private condominium complex which initially opened in 1979, and contains 171 rooms with AC, mini-bar, music, and cable television. Facilities include 2 pools, 2 tennis courts, 2 restaurants, and a coffee shop. Some rooms offered all inclusive.
Visit tesororesorts.com

Time Share

Coral Ixtapa: ☎ 553-1746

Green **Ixtapa:** ☎ 553-0025

Ixtapa Palace: *Esq. Paseo de las Garzas y Paseo del Rincón.* ☎ 553-1359. This **time-share** complex has over 400 units. The complex has *Emilio's Pizza* take-out. There is a mini-golf course, olympic-sized pool, beauty salon, and really nice gym.

Visit **www.ixtapapalaceresort.com**
or ✉ **ixtapapalace@hotmail.com**

La Quinta Ixtapa: Golindrinas #136. ☎553-1248.

Pacífica: Paseo de la Colina s/n. ☎ 555-2500 or 01(800)711-1934. This time-share complex is located on the mountain above *Las Brisas* and has the best view of the bay. The complex contains the *El Faro* restaurant, which is open to the public. Visit **www.pacifica.com**

Puerta del Mar: Esq. Paseo de las Gaviotas y Agua de Correo. ☎ 553-2045/2105. There are 45 suites surrounding a pool. Within walking distance of beach. Located behind the Ixtapa shopping center.

Villas Sol Pacífica: Retorno de las Alondras #270. ☎553-1283.

Other Accommodations
(Apartments, Houses, Condos, and Small Villas)

Generally, the hotels, villas, and houses in Ixtapa are much more formal than in *Zihua.*

For the months of December through May, most hotels and other lodgings are booked to capacity and charge premium rates. Bargain hunters do not belong in Ixtapa during high season—attractive packages are available off-season.

As in *Zihua,* there are many houses for rent or for sale depending on time of year. Most of the homes for sale or lease are around the golf courses. For more information, contact one of the very fine real estate firms listed under **Real Estate**.

Expect to pay at least $1,000 U.S. per month for a home during high season (most homes have pools). If interested in buying, expect to pay no less than $100,000.

Small Hotels and *Villas*

For those individuals who like luxury accommodations but don't care for the impersonality of the large high-rise hotels, there are numerous smaller hotels and villas in Ixtapa to choose from. Most, not all, are situated around the golf course on the *Paseo de las Golondrinas.* The following are the only ones I could verify. It would be advisable to use one of our local websites or a real estate agent.

Capella Hotel & Spa: ★ ★ ★ ★ ☎ 555-1112 (local). In U.S. (877) 2968889. In Mexico 01(800)838-6501. *Paseo Playa Linda.* Fabulous small boutique hotel voted best in Ixtapa by Trip Advisor. Marvelous restaurants—*Amares,* Seafood Terrace, and the daytime eatery *Las Rocas.* Visit www.capellahotels.com

Flamingo Golf Villas: ★★★★ (Map I25). ☎ 553-1297. In U.S (210)563-6310. or local 553-1297. A lovely spot close to the beach and shopping. No hills to climb! There are three condos available of two, three, or four bedrooms. All amenities. Right on the golf course with a huge swimming pool. My personal favorite.
✉ Gloria Bellack **flamingogolf@zihuatanejo.net**

Tres Puertas: ★★★ (Map I33). ☎ 553-0610 or Fax 553-0573. Four suites available with full kitchen and amenities. Quite lovely but a little off the beaten path requiring taxis for transportation, unless you are in really good physical shape.
✉ **3puertasixtapa@prodigy.net.mx**

Villas Ixzi: ★★★ *Paseo de las Golindrinas* #27. ☎ 553-2297. There are 40 guestrooms. They have a pool and tennis court for guests. Very nice and moderately priced. Visit **www.villasixzi.com** or
✉ **reservations@villasixzi.com**

Villas Paráiso: ★★*Paseo de Rincon s/n.* ☎ 553-0194/34. There are 7-master suites and 49 suites available with full amenities and reasonably priced. (The suites have phone numbers different from regular rooms—go figure?) Visit **www.villasparaiso.com**
✉ **villasparaisoixtapa@prodigy.net.mx**

Condos

Amara:★★★★ ✉ **info@condoixtapa.com**

Casa Bonita: ★★★★ *Blv.* Ixtapa #1. Lovely condos at the south entrance to Ixtapa coming from *Zihua.* No bay view and quite a walk to the beach. Several are offered online by individuals. Couldn't find onsite property manager for rentals.

Bay View Grand Residencias: ★★★★ (Map I37). Luxury high-rise condos on the beach.

Marina Ixtapa: ★★★★ This is an impressive condo hotel complex built around the marina at the end of *Playa Palmar.* Some of the condos surround the *Marina* Golf Course.

Monarca: ★★★★ (Map I37), ☎ 553-0210. This complex is right on the beach. It has four vertical towers, each containing 90 condos. Visit **www.monarca.ixtapa.com**
or ✉ **mme@cuidadargentum.com**

Real de Palmas: ★★★ (Map I13). Always condos for rent by owners so must check on the web. I pulled up a list of 6 different condos on one of our local websites.

Selva del Mar: ★★★★ (Map I39). There are ten beautiful units here in the vicinity of *Las Brisas*, with a fabulous bay view but a taxi ride to the beach.

Trapachi: ★★★★ *Paseo de la Roca*. This high-rise condo building contains luxurious large suites with all amenities. Commanding a magnificent view of the bay. No website or contact number except for real estate agents with listings.

Vista de las Rocas: ★★★★ *Paseo de las Rocas*. This is an 8-unit complex with 2 houses of 3-bedroom/2 baths, 4 condos of 2-bedroom/2 bath, and 2 penthouses. They are for sale or rent.

This is a very short list of condo offerings. Again, the services of one of the real estate agents listed in the Zihuatanejo part of the book is the best way to go if looking for a condo to buy or rent or check out one of the listed websites for the area—people are paying to advertise their places and you can find individual rentals on these sites.

Restaurants

Naturally, all the **and Bars** hotels host numerous restaurants and lobby bars. Each hotel also hosts a Mexican Fiesta Night. These are held on different nights of the week so check with the hotel. Mostly, I mention the bars and restaurants I know personally or know from trusted friends. I never go to Ixtapa except to eat with friends on rare occasions and see the vet!! Since the type of person that frequents Ixtapa rarely buys my book, I see no reason to really do detailed explanation about the area. It's a prejudice thing.

Al Cilantro: ⬤⬤ (Map I15). ☎ 553-0610. Fantastic food and a lovely setting.

Bogart's: ⬤⬤⬤⬤ (Map I8). ☎ 553-0333. Located in front of the *Hotel Krystal,* this is a fantasy restaurant designed to resemble a set from the movie "Casablanca." Rattan furniture, white ceiling fans, plants, and fountains, together with soft lighting and looms hanging from the roof give a pleasantly fresh and exotic feeling to the restaurant. Specializing in Marrakesh dishes combining meat and seafood. A musician plays a white grand piano on a dais and, as is the custom in many grand restaurants in Europe, women are requested to remove their shoes and a velvet cushion is placed under their feet. Dinner only and reservations recommended.

I won a bet once with friend, Martha Gordon of the *Villa de la Roca,* and she had to treat me to dinner at the "restaurant of my choice." I chose *La Margarita* in the *Los Patios* shopping center and we had a delightful meal costing under $30.00 for two. Feeling magnanimous (as I sometimes do after a couple of drinks), I invited Martha for an after-dinner drink and dessert at Bogart's. When the bill arrived I didn't know whether to laugh or cry—one after dinner drink each with coffee and a shared dessert was even more than our lovely dinner with margaritas!

Beccofino: ⬤⬤ *(Marina Plaza).* ☎ 553-1770. This is considered one of the finest dining spots in Ixtapa.

Bucaneros: ⬤⬤ *(Marina Plaza).* ☎553-0116. This is a favorite of locals. The food is quite good and you have a lovely view of the marina.

Che Mangiamo: ⬤⬤ *Marina* Ixtapa. ☎553-0690. Owner Miguel De Quevedo wants to make sure you have a really good time and really good food. Live music often during high season. Open only for dinner.

Cocobie: Marina Ixtapa. 553-0425/6. Lovely restaurant featuring international cuisine. Open for breakfast, lunch and dinner.

El Faro: *(Marina Plaza).* 553-2090. Located on top of the *Marina* tower with a piano lounge. Singing and dancing nightly.

El Faro: (Map I44) 553-1027, ext. 124. This is part of the *Pacífica* complex with a breathtaking view of the bay. You go for the view.

El Galeon: *(Marina Plaza).* 553-2150. Great view of the marina and good seafood.

Entresol: *(Marina Plaza).* Can't find anyone knowledgeable about this restaurant and they were not open when I was doing my review for Ixtapa.

Fishers: *(Marina Plaza).* 553-3270. Chain from Mexico City with pricey but delicious seafood. (From 9:00 a.m.-1:00 p.m. there is a "special" menu with great food selections and very inexpensive prices). At night, the prices go way up.

Soleiado: *Paseo de Ixtapa—Plaza Ambiente.* Across from *Park Royale.* 553-2101. Without a doubt the best in Ixtapa. The food is fabulous and moderate to expensive. The presentation is wonderful and the decor lovely. Open lunch and dinner during high season.

Subway: 553-1921. Located on Blvd. Ixtapa by Hotel *Fontán.* Daily special of ½ full sub for $29.00 pesos—that's a deal!

Villa de la Selva: (Map I47). 553-1190. This most fashionable restaurant was formerly the home of past President Luis Echeverría Alvarez. It's a wonderful spot for sunset cocktails and dinner. The ocean view is spectacular and due to the special lighting, the ocean can be seen after sundown. The *tejones* come out at dusk and roam the mountainside. The food is nothing to write home about but it is the romantic spot for wining and dining. Reservations a must if you want to eat close to the water.

Shopping Center Restaurants

There are many fine restaurants in the Ixtapa shopping center, many of which are quite good.

Casa Morelos: ⦿⦿ *Las Puertas* shopping center. Cute decor and quite good Mexican dishes.

Chili Beans: ⦿⦿ Blvd. Ixtapa. Moderately priced cute restaurant serving "American style" Mexican food. (A gentle touch on the spices and chiles).

Da Baffone: ⦿⦿ *Las Puertas.* ☎ 553-1122. An Italian eatery, serving lunch and dinner from 12 until 12. The pasta and bread are homemade and sauces follow traditional recipes. Extensive menu selection and moderately priced.

Dal Toscano: ⦿⦿ Excellent Italian food and thin crust pizza.

Domino's Pizza: ⦿⦿ ☎ 553-1333. You get **exactly** the same as Stateside. If you don't like their pizzas at home, you won't like them here.

Emilio's: ⦿⦿⦿⦿ *Plaza Ixsol.* ☎ 553-1585. If I want ribs or fantastic pizza, this is the place. Huge portions and excellent food although I can't seem to get away from ordering the house salad and ribs every time I go.

Fragolino: While not a restaurant per se; they do have wonderful Italian ice creams or gelatos in some mouthwatering flavors.

Franks: ⦿⦿ *Ixpamar Plaza.* A favorite of the foreign population—Frank serves good pizzas and pasta. He's know for his sports bar and gets a really good crowd on the weekends.

La Gloria del Infierno: ⦿⦿ In the shopping center close to *Señor Frogs.* Cute cantina with live music serving a hodge podge of pretty tasty Mexican dishes.

Lobster House: ⦿⦿⦿ Ixtapa *Plaza.* ☎ 553-2494. Serving up lobster and other goodies from the sea.

Mama Norma's & Deborah: ⦿⦿ *Las Puertas.* ☎ 553-0275. A Canadian, Debra, owns this popular restaurant and she has quite a diverse menu with some unusual items.

Nueva Zelanda: ⦿⦿ *Centro Comercio Kiosko.* ☎ 553-0838. They serve fresh fruits, juices, coffee, eggs, and sandwiches. Very clean.

Raffaello's: ⦿⦿ ☎ 553-0092. This is a very successful Italian chain restaurant located in a rustic setting with a terrace surrounded by a beautiful garden. The specialty is a blend of Italian and Latin American cuisine. The chefs have many years of experience resulting in a very popular dining spot. Open evenings and moderately priced.

Ruben's Hamburgers: ❙●❙❙●❙*Plaza Flamboyant.* ☎ 553-0027. Just about the best hamburger around. You can order a baked potato, baked *chayote*, baked squash, and baked sweet potato.

Senor Frog's: ❙●❙❙●❙❙●❙ ☎ 553-0692. Better known for its late hour disco dancing than food, this is a very popular spot for the young and young at heart.

Please note: Most restaurants are open for dinner beginning at 5:00 or 6:00 p.m. Remember, Mexicans have their big meal during the siesta hours between 2 and 4 p.m. Therefore, they eat dinner very late— usually around 9:00 or 10:00 p.m. Just because the restaurant is deserted (which it is likely to be in the early evening), it doesn't indicate the food is not good and that local residents don't patronize the establishment.

Shopping Center

The Ixtapa Shopping Plaza is large and divided into separate shopping "malls." They are: *Galerias Center, La Puerta, Ixpamar, Las Fuentes,* Ixtapa *Plaza,* and *Los Patios.* Each contains dining establishments, car rentals, pharmacies and mini-grocery stores. The largest grocery store is **Scruples** and has the basics for a vacation stay. There is also a laundromat in Ixtapa *Plaza.* There are banks— ***Bancomer,*** on the backside of the shopping mall. ***Banamex*** is found on *Blvd.* Ixtapa on the south entrance. The ***Flamingo*** movie theater ($60.00 pesos) and a miniature golf course are on the backside of the mall. The telephone office of ***Telcel*** is next to the theater and you need to come here to reactivate phones or put in new SIM cards. Also on the backside of this shopping center is ***Intercam***, where one can cash U.S. personal checks after registering with them. The **Century 21/Alpha 2000 Real Estate** is located near *Intercam.* Of some import is the Ixtapa bus station located in the *Ixpamar* mall. Bus tickets to far away places can be purchased here as well as boarding a bus here as opposed to traveling to *Zihua.* ☎553-3315/0757. One can easily spend an hour wandering around this large complex. (At one time, I wrote you could spend a day wandering around the complex but with about 60% or more of the shops closed, it doesn't take long to cruise through). A person on vacation can generally find life's little necessities here. There are dozens of clothing stores ranging from moderately priced to very expensive. In my humble opinion, the finest clothing stores are **MicMac** (close to *Mama Norma's), ***Siboney*** (front side of shopping center carrying expensive swimwear), **Tandor** (very nice and expensive menswear), and ***El Fuente*** in *Los Patios* mall.

Sports & Entertainment

Please check the *Zihua* listing as most activities overlap, with few exceptions. In Ixtapa we now have *Delfiniti.* ☎ 102-8032 or ✉ mkt@delfiniti.com This is "entertainment" according to some folks. You have an opportunity to swim for 45 minutes with captured dolphins in a swimming pool. They are open from 10:00 a.m. until 2:00 p.m. and again between 4:00 and 6:00 p.m. The current price is $1,439.00 pesos or a little more than $100.00 U.S.

Magic World: Next to Ixtapa Palace. An entertainment complex for children of all ages.

If you prefer "group" activities, you might want to call **Eco-Excursions.** ☎ 553-1069/556-3322. They will arrange hiking, biking, kayaking, fishing, etc., for a premium price.

Nightlife is centered on the very late-opening discos, and **Señor Frog's.**

Entertaining and kinda corny are the carriage rides—operating during evening hours in the back of the shopping center.

Of special interest is Ixtapa *Guau! Hotel* for pets. *Comercial Ixtapa* close to *Intercam and Century 21.* ☎ 553-0379 or ☎ (755)553-0379. Visit www.ixtapaguauhotel.tk or
✉ hotel_ixtapa_guau@hotmail.com

There are numerous discos including *Christine* and *Le Rouge.*

My favorite Ixtapa place to imbibe is **La Cohiba** next to the *Flamingo* movie theater. Its air conditioned, has great *botanas*, reasonably priced drinks, and satellite TV for sports' fans.

That pretty much covers the Ixtapa area—I've think I've pretty much covered all the areas in and around Zihuatanejo and Ixtapa. This guidebook could be hundreds of pages longer but I had to make some tough decisions on what to include and what to exclude. I've done my best and hope you enjoyed.

A NOTE FROM THE AUTHOR

My love affair with Zihuatanejo began over four decades ago. Writing a travel guide is a reflection of personal taste and I'm obviously very prejudiced toward Zihuatanejo as opposed to Ixtapa.

Specific questions from tourists and ex-patriots living here provided the skeleton for my book. I've tried to give helpful information and address the many questions tourists have asked me. If you, the reader, have questions or suggestions regarding this book, I would greatly appreciate hearing from you.
E-mail **lrfox2@yahoo.com**.

I am still making formatting errors. I am not a very knowledgeable computer person. My go-to people are no longer around and I couldn't find anyone that knew how to properly format.

Also, Victoria Priani edited with a fine-toothed comb and we went over and over and over the grammar and spelling. I noticed that when I would make a correction she suggested, sometimes it would result in a new mistake! All mistakes are entirely mine. Also, I used a Create Space template and it did some weird things when I plugged the book into the template.(Such as inserting part of a page instead of the whole page. Simply can't figure out why and spent dozens of hours trying to correct this problem to no avail.)

After publication of my first edition in 1989, I was cocky enough to think I had "covered it all." I simply couldn't imagine that there was any area that I had not touched upon, however briefly.

For a while, I maintained a tourist information office in front of the now defunct "Captain's Table Restaurant", dispensing advice, giving information and directions, and promoting my book. Onc afternoon, a fashionably dressed woman with a grim look on her face paid me a visit. "I purchased your book and read the entire text. It's really quite good; however, Linda, you failed to include something really important." "I'm terribly sorry," I replied. "Perhaps I can help you now." The woman said, "I have runs in all my stockings and need a new pair of panty hose. It wasn't mentioned in the book and I've looked everywhere." I, who am never speechless, was absolutely dumbfounded. I'd never seen a woman in Ixtapa or Zihuatanejo wearing stockings much less encountered them in a store. I simply had no answer to give her and she left in a huff. Oh well, "You can please some of the people some of the time but not all the people all the time."

Notes

Mapa de Orientación

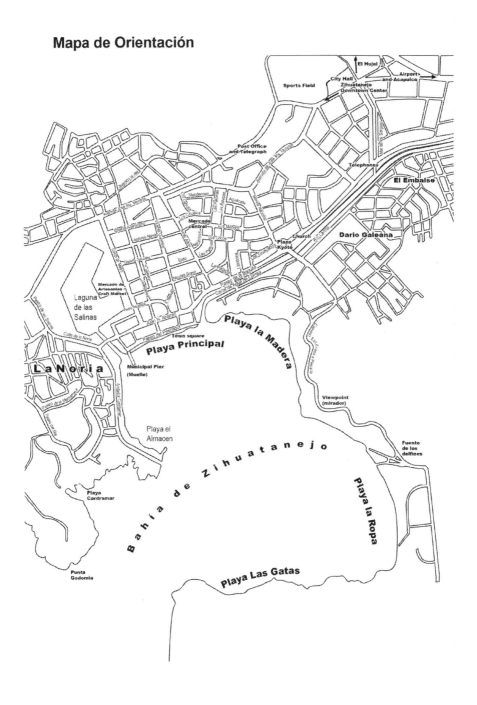

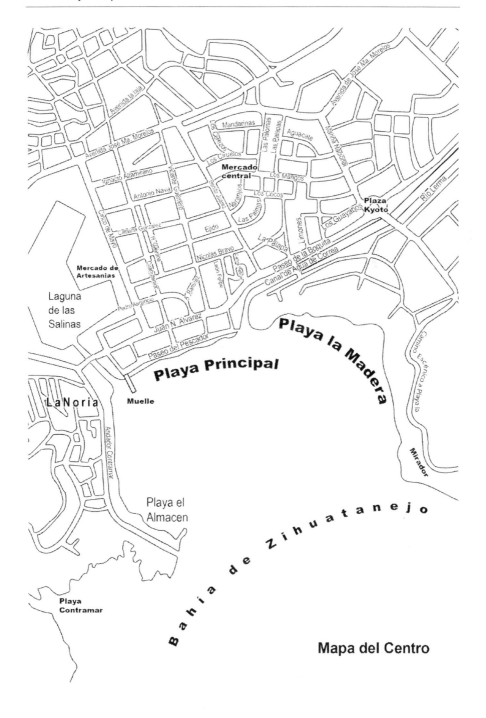

Mapa del Centro

Playa La Madera Notes

Mapa de Playa La Madera

Mapa de Playa La Ropa (LR)

Amuleto	9	Las Urracas	16
Los Arcos	26	La Villa	13
Búngalos Tucanes	2	Marlin	24
Búngalos Vepao	3	Manglar	53
Casa de Arbol	22	Mi Casita	51
Casa Buenaventura	47	Parthenon	38
Casa Cuitlateca	4	Paty's Mar y Mar	45
Casa de las Pierdra/Bamb	5	Puesta del Sol	42
Villas Guadalupe	6	Punta Marina	33
Casa Larga	29	Punta Punesca	34
Casa Luna & Búngalos Azul	8	Quinta Troppe	18
Cascada	31	Resi. Sotovento	20
Club Interwest/ZI Restaurant	35	Resi. Villa del Sol	24
Crocodile Café/Casa del Mar	17	Rossy's Hotel	19
Don Francisco Hotel	11	Rossy's Restaurant	19
Doña Prudencia	28	Suites La Ropa	21
El Tamarindo de Zihngaras	12	Tango	37
Elvira	40	Villas Carolina	27
Gal Art	24	Villas Ema	39
Gaviota	41	Villas de la Palma	36
Gloria Maria Búngalos	14	Villas de Palmar	56
Hotel Casa Blanca	1	Villas Palmera	24
Hotel Catalina	10	Villa de la Roca	23
KauKan	52	Zanzibar	30
Il Mare	46		
La Casa Que Canta	15		
La Escollera	54		
La Perla	43		

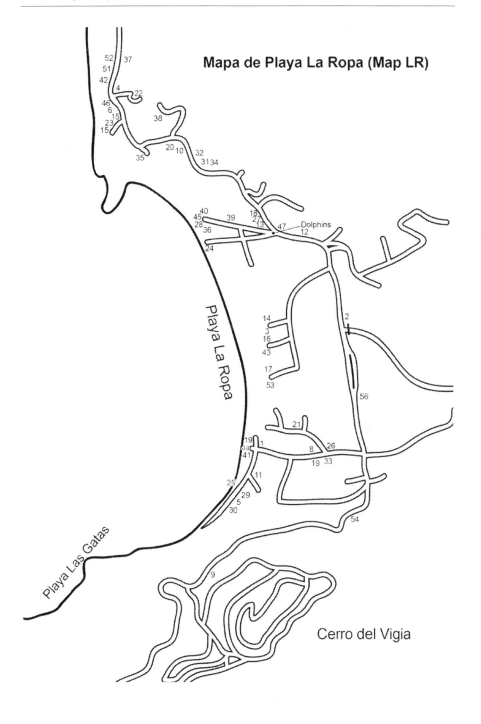

Mapa de Playa La Ropa (Map LR)

Mapa I—Ixtapa

Al Cilantro	15
Bancomer	19
Bay View Grand	37
Barcelo	2
Bogart's	8
Casa Bonita	1
Casa Golondrinas	23
Casa Ixtapa	24
Casa Pelicanos	27
Casa Sol	28
Delfiniti	22
DIF	12
Dorado Pacifico	7
El Faro	44
Emporio Ixtapa	6
Flamingo Golf Villas	25
Flamingo Movie Theater	20
Hotel Fontán	3
Hotel Presidente	4
Ixtapa Palace	45
Krystal	8
Las Brisas	1
Mansion Galandon	31
Marina Ixtapa	41
Monarca	37
Pacifica	44
Paraiso	32
Posada Real Ixtapa	10
Puerta del Mar	46
Park Royal	9
Real de Palmas	13
Selva del Mar	39
Trapiche	42
Tres Puertas	33
Villa de la Selva	47
Villa Driana	35

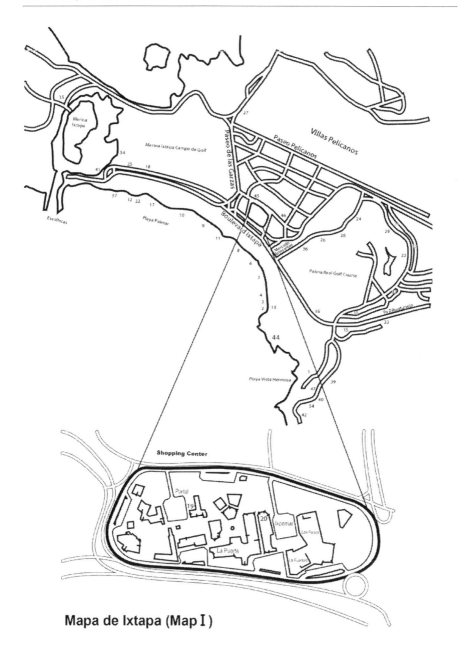

Mapa de Ixtapa (Map I)

Made in the USA
Charleston, SC
28 November 2012